THE RAID
LOCKED UP

SCRIPT
OLLIE MASTERS
(CHAPTERS ONE AND TWO + PLOT FOR THREE AND FOUR)
ALEX PAKNADEL
(CHAPTERS THREE AND FOUR)

ART
BUDI SETIAWAN

COLORS
BRAD SIMPSON

LETTERING
JIM CAMPBELL

FOREWORD

When we made *The Raid*, we had no idea the kind of impact it would have – not just for an audience, but for ourselves also. Working in our own bubble, we never dreamed it would reach an audience as widely as it has. We simply spent each day doing everything we could to maximise the low budget: from recycling the wood of struck sets, to wiping the chalk numbers off the doors in order to suggest we had a 5th, 6th, 15th floor...

Nothing could have prepared us for the reaction we would get when the film premiered to a packed crowd at Midnight Madness in 2012.

It was palpable from the moment we got our first cheer of the screening, as Rama went to work on the punchbag. Sat next to me, an excited Iko shoved his elbows into my side – it was the first of many cracked ribs that night.

Both of us, along with Joe Taslim (Jaka) and Director of Photography Matt Flannery would go on to spend the rest of the night stalking Twitter as reactions came flooding in. Giddy, we stayed up til 4am unable to comprehend what had just happened.

And then we had to do it all over again. But this time on a much larger canvas. And this time without the element of surprise. Back into our bubble we went...

With *The Raid 2*, we knew we wanted to expand the scale and scope of the story. We wanted to create its own universe with elements that would tie into the first film: small trivial things such as the recurring bull paintings in Bangun's office as seen in Tama's office in the first film – the suggestion being that Tama's painting was a gift from Bangun. More importantly, we had an opportunity to create a rogues gallery of iconic characters and villains. They had to be memorable, unique and say a lot about themselves with little to no exposition. Comic books have long provided me with inspiration. The ability to use just a few panels to tell a reader all they need to know about someone is a true art. We sought to achieve this same economical storytelling with our trio of assassins - The Assassin (I'm terrible with names), Baseball Bat Man (I told you) and Hammer Girl.

Played enigmatically by the actors, they embodied those roles and elevated the simple back-stories we had written. Finding eccentricities, affectations and off-kilter yet relatable mannerisms, they made each feel somewhat grounded despite ultimately being part of a heightened world.

A heightened world that the team at Titan Publishing have continued to explore in wonderfully realized detail through this series of comics. It has been a pleasure to dig out those old character bios and see the striking visuals and sublime panel designs used to tell these tales. They have captured that raw energy and drive of the action beautifully.

I sincerely hope you enjoy these continued adventures – it seems Rama isn't done quite yet.

Gareth Evans
December 2018

THE RAID

LOCKED UP

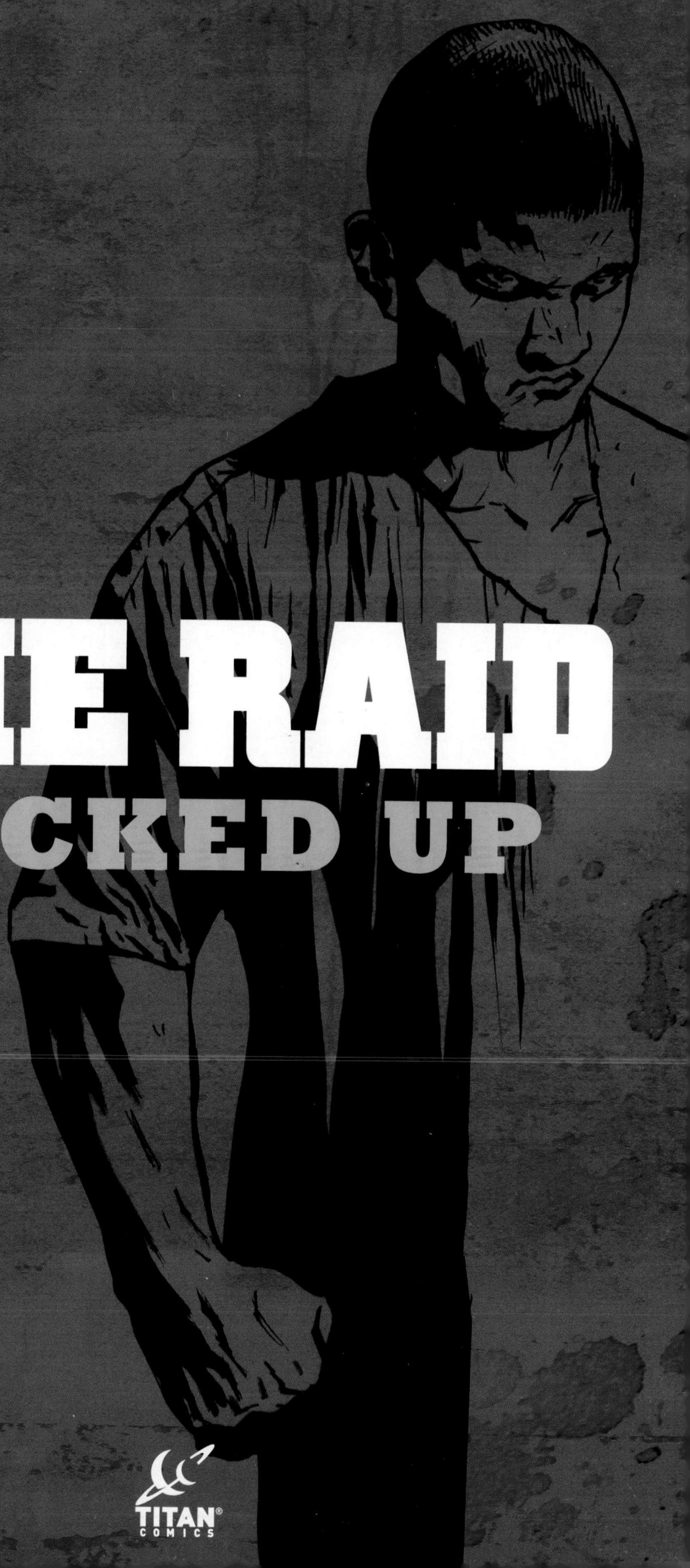

TITAN COMICS

TITAN COMICS
MANAGING EDITOR Martin Eden
PRODUCTION CONTROLLER Peter James
SENIOR PRODUCTION CONTROLLER Jackie Flook
ART DIRECTOR Oz Browne
SALES & CIRCULATION MANAGER Steve Tothill
PRESS OFFICER Will O'Mullane
COMICS BRAND MANAGER Chris Thompson
COMMERCIAL MANAGER Michelle Fairlamb
HEAD OF RIGHTS Jenny Boyce
PUBLISHING MANAGER Darryl Tothill
PUBLISHING DIRECTOR Chris Teather
OPERATIONS DIRECTOR Leigh Baulch
EXECUTIVE DIRECTOR Vivian Cheung
PUBLISHER Nick Landau

THANK YOU TO: Gareth Evans for all his input and help with this series. Everyone at XYZ Films for all their help, including Aram Tertzakian, Nick Spicer, Alex Williams, and Francesca Musumeci.

FOR RIGHTS INFORMATION CONTACT: jenny.boyce@titanemail.com

Published by Titan Comics
A division of Titan Publishing Group Ltd.
144 Southwark St.
London
SE1 0UP

 A CIP catalogue record for this title is available from the British Library

First edition: May 2019
Collects The Raid issues 1 to 4

ISBN: 9781785858659

10 9 8 7 6 5 4 3 2 1

Printed in China.

www.titan-comics.com

Follow us on **Twitter @ComicsTitan**

Visit us at **facebook.com/comicstitan**

CAST OF CHARACTERS

RAMA

A tough special forces Jakartan cop. To try and bring down a criminal empire, he has gone undercover – in prison… He is currently under the alias 'Yuda'.

BEJO

An ambitious and ruthless Jakartan crime boss.

THE ASSASSIN

Out of Bejo's three main hitmen, The Assassin is perhaps the most high-ranking.

HAMMER GIRL

A brutal assassin who uses claw hammers to destroy her enemies…

BASEBALL BAT MAN

Hammer Girl's brother. BBM and Hammer Girl are two of Bejo's top assassins.

UCO

A mobster – the son and heir to the head of the police's internal investigation unit. In this story, Uco is in prison.

TEJA

A special operations officer – new to the *Raid* saga.

THE STORY

Jakarta is under constant threat from ambitious crimelords and their deadly henchmen... The police special forces do whatever they can to quash the threats but it's a deadly challenge... It takes a special, determined, skilled, and tough individual to rise to that challenge...

• This story takes place during *The Raid 2*...

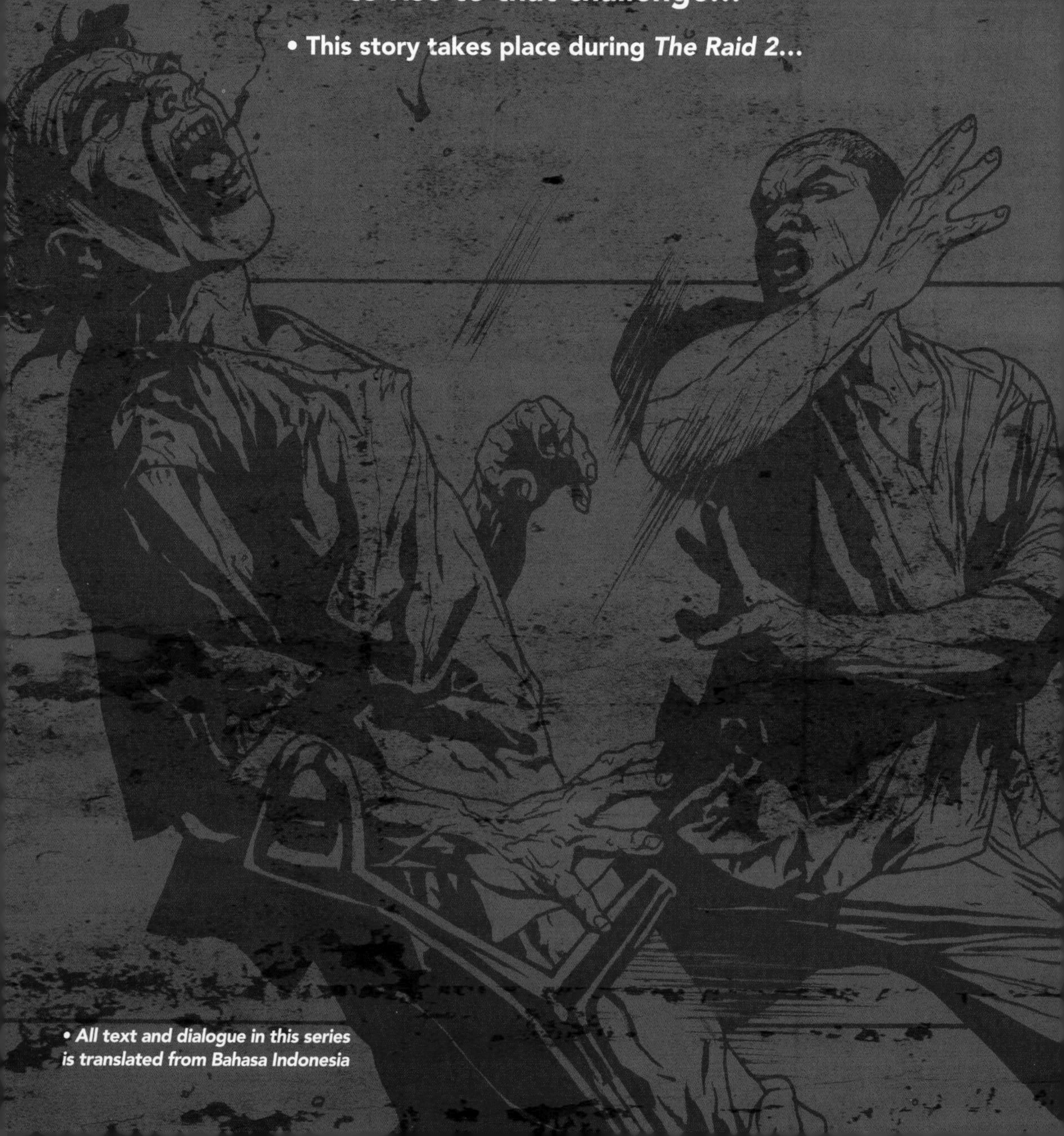

• All text and dialogue in this series is translated from Bahasa Indonesia

CHAPTER 1

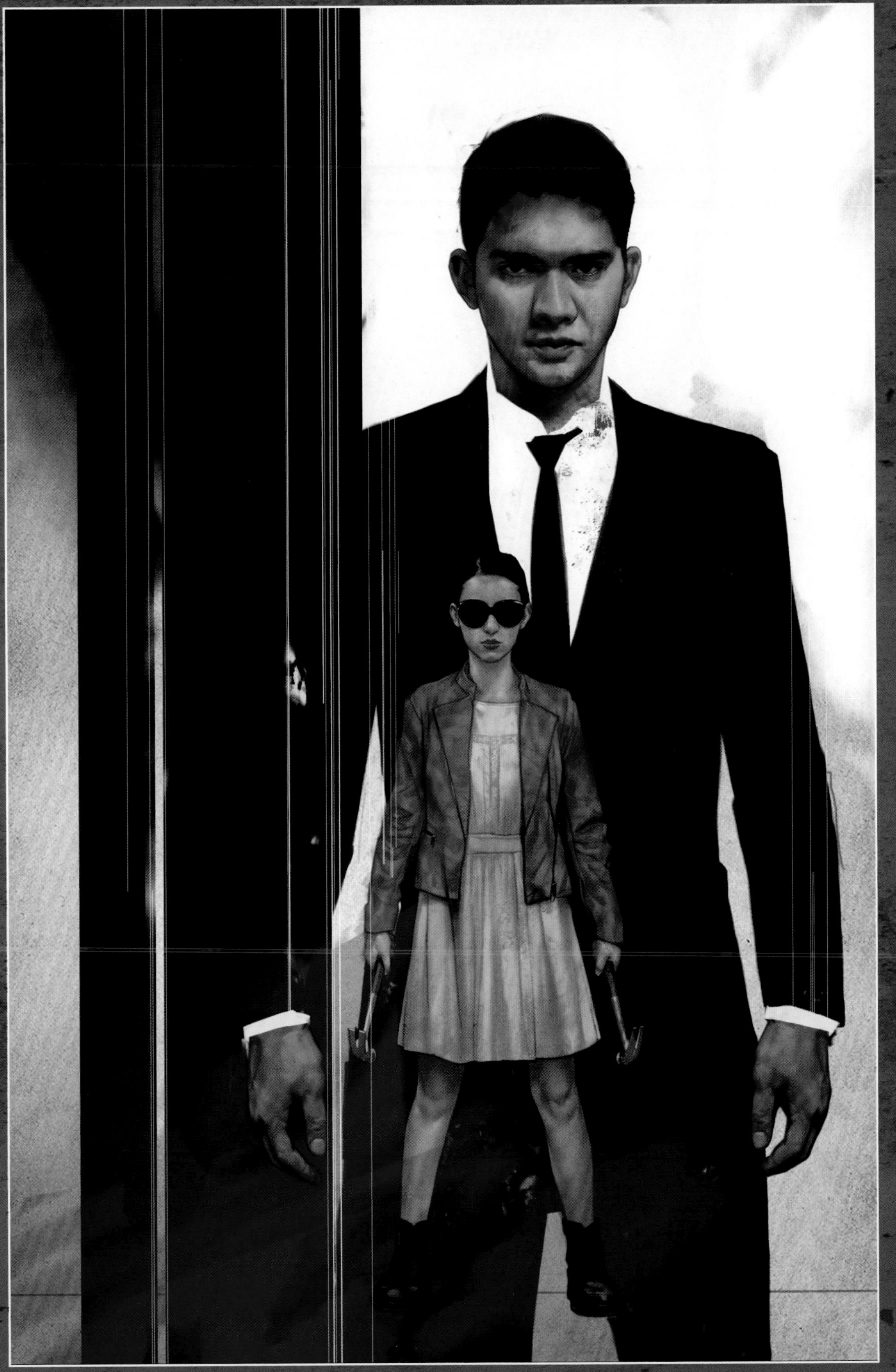

Illustration by **Ben Oliver**

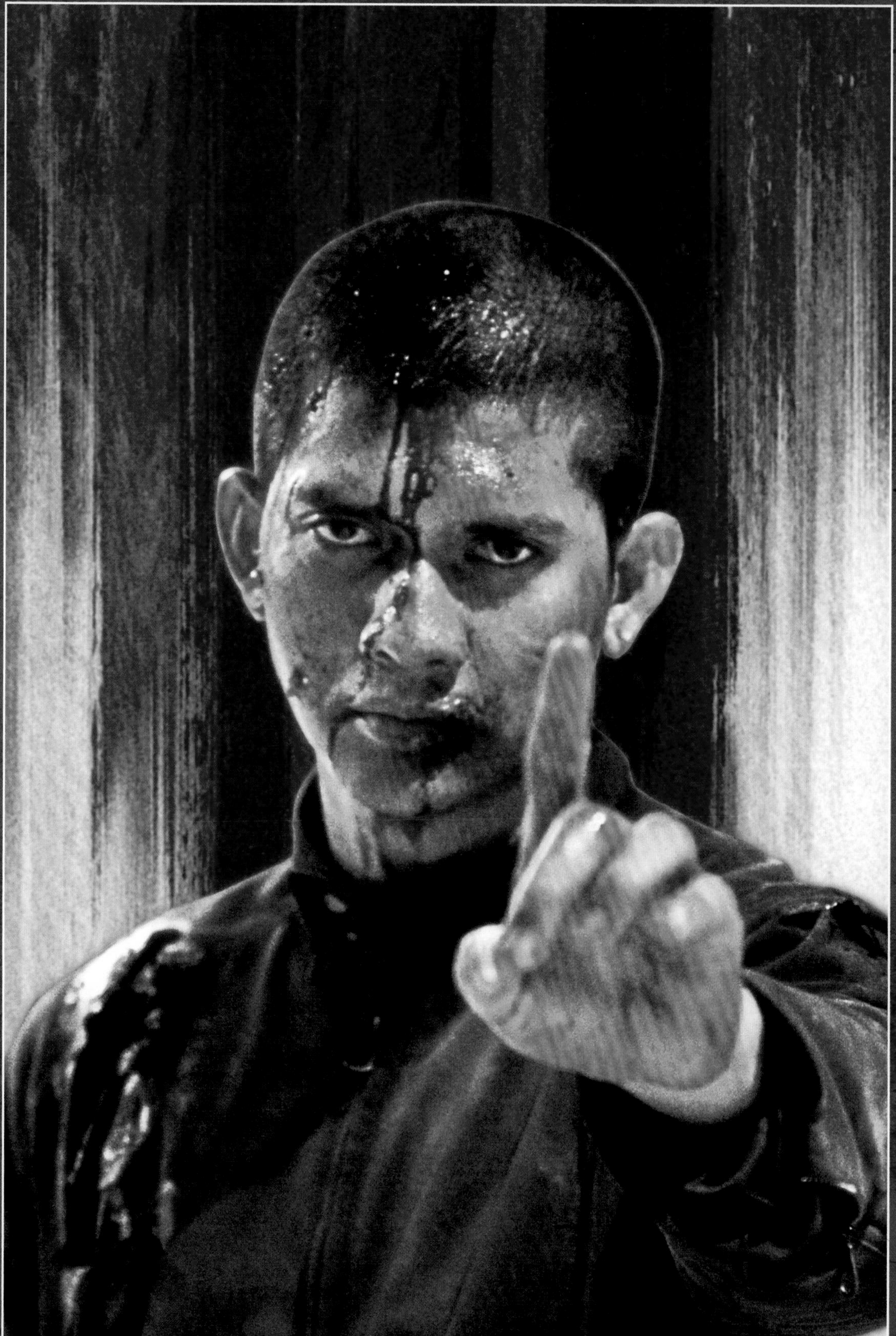

Cover 1b

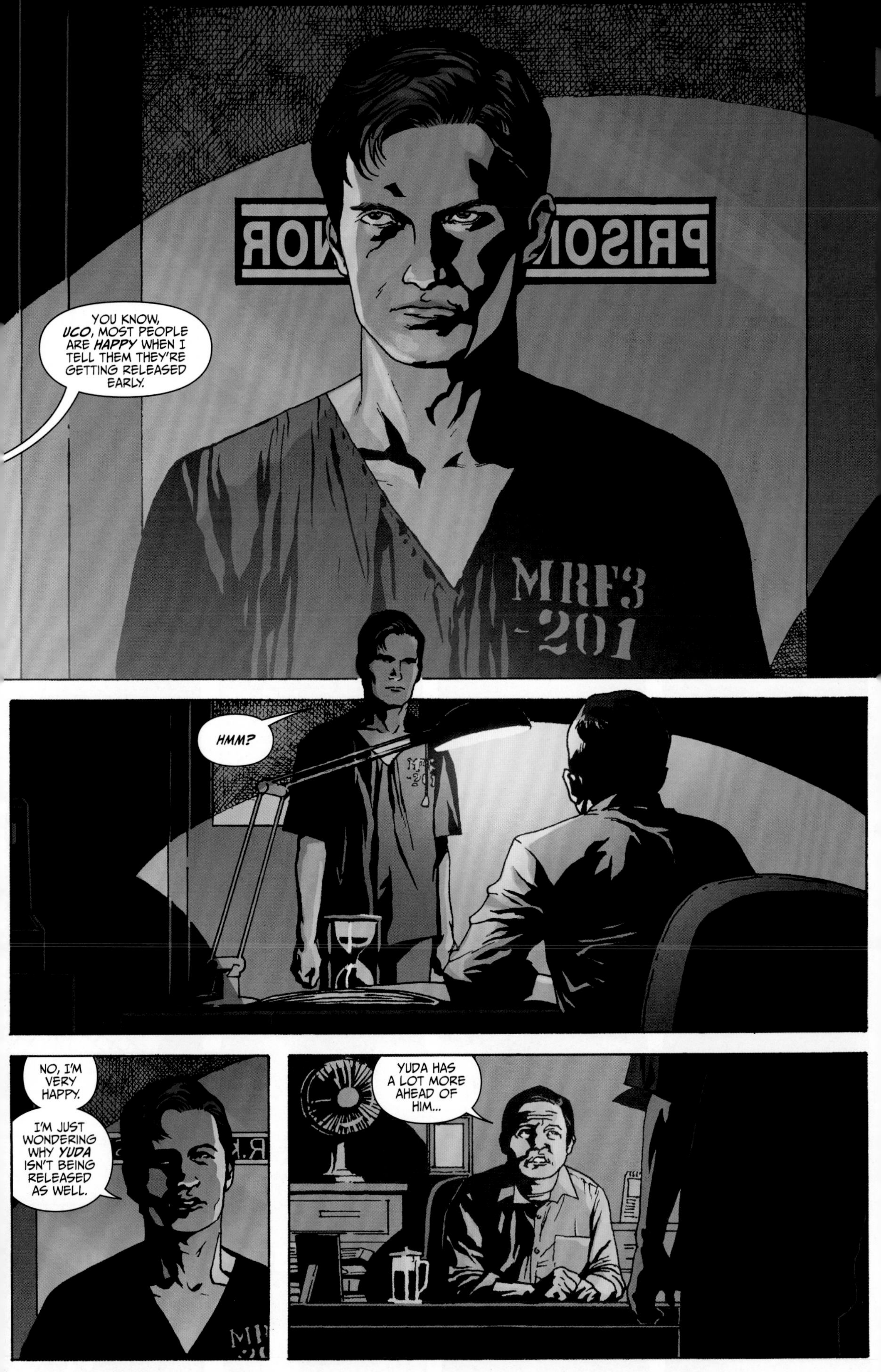

PRISONER (mirrored)
YOU KNOW, UCO, MOST PEOPLE ARE HAPPY WHEN I TELL THEM THEY'RE GETTING RELEASED EARLY.
MRF3 -201
HMM?
NO, I'M VERY HAPPY.
I'M JUST WONDERING WHY YUDA ISN'T BEING RELEASED AS WELL.
YUDA HAS A LOT MORE AHEAD OF HIM...

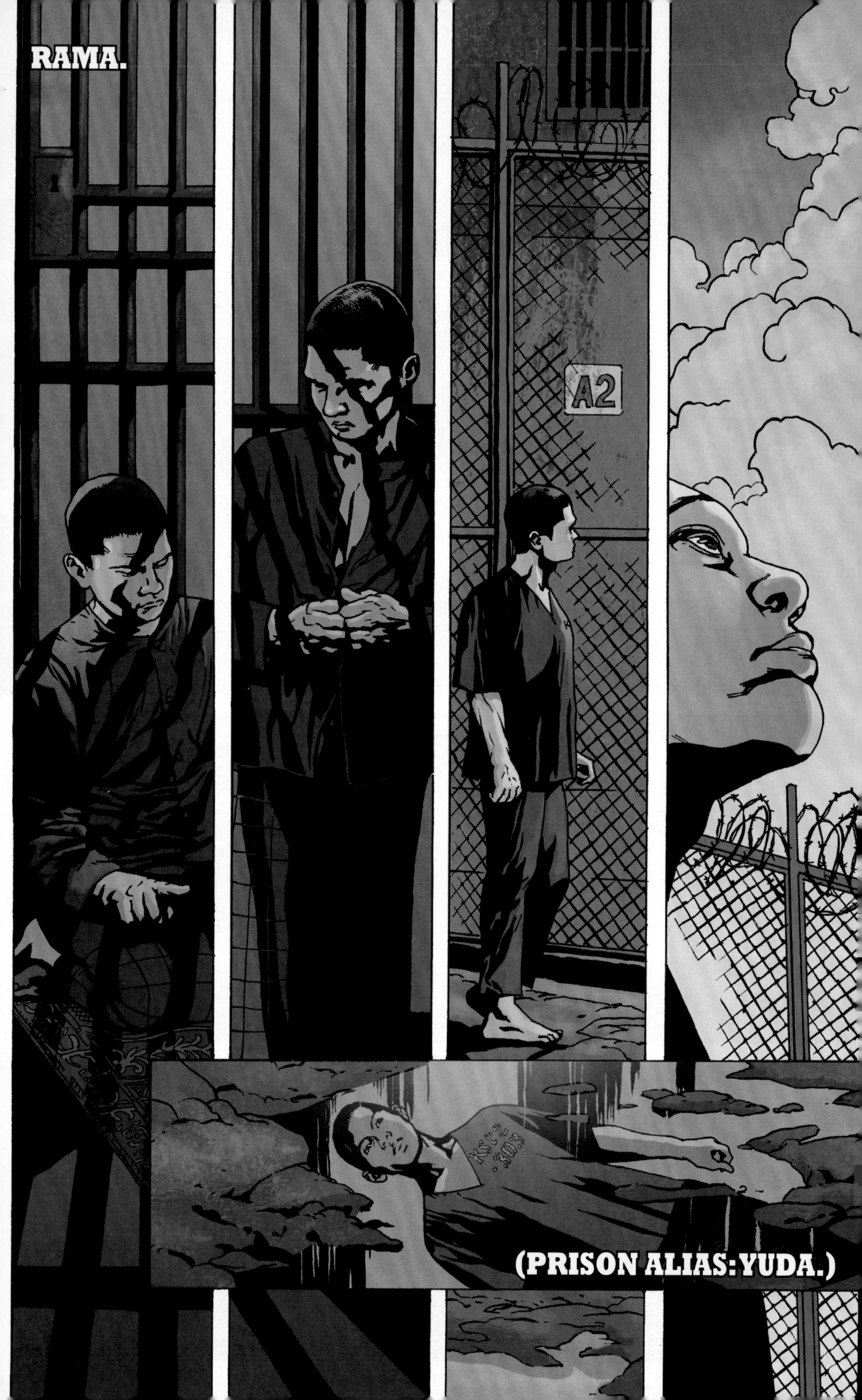
RAMA.
A2
(PRISON ALIAS: YUDA.)

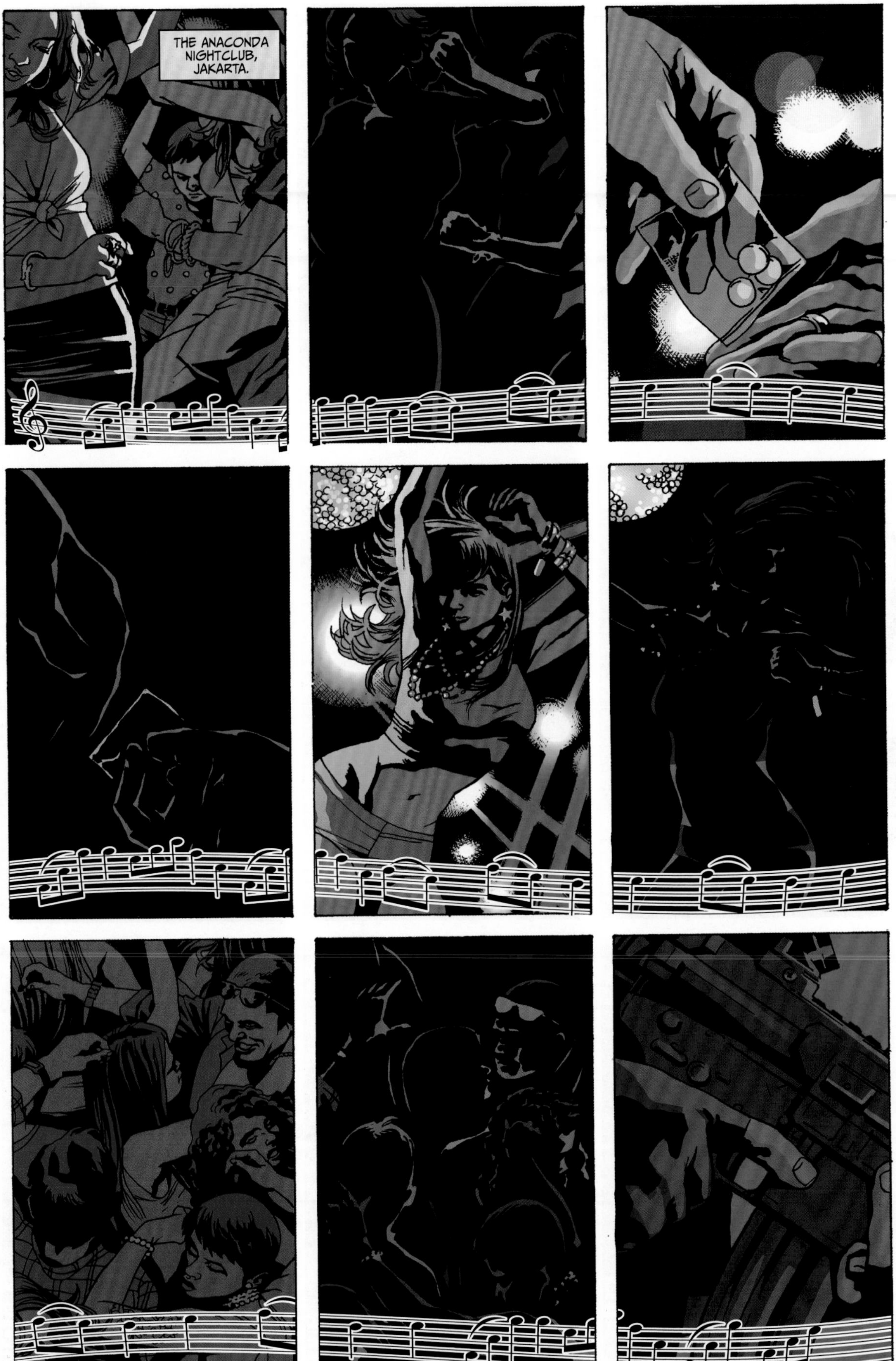
THE ANACONDA NIGHTCLUB, JAKARTA.

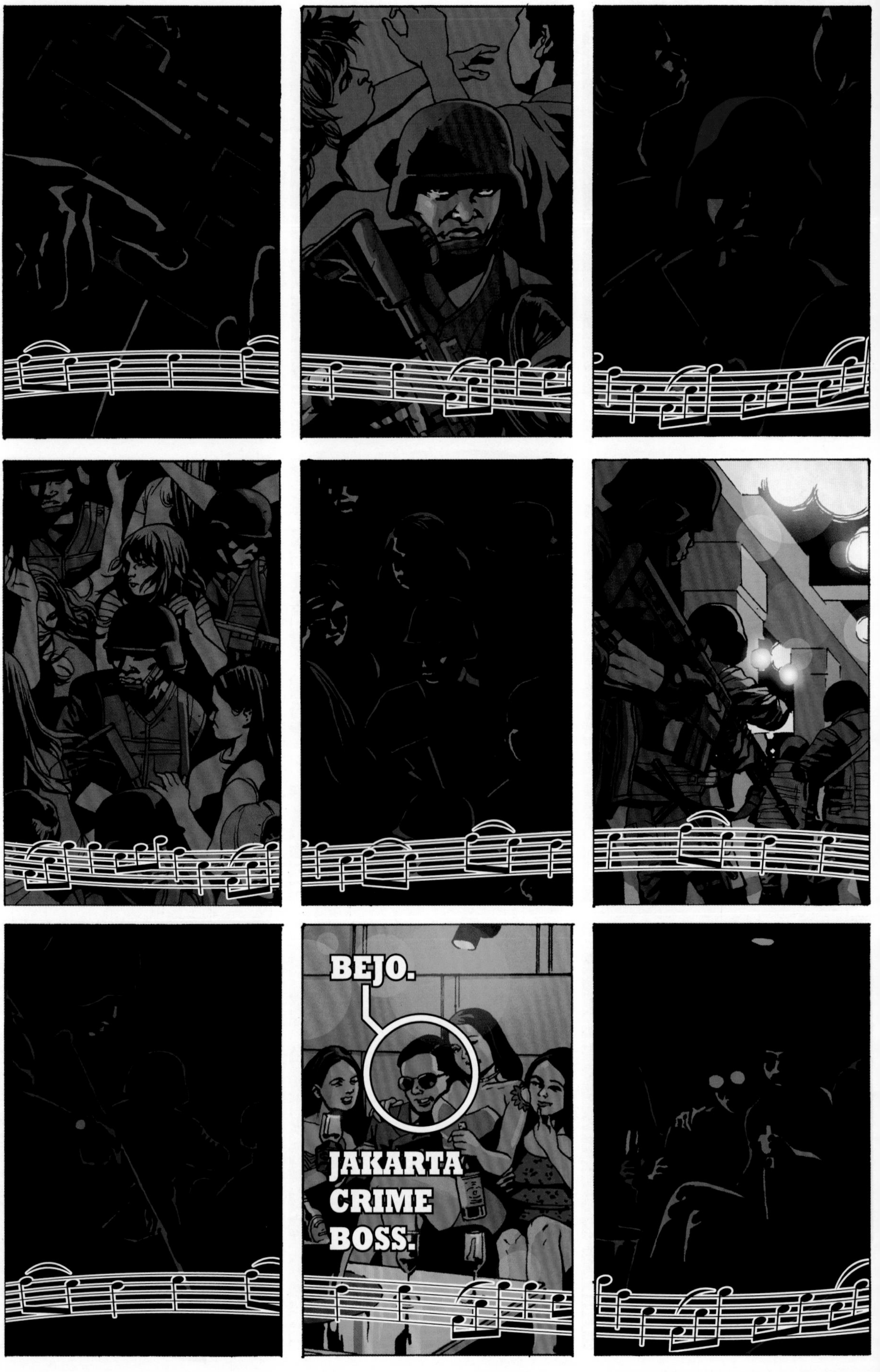
BEJO.
JAKARTA CRIME BOSS.

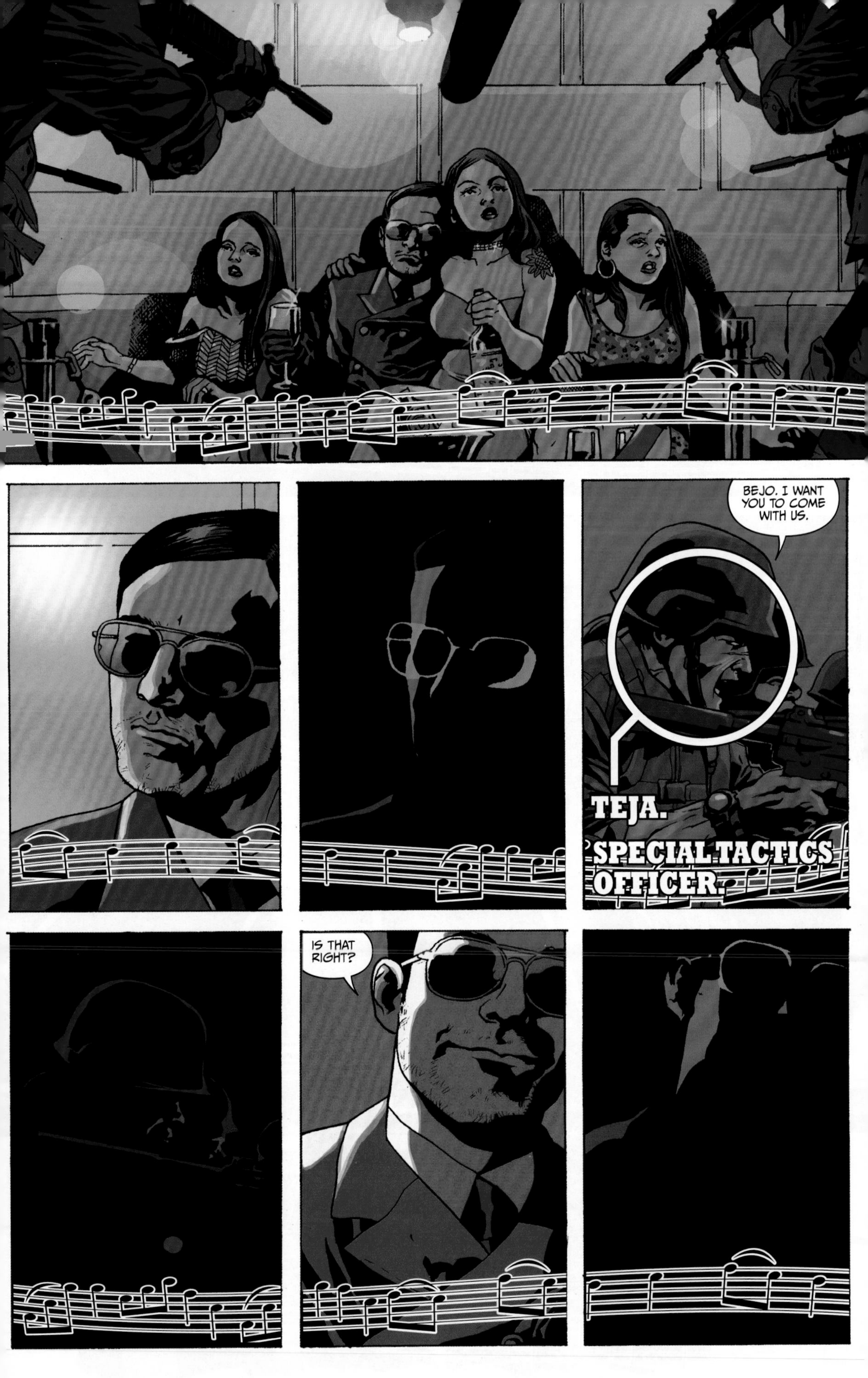
BEJO. I WANT YOU TO COME WITH US.
TEJA.
SPECIAL TACTICS OFFICER.
IS THAT RIGHT?

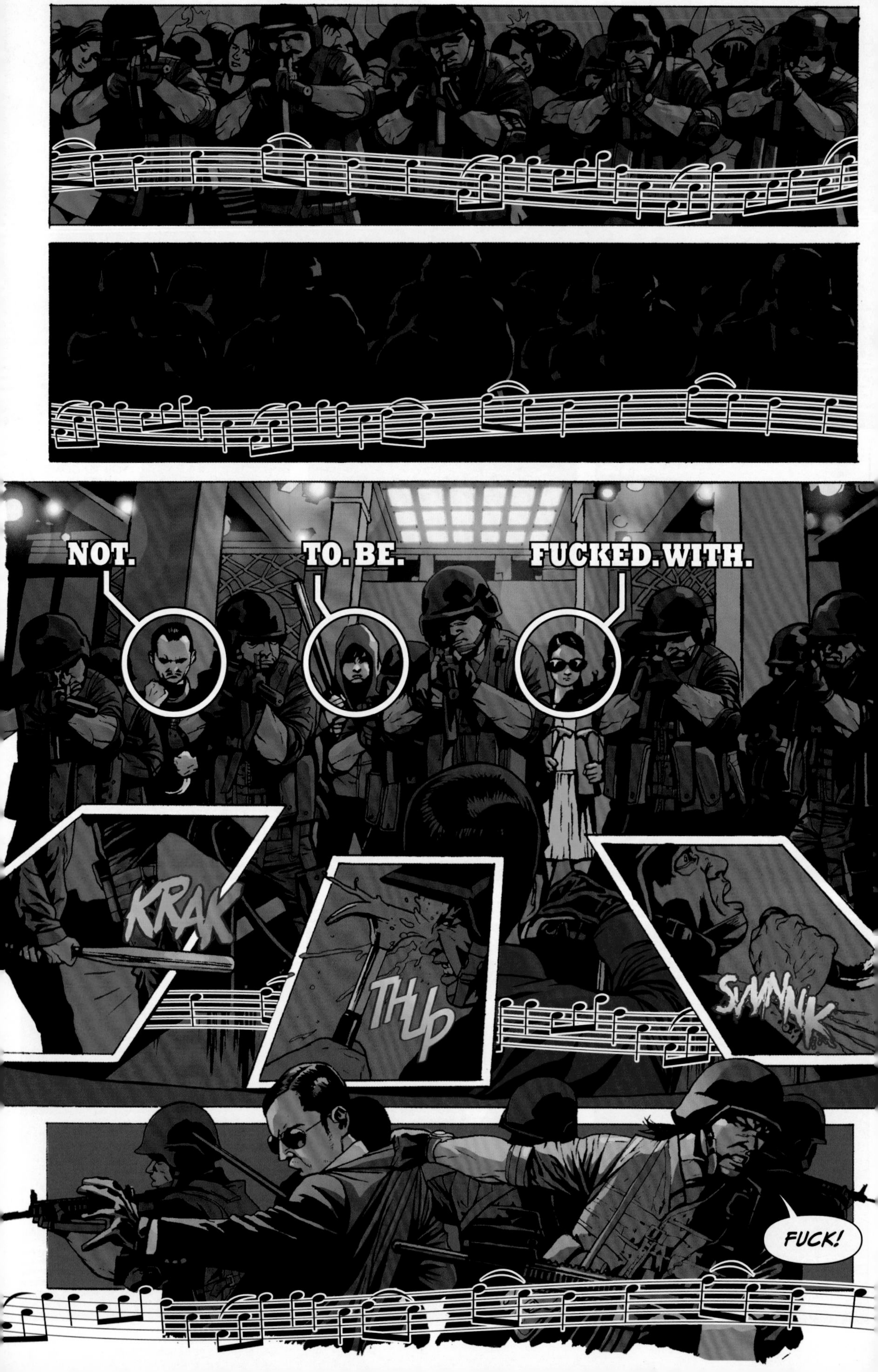
NOT.
TO. BE.
FUCKED. WITH.
KRAK
THUP
SWNNK
FUCK!

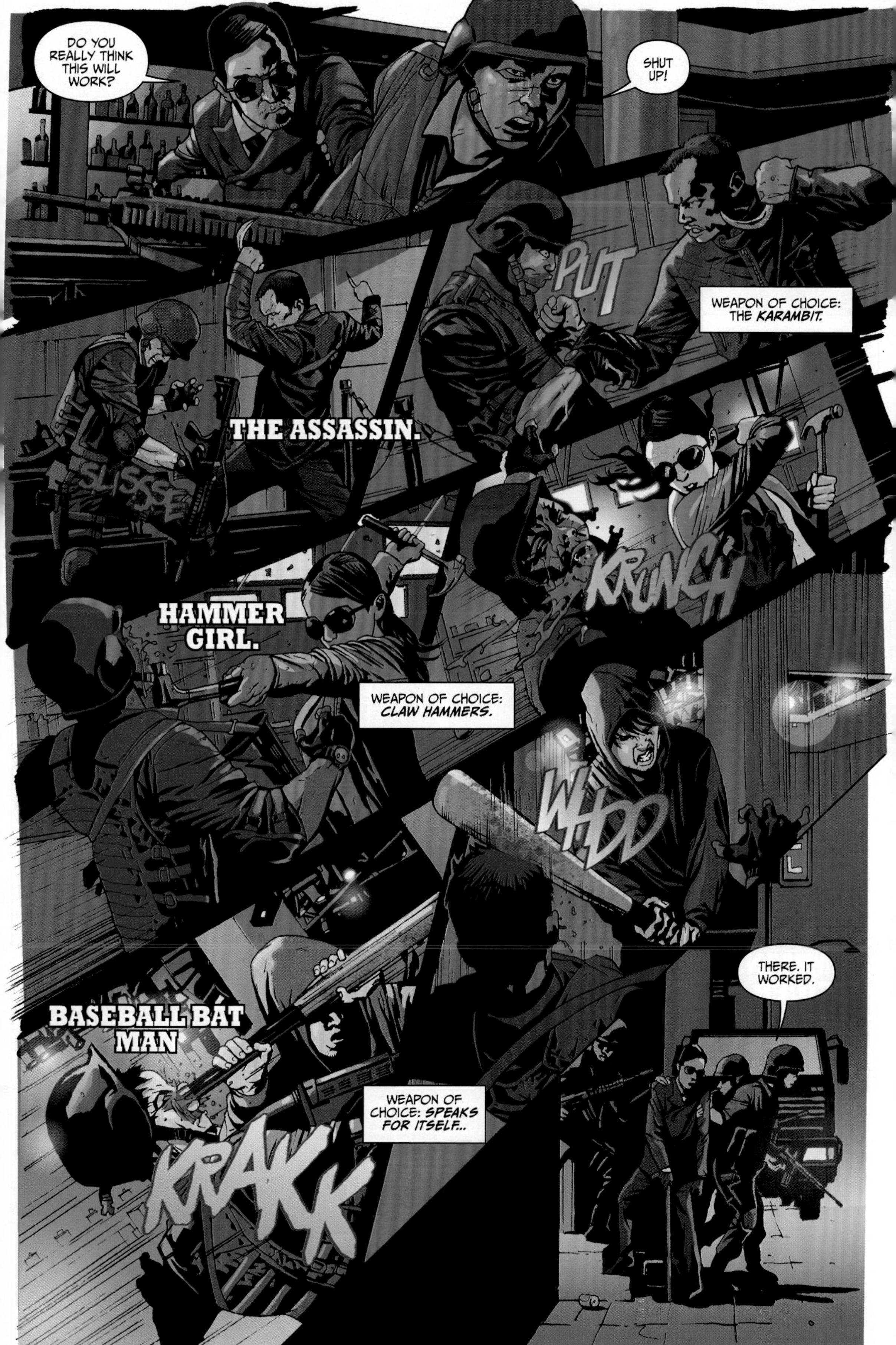
DO YOU REALLY THINK THIS WILL WORK?
SHUT UP!
PUT
WEAPON OF CHOICE: THE *KARAMBIT.*
THE ASSASSIN.
SLISSSE
KRUNCH
HAMMER GIRL.
WEAPON OF CHOICE: *CLAW HAMMERS.*
WHDD
THERE. IT WORKED.
BASEBALL BAT MAN
WEAPON OF CHOICE: *SPEAKS FOR ITSELF...*
KRAKK

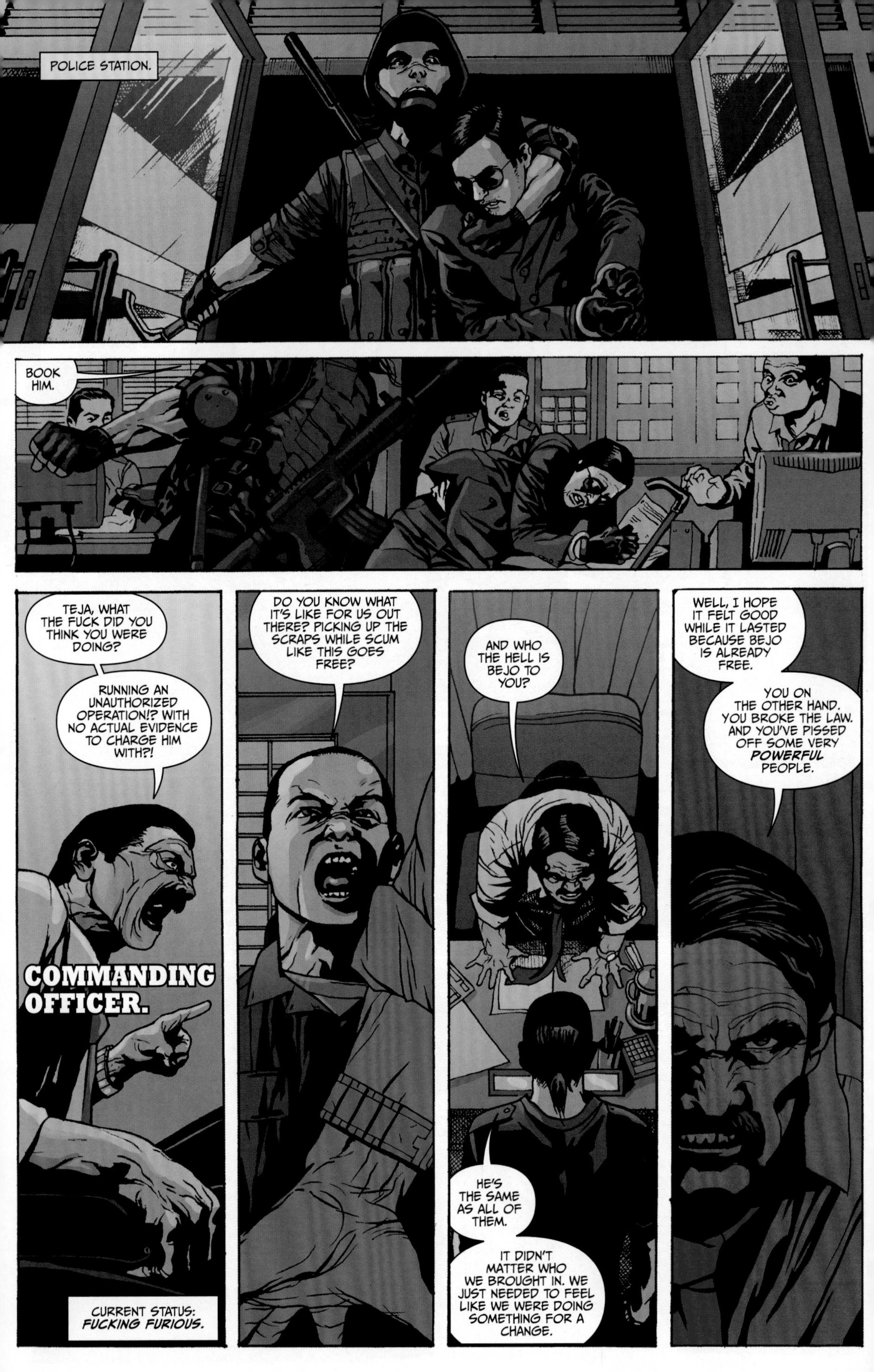
POLICE STATION.
BOOK HIM.
TEJA, WHAT THE FUCK DID YOU THINK YOU WERE DOING?
RUNNING AN UNAUTHORIZED OPERATION!? WITH NO ACTUAL EVIDENCE TO CHARGE HIM WITH?!
COMMANDING OFFICER.
CURRENT STATUS: *FUCKING FURIOUS.*
DO YOU KNOW WHAT IT'S LIKE FOR US OUT THERE? PICKING UP THE SCRAPS WHILE SCUM LIKE THIS GOES FREE?
AND WHO THE HELL IS BEJO TO YOU?
HE'S THE SAME AS ALL OF THEM.
IT DIDN'T MATTER WHO WE BROUGHT IN. WE JUST NEEDED TO FEEL LIKE WE WERE DOING SOMETHING FOR A CHANGE.
WELL, I HOPE IT FELT GOOD WHILE IT LASTED BECAUSE BEJO IS ALREADY FREE.
YOU ON THE OTHER HAND. YOU BROKE THE LAW. AND YOU'VE PISSED OFF SOME VERY *POWERFUL* PEOPLE.

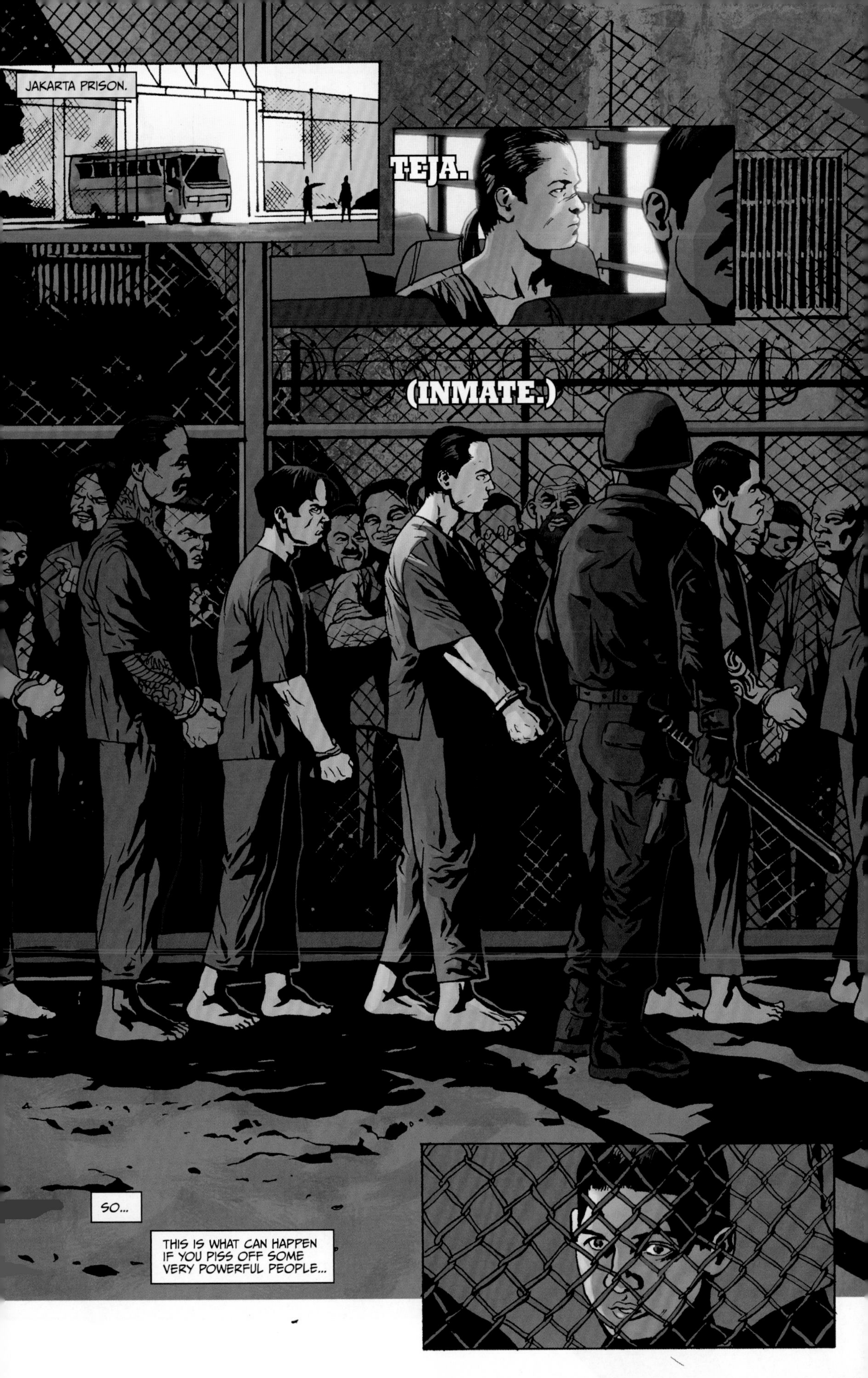

JAKARTA PRISON.
TEJA.
(INMATE.)
SO...
THIS IS WHAT CAN HAPPEN IF YOU PISS OFF SOME VERY POWERFUL PEOPLE...

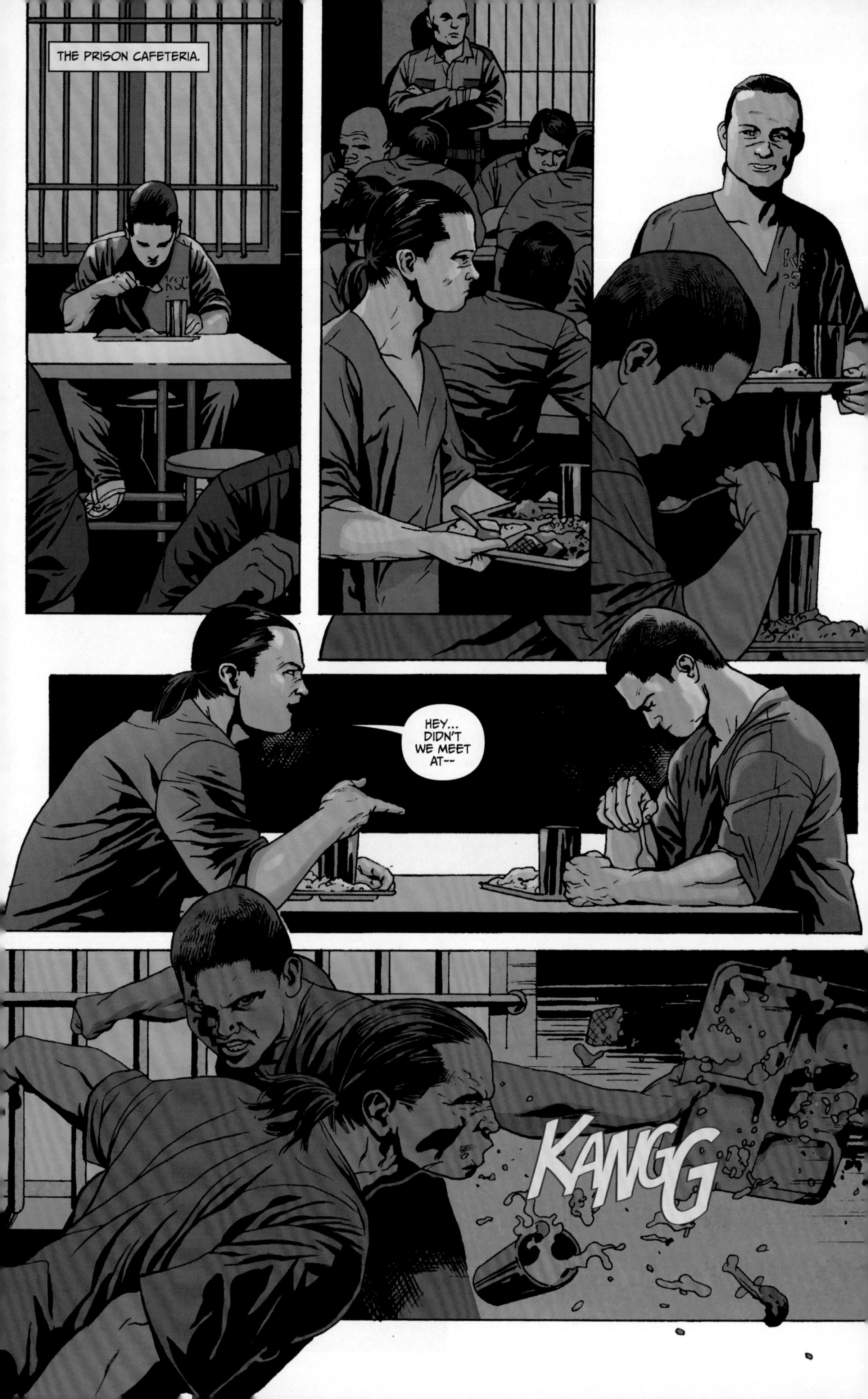
THE PRISON CAFETERIA.
HEY... DIDN'T WE MEET AT--
KANGG

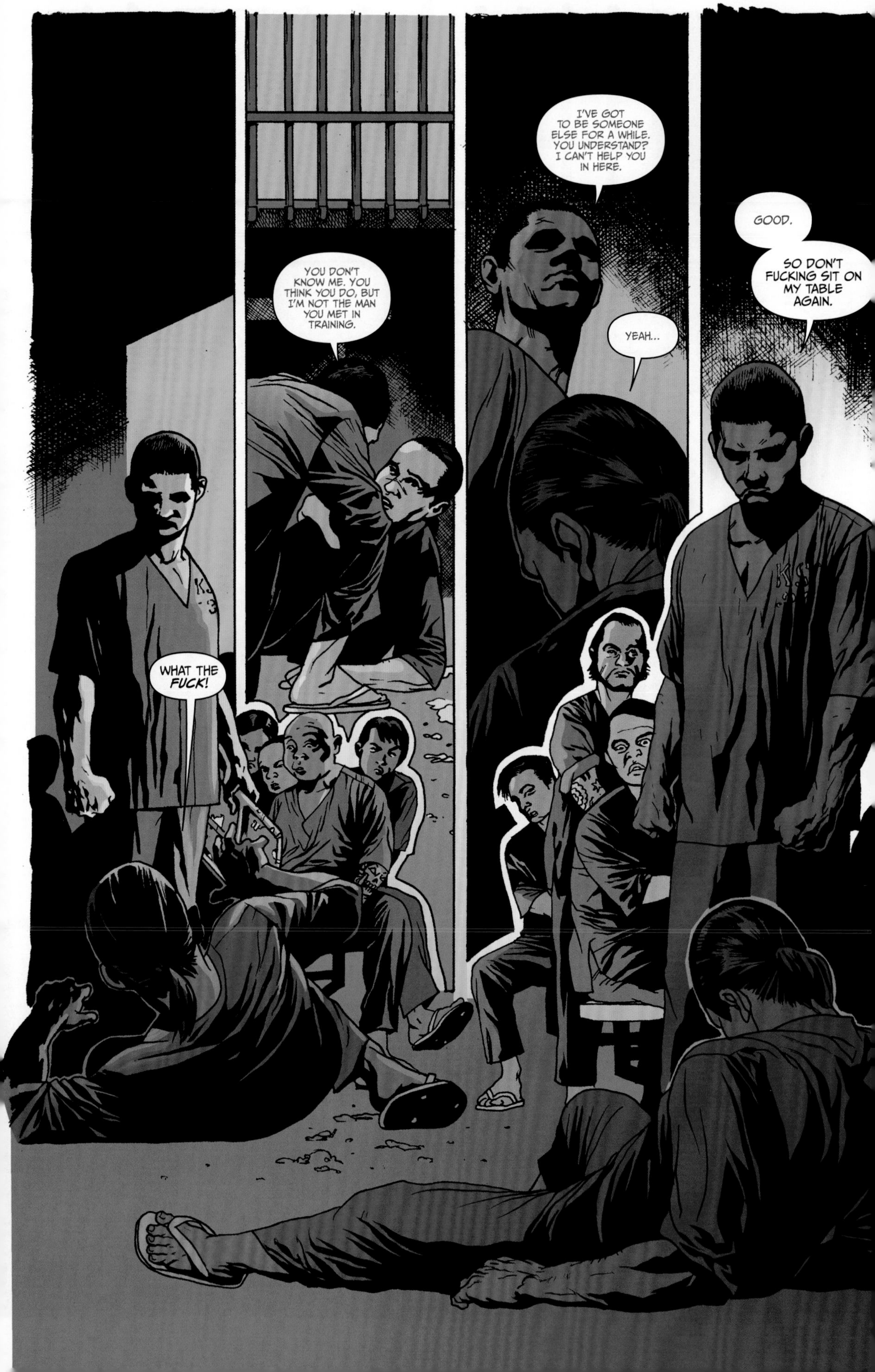
WHAT THE FUCK!
YOU DON'T KNOW ME. YOU THINK YOU DO, BUT I'M NOT THE MAN YOU MET IN TRAINING.
I'VE GOT TO BE SOMEONE ELSE FOR A WHILE. YOU UNDERSTAND? I CAN'T HELP YOU IN HERE.
YEAH...
GOOD.
SO DON'T FUCKING SIT ON MY TABLE AGAIN.

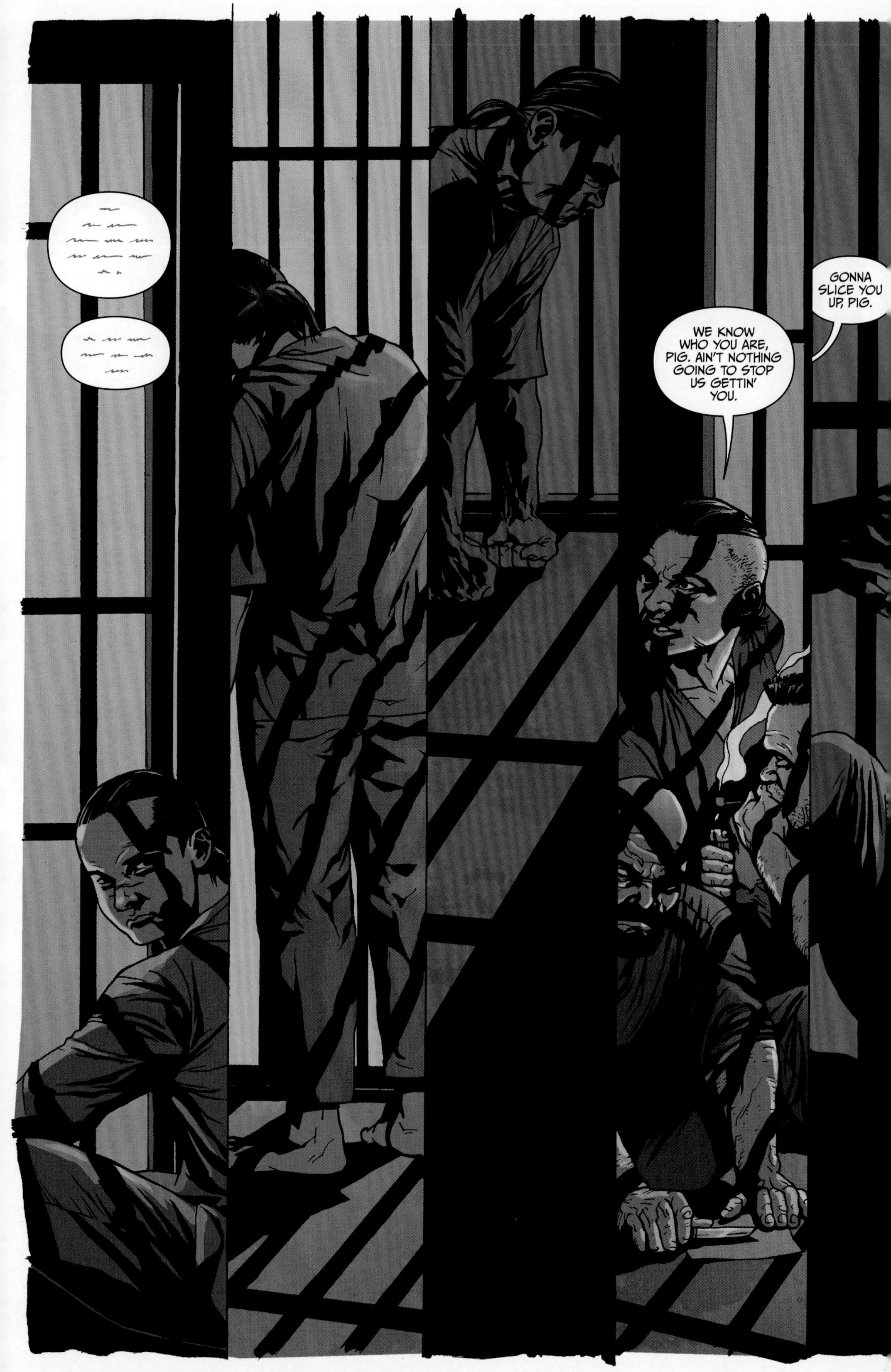
WE KNOW WHO YOU ARE, PIG. AIN'T NOTHING GOING TO STOP US GETTIN' YOU.
GONNA SLICE YOU UP, PIG.

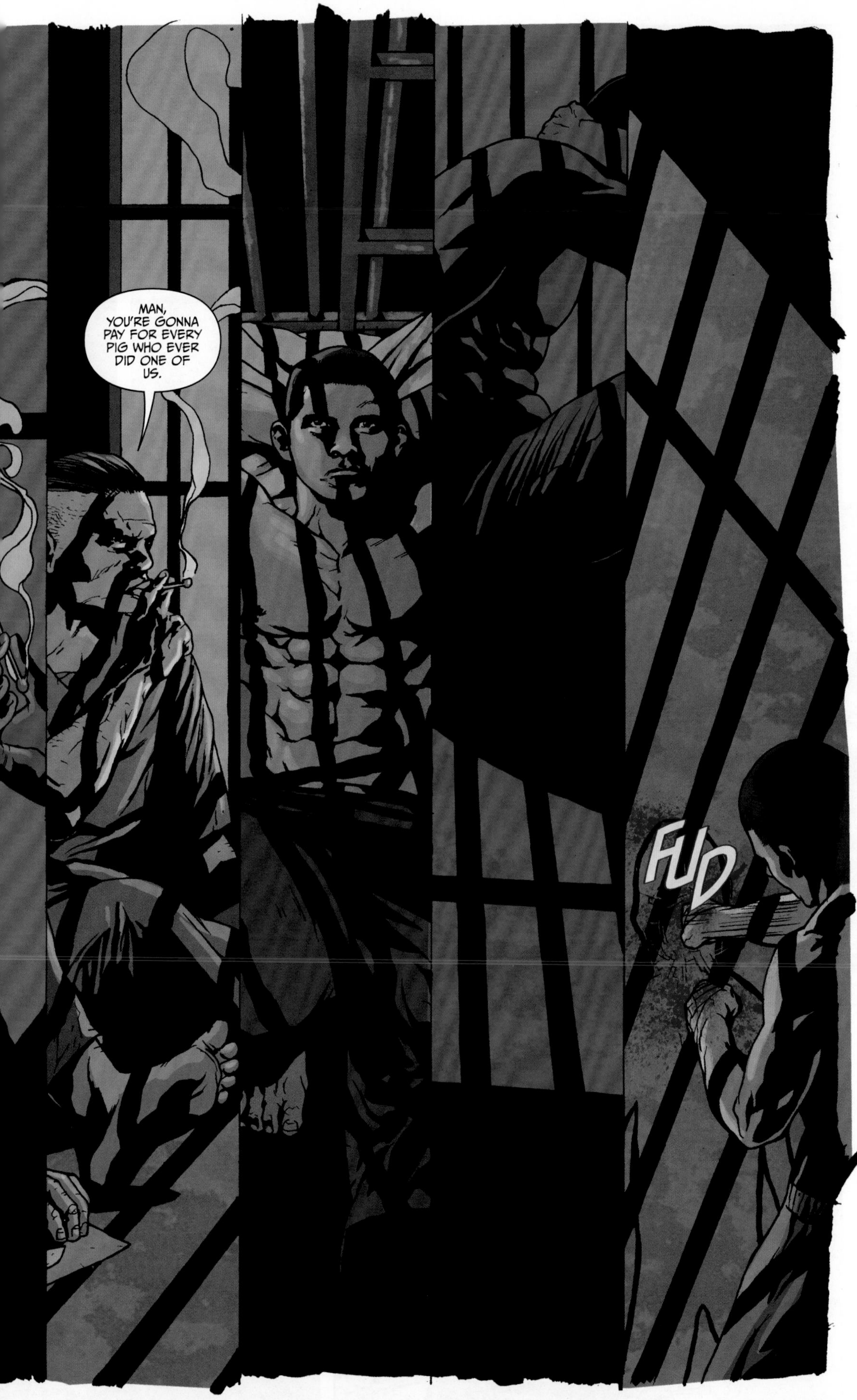
MAN, YOU'RE GONNA PAY FOR EVERY PIG WHO EVER DID ONE OF US.
FUD

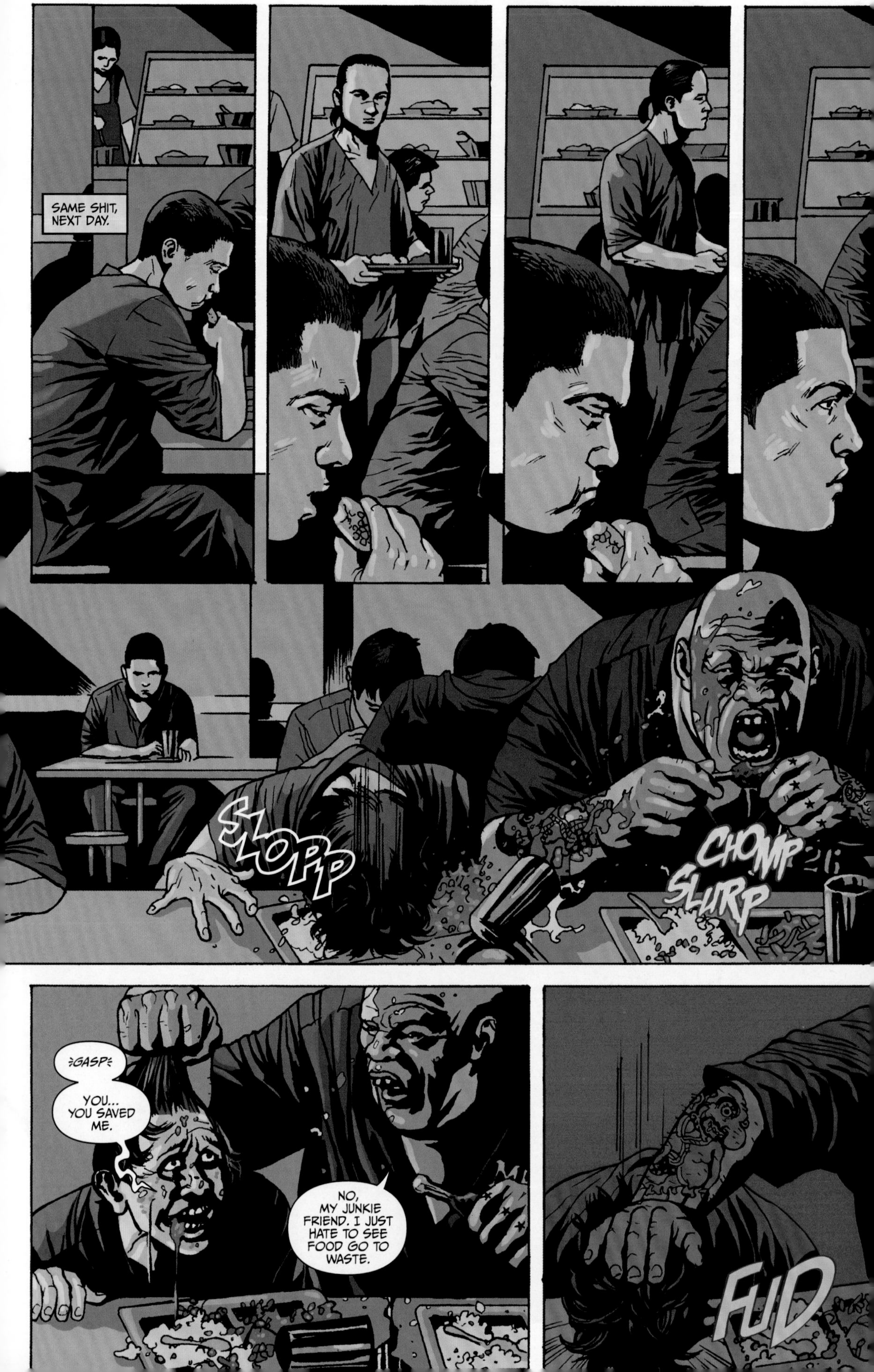
SAME SHIT, NEXT DAY.
SLOPP
CHOMP
SLURP
GASP
YOU... YOU SAVED ME.
NO, MY JUNKIE FRIEND. I JUST HATE TO SEE FOOD GO TO WASTE.
FUD

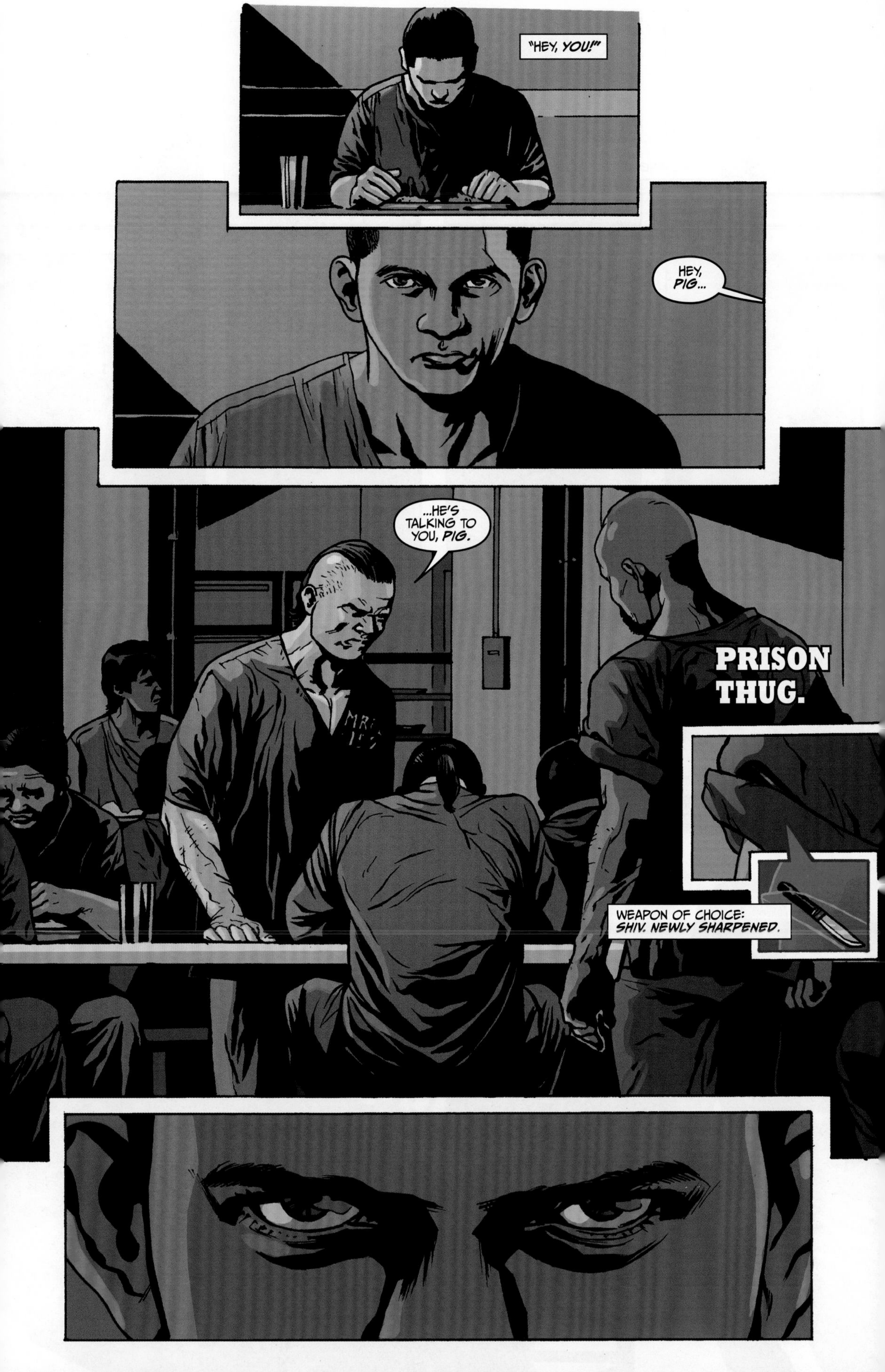
"HEY, *YOU!*"
HEY, *PIG*...
...HE'S TALKING TO YOU, *PIG*.
PRISON THUG.
WEAPON OF CHOICE: *SHIV. NEWLY SHARPENED.*

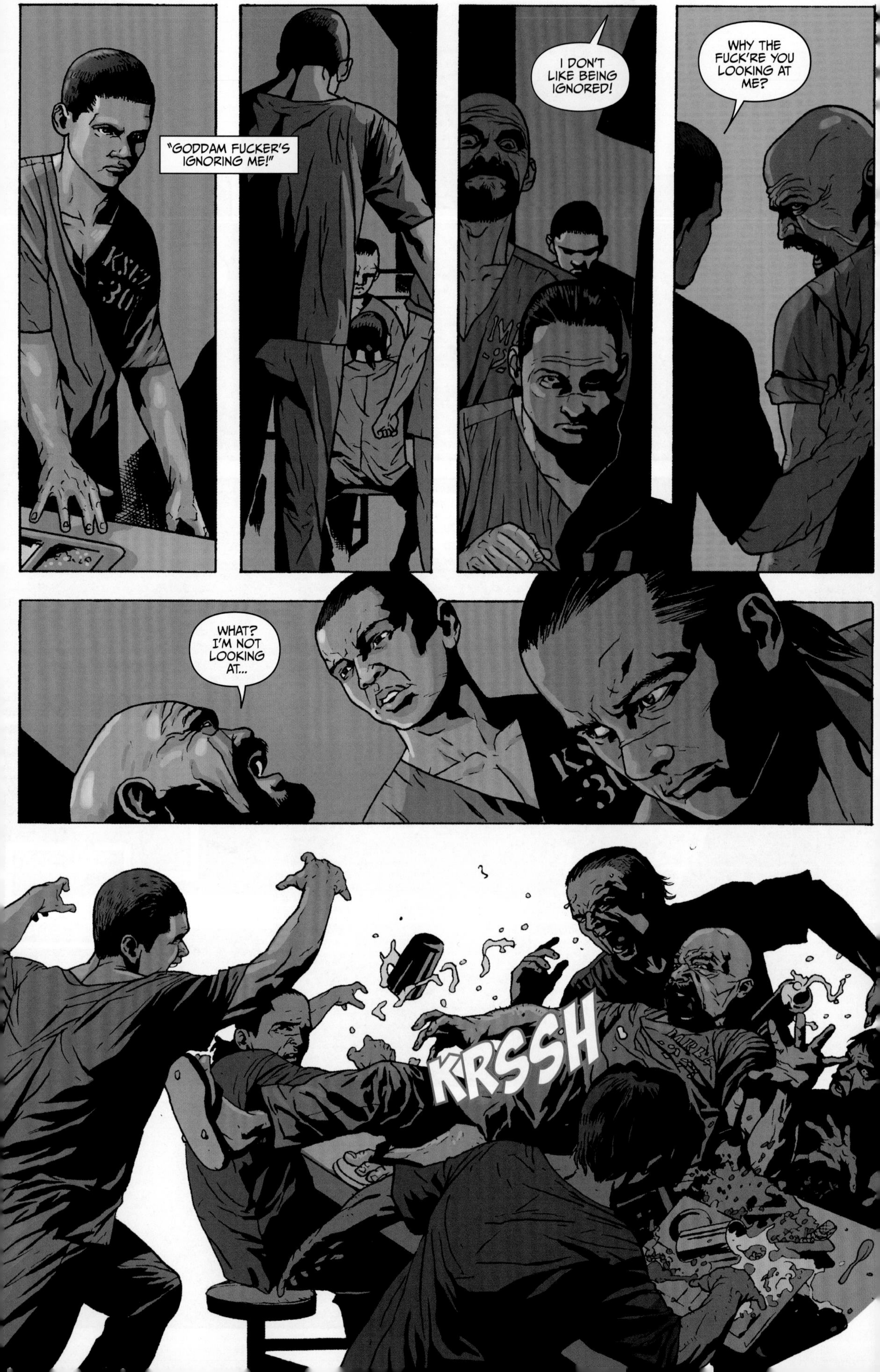
"GODDAM FUCKER'S IGNORING ME!"
I DON'T LIKE BEING IGNORED!
WHY THE FUCK'RE YOU LOOKING AT ME?
WHAT? I'M NOT LOOKING AT...
KRSSH

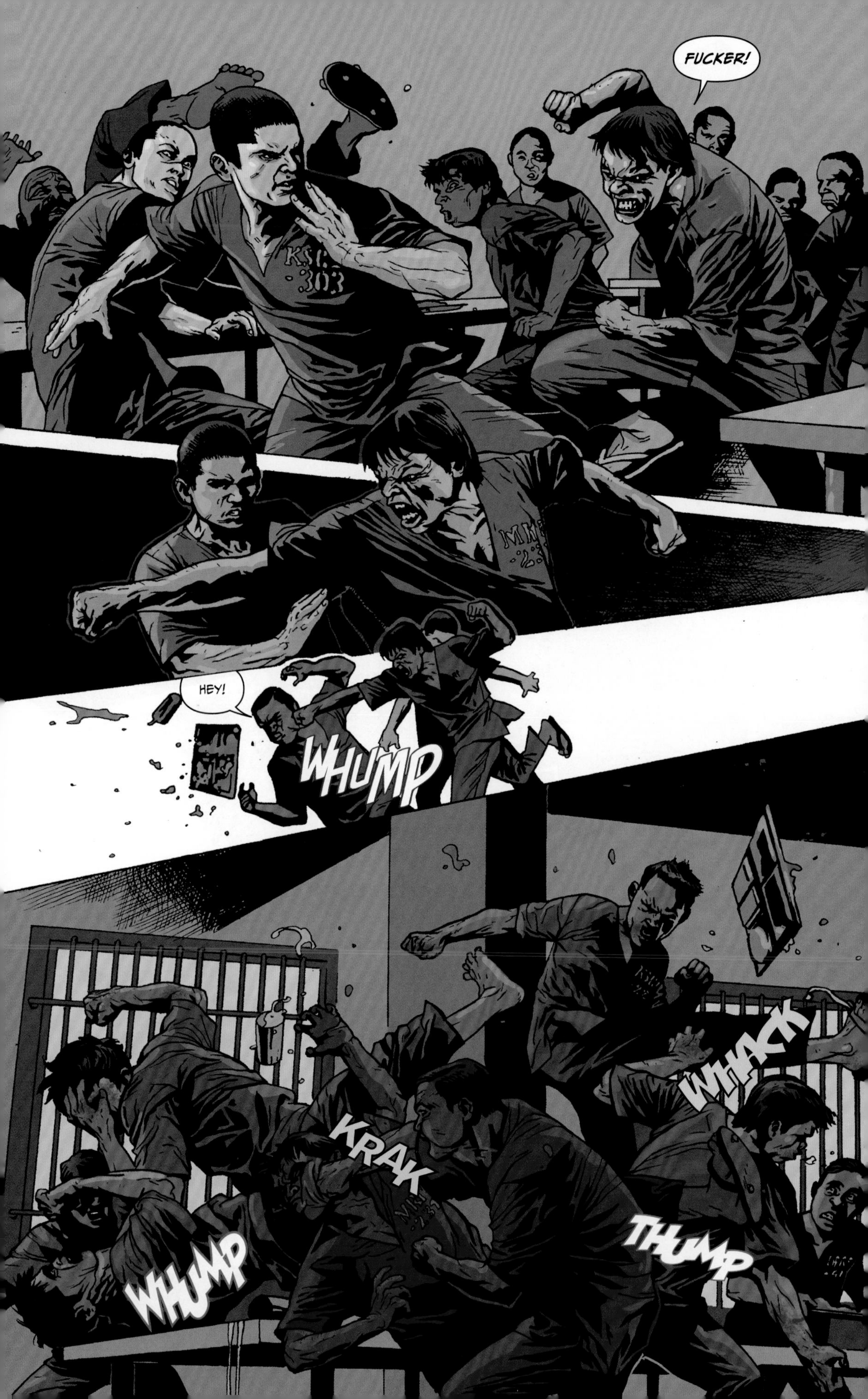
FUCKER!
HEY!
WHUMP
WHACK
KRAK
WHUMP
THUMP

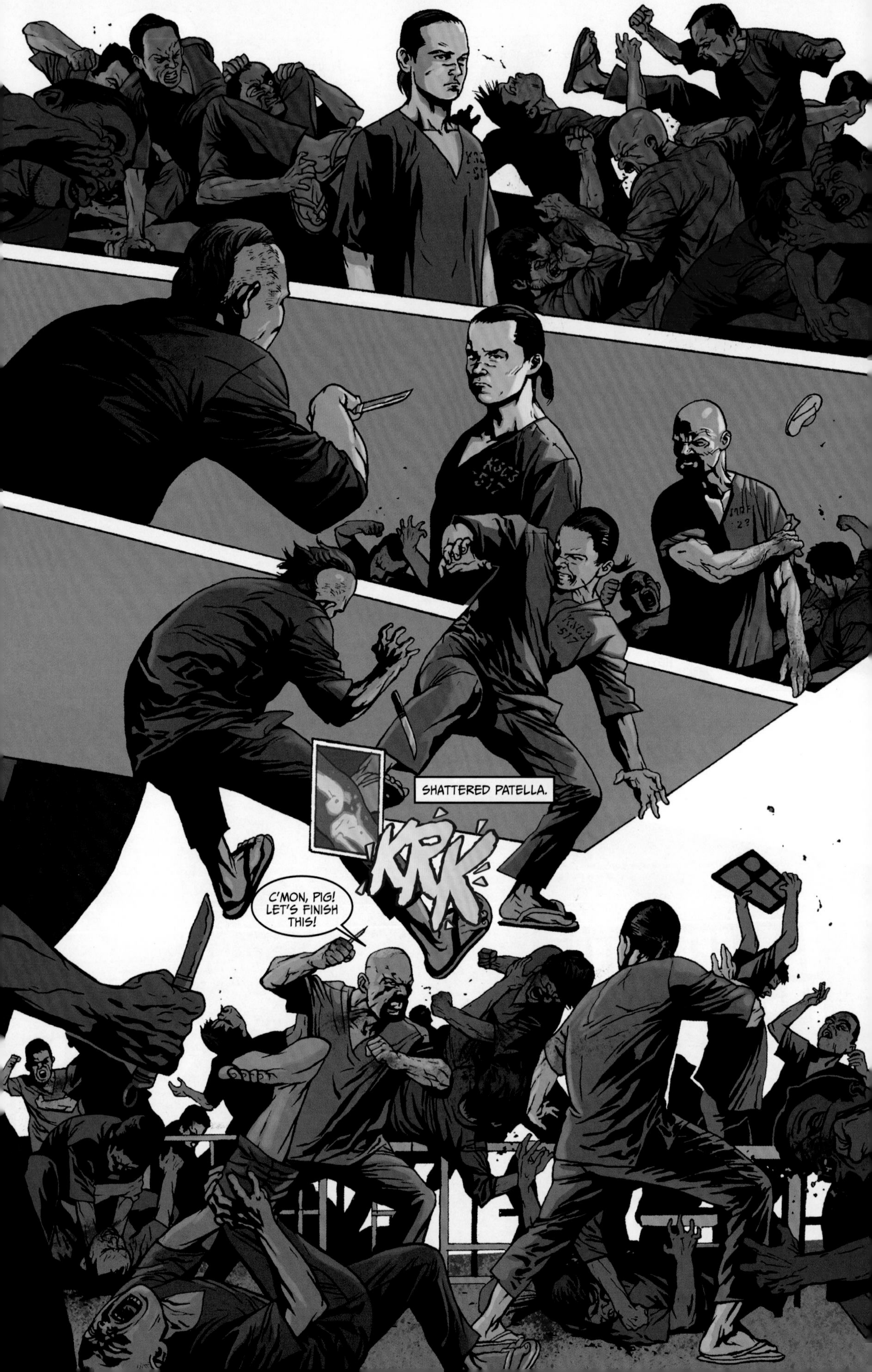
SHATTERED PATELLA.
KRK
C'MON, PIG! LET'S FINISH THIS!

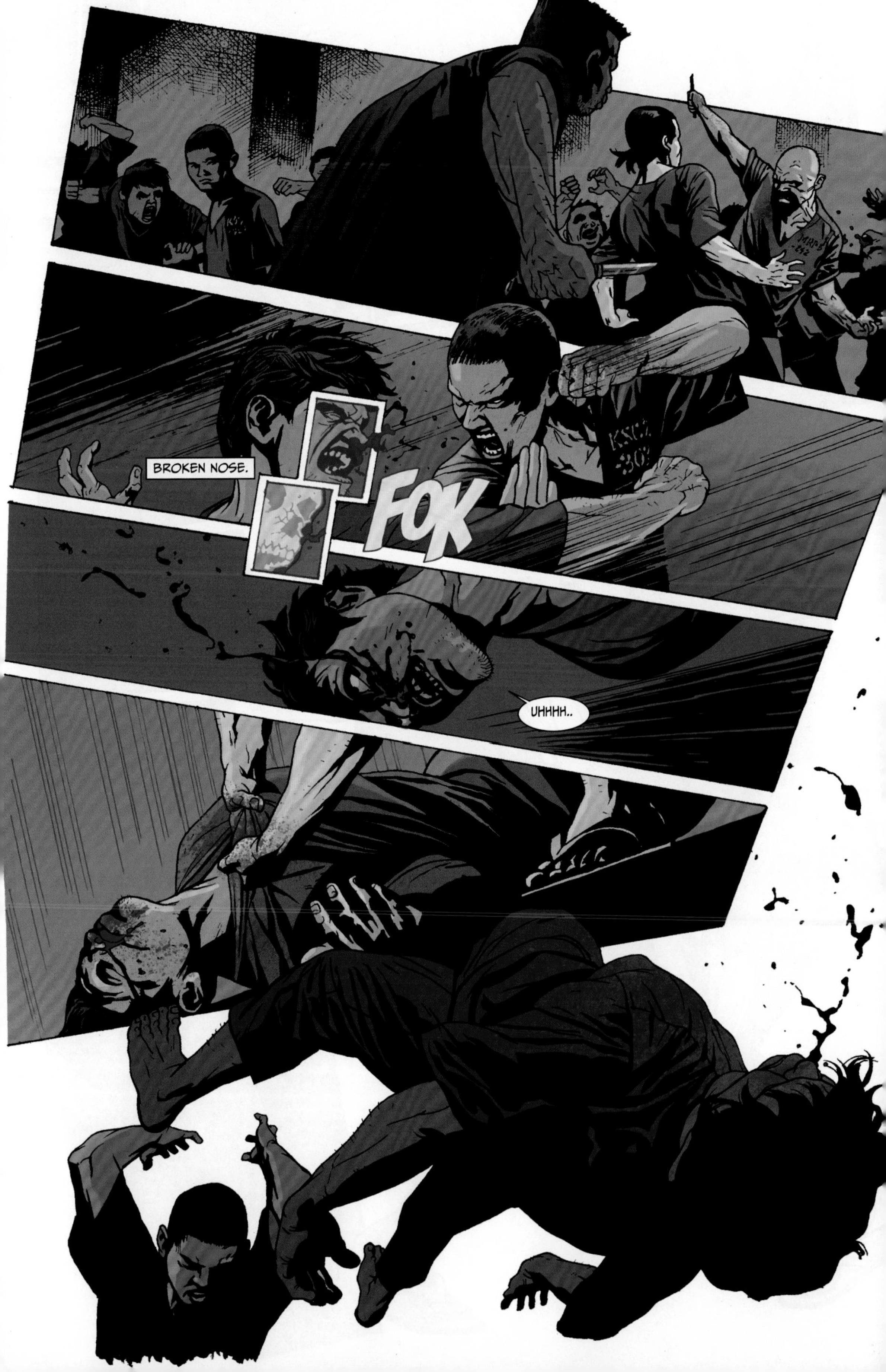
BROKEN NOSE.
FOK
UHHHH..

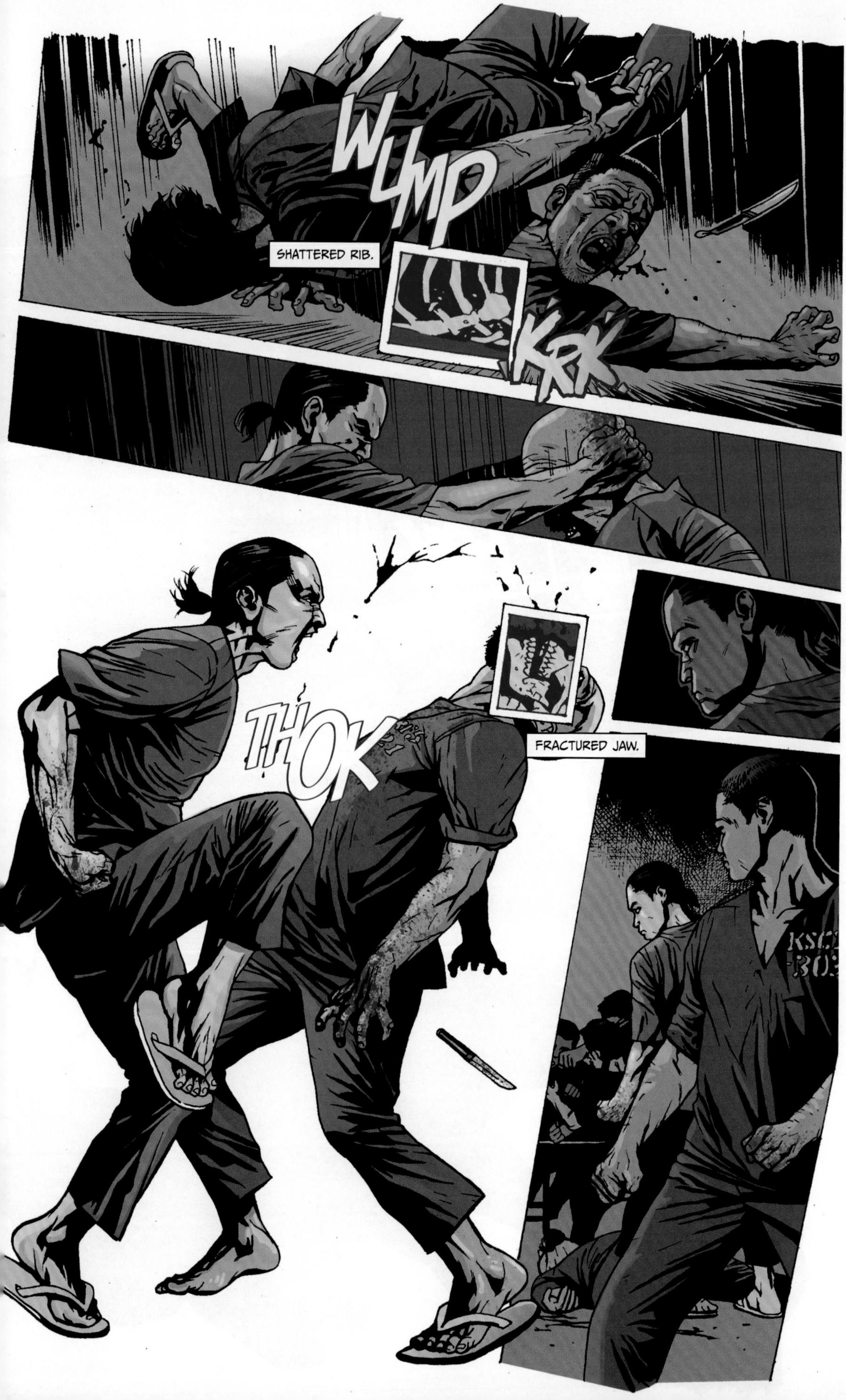
WUMP
SHATTERED RIB.
KRK
THOK
FRACTURED JAW.

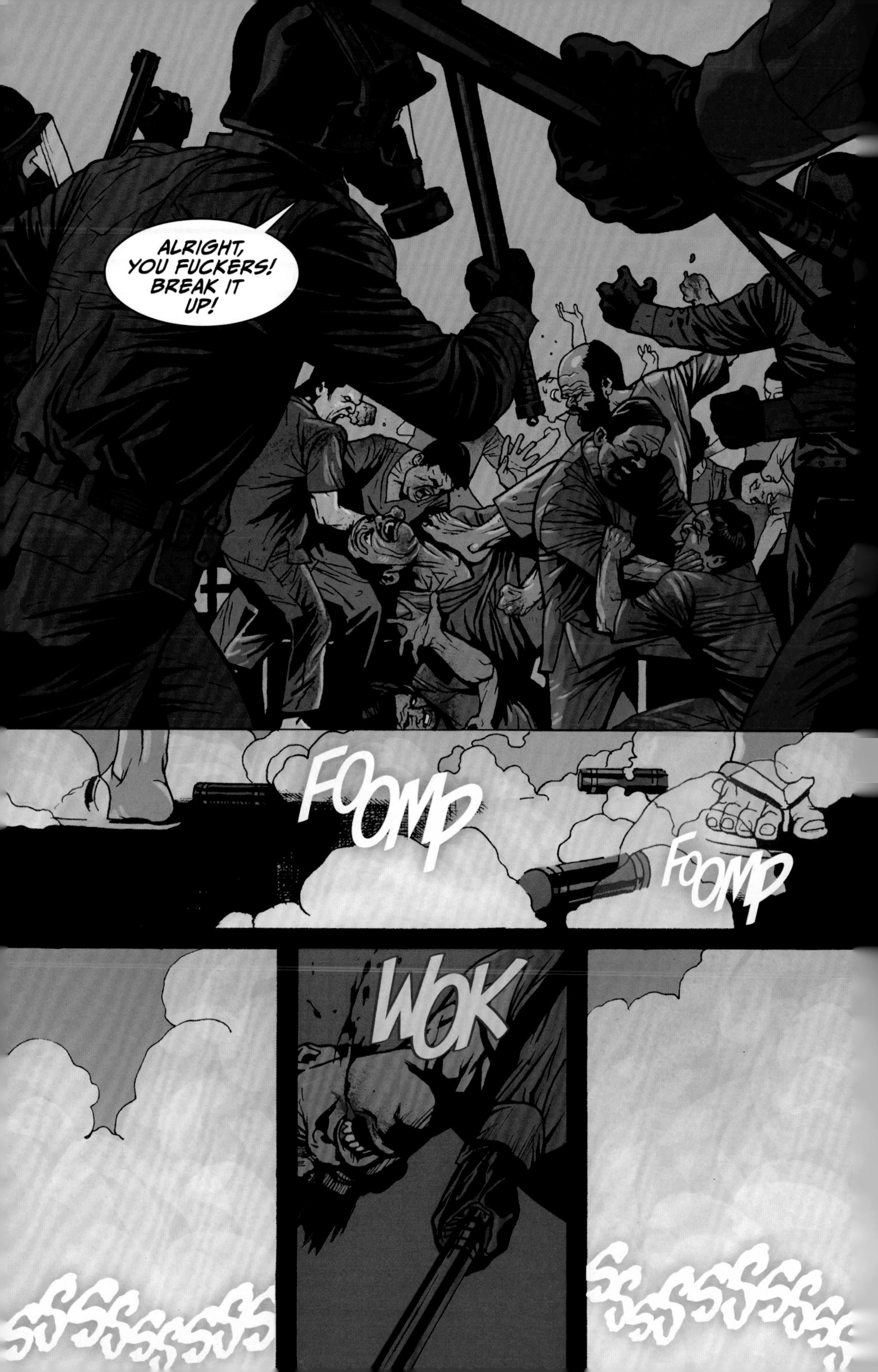
ALRIGHT, YOU FUCKERS! BREAK IT UP!
FOOMP
FOOMP
WOK
SSSSSSSSS
SSSSSSSSS

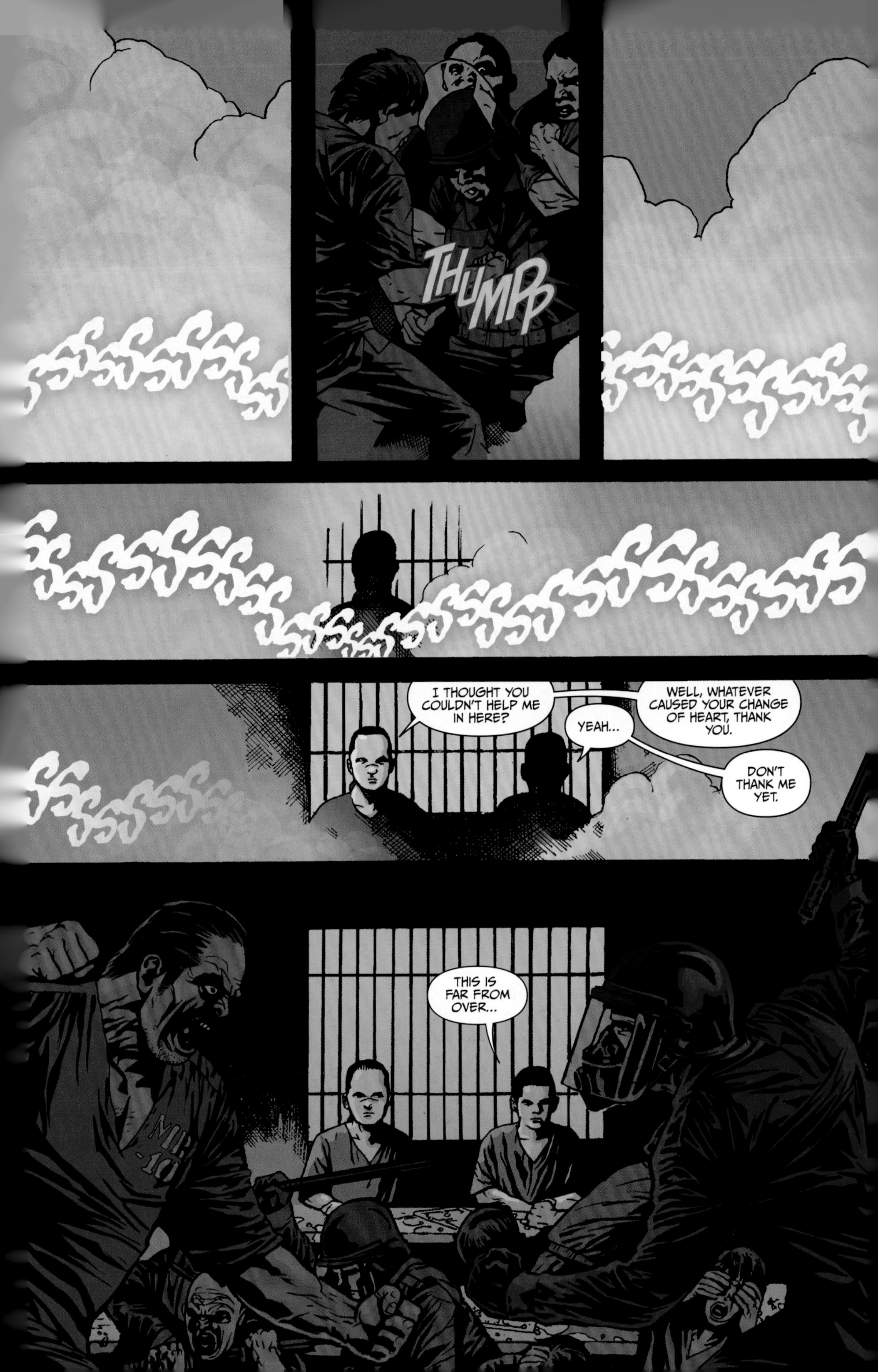
THUMPP
I THOUGHT YOU COULDN'T HELP ME IN HERE?
YEAH...
WELL, WHATEVER CAUSED YOUR CHANGE OF HEART, THANK YOU.
DON'T THANK ME YET.
THIS IS FAR FROM OVER...

CHAPTER 2

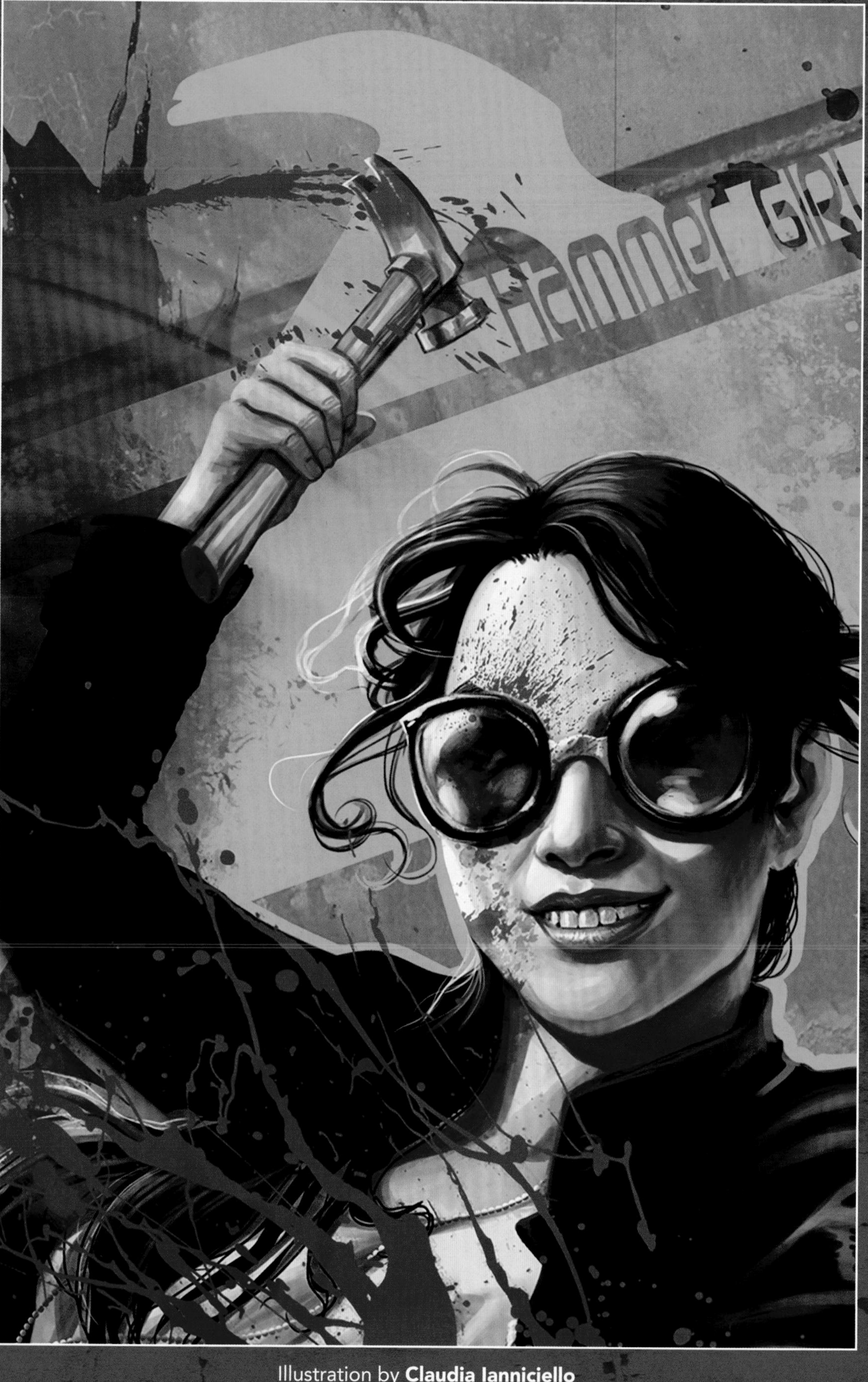
Hammer Girl

Illustration by **Claudia Ianniciello**

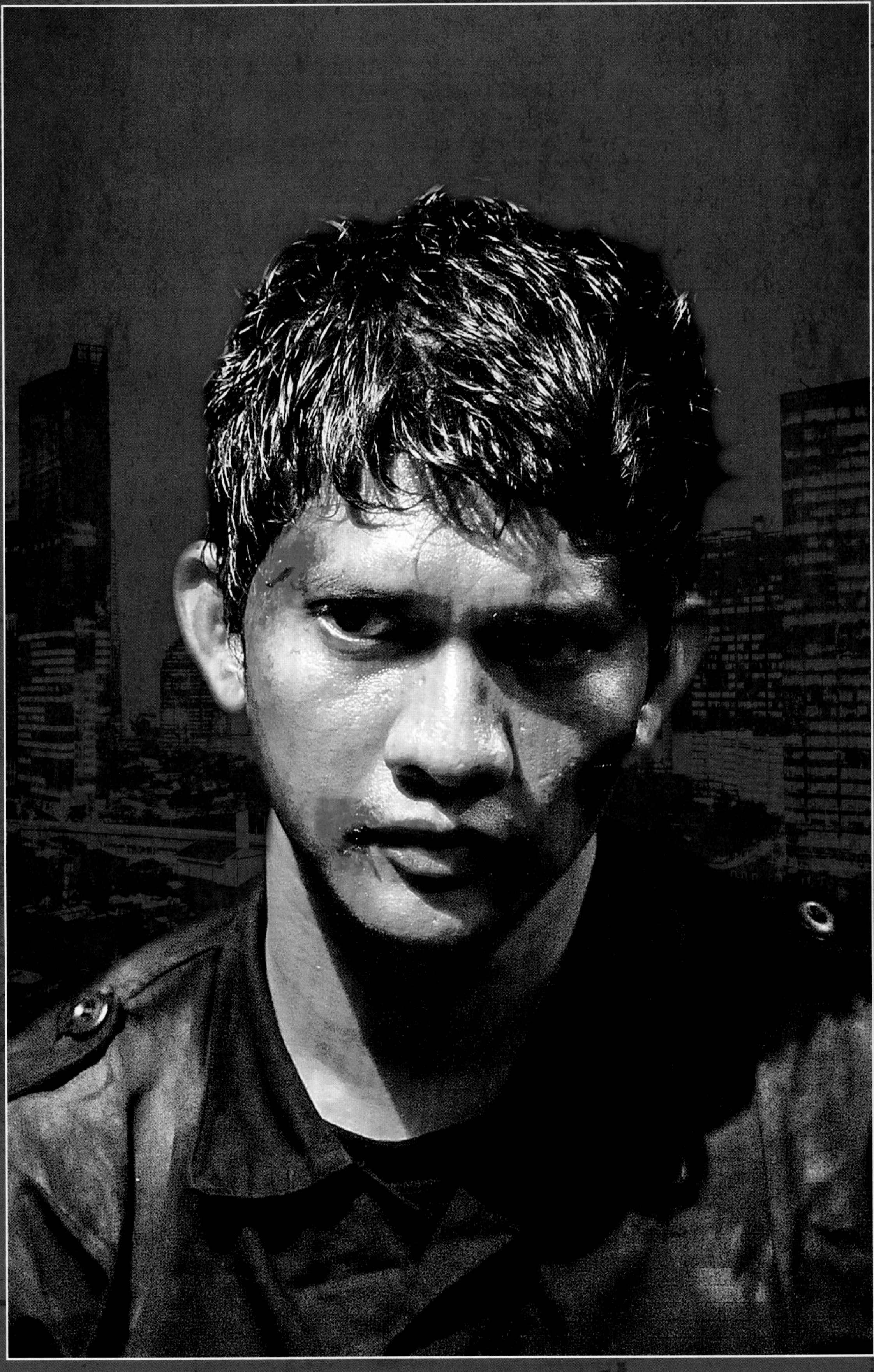

Cover 2b

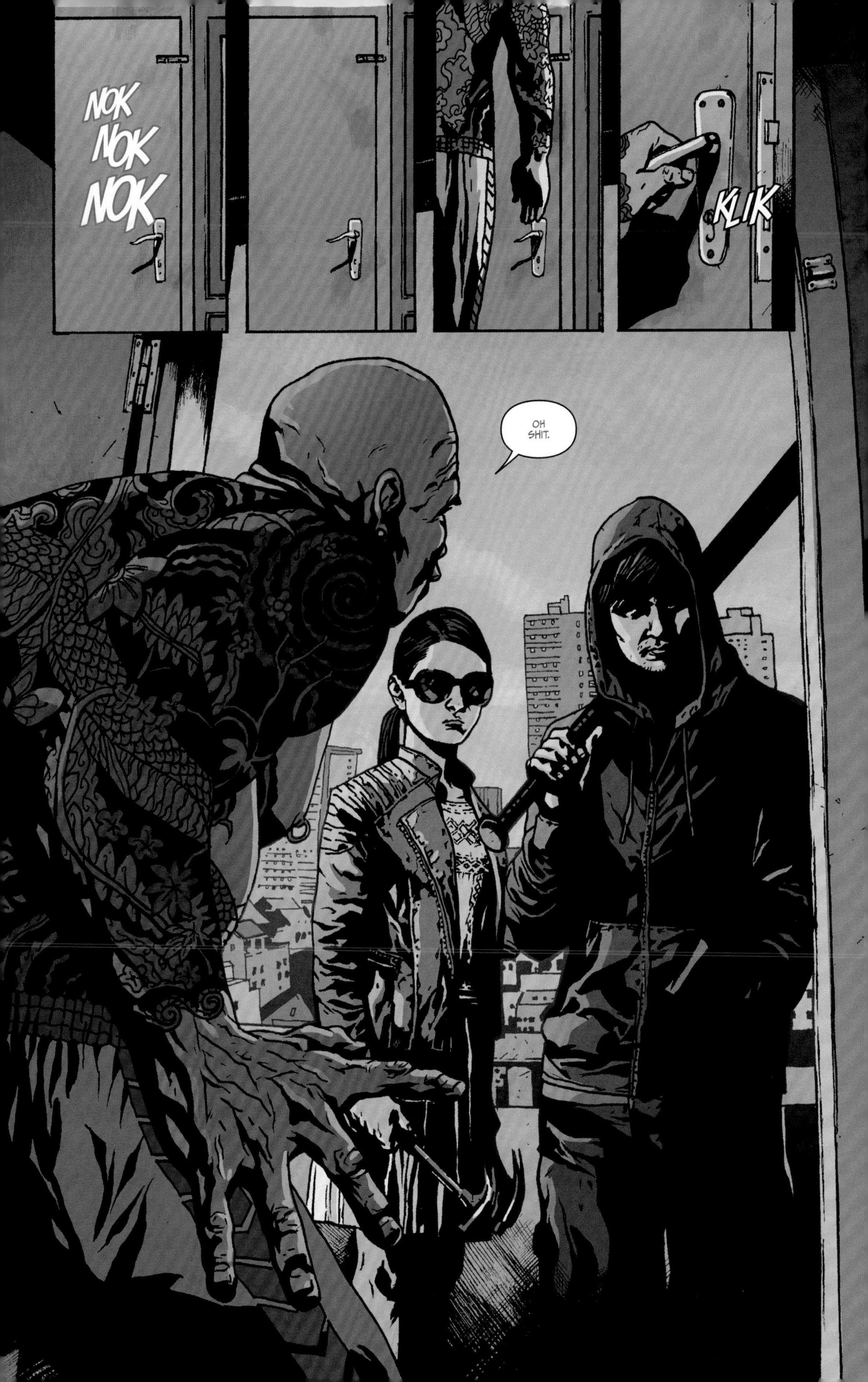
NOK
NOK
NOK
KLIK
OH SHIT.

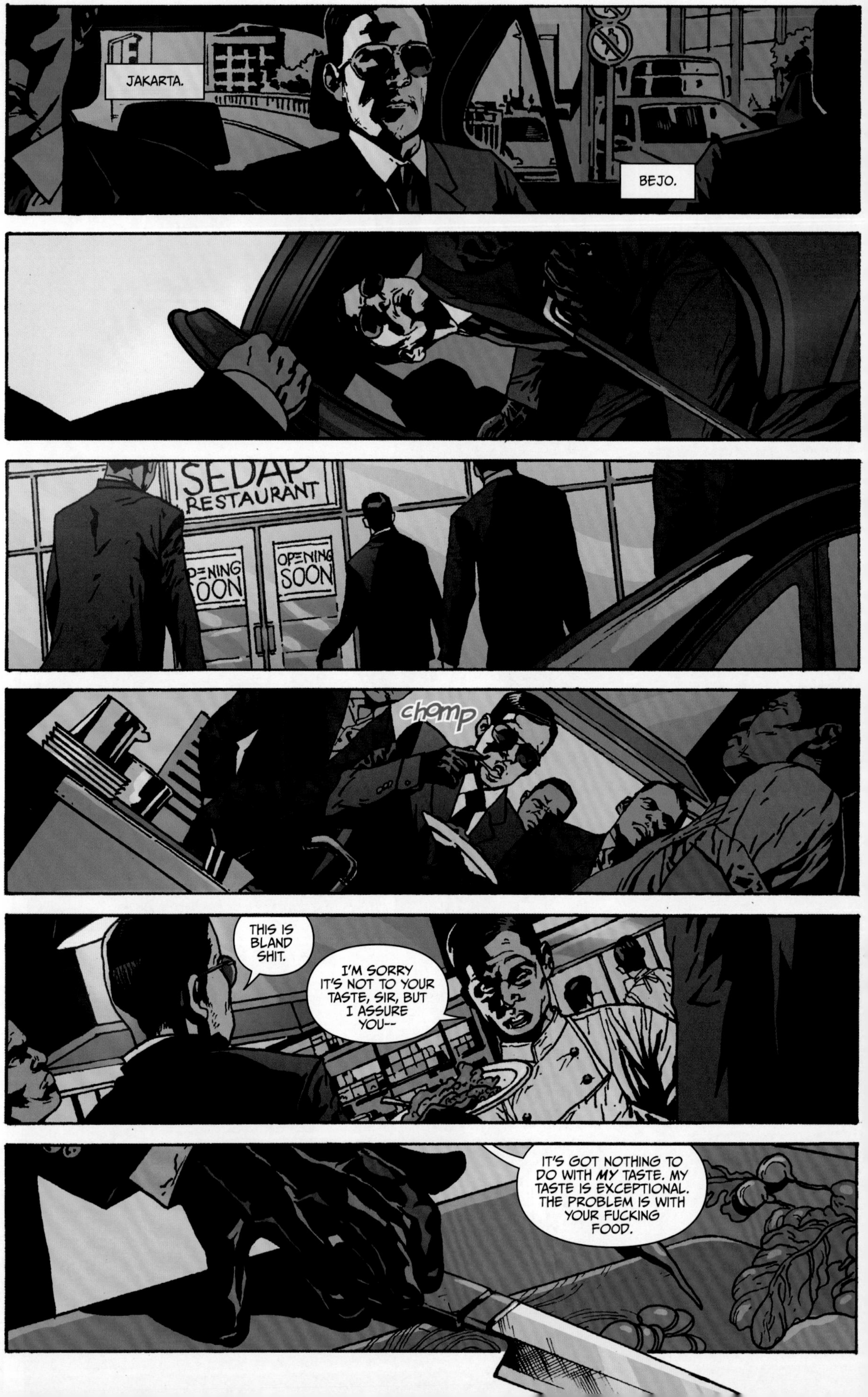
JAKARTA.
BEJO.
SEDAP RESTAURANT
OPENING SOON
OPENING SOON
chomp
THIS IS BLAND SHIT.
I'M SORRY IT'S NOT TO YOUR TASTE, SIR, BUT I ASSURE YOU--
IT'S GOT NOTHING TO DO WITH MY TASTE. MY TASTE IS EXCEPTIONAL. THE PROBLEM IS WITH YOUR FUCKING FOOD.

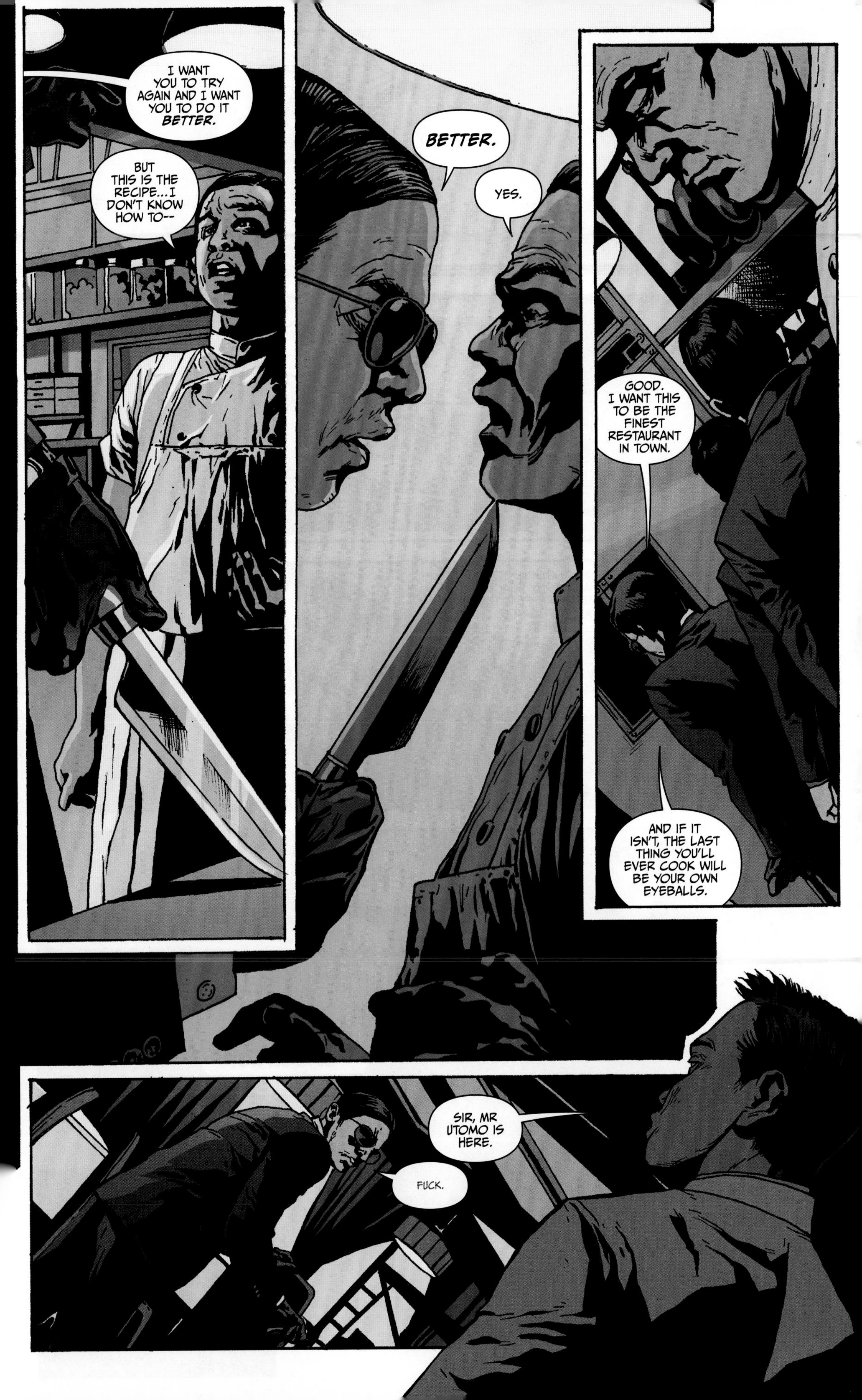
I WANT YOU TO TRY AGAIN AND I WANT YOU TO DO IT *BETTER.*
BUT THIS IS THE RECIPE...I DON'T KNOW HOW TO--
BETTER.
YES.
GOOD. I WANT THIS TO BE THE FINEST RESTAURANT IN TOWN.
AND IF IT ISN'T, THE LAST THING YOU'LL EVER COOK WILL BE YOUR OWN EYEBALLS.
SIR, MR UTOMO IS HERE.
FUCK.

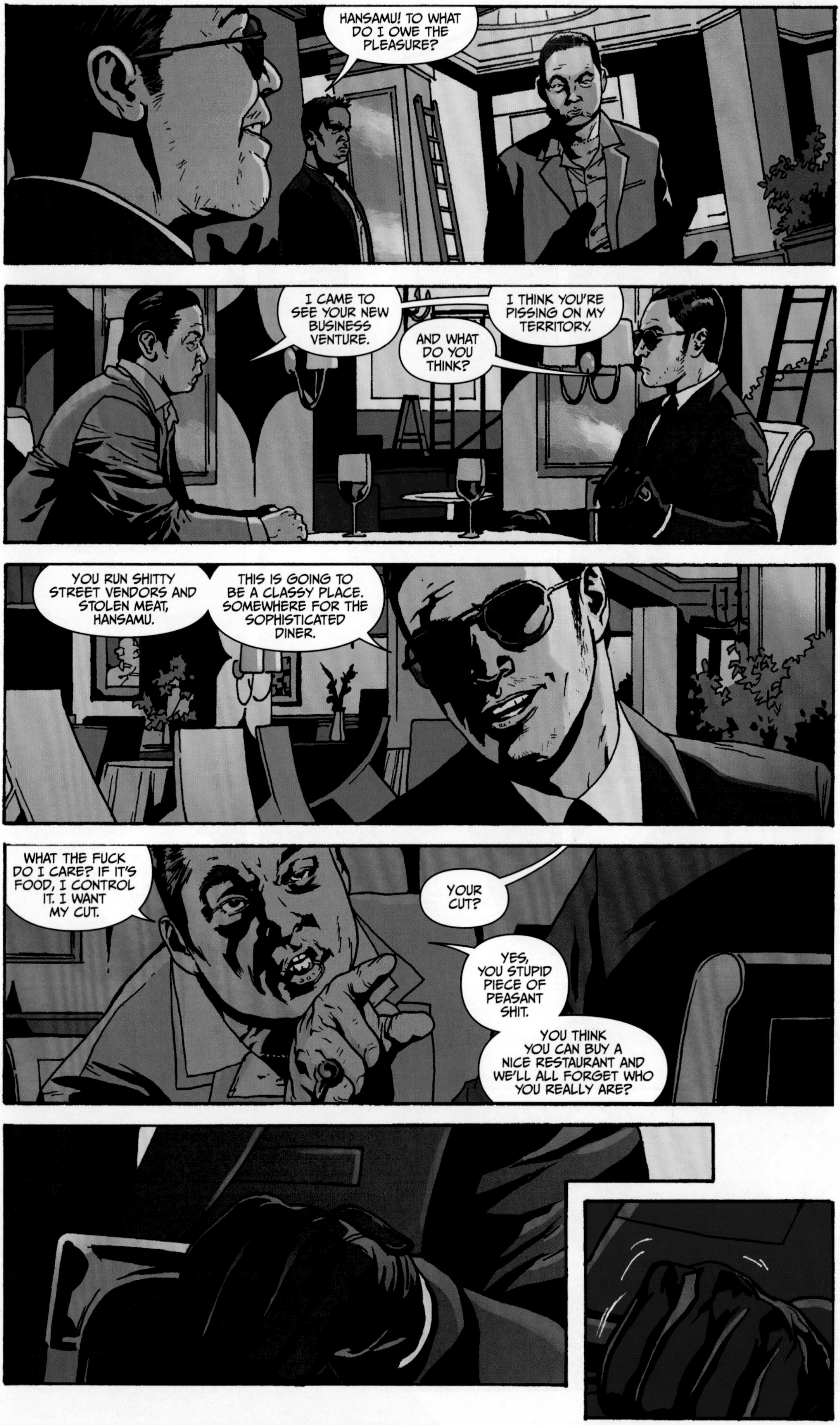
HANSAMU! TO WHAT DO I OWE THE PLEASURE?
I CAME TO SEE YOUR NEW BUSINESS VENTURE.
AND WHAT DO YOU THINK?
I THINK YOU'RE PISSING ON MY TERRITORY.
YOU RUN SHITTY STREET VENDORS AND STOLEN MEAT, HANSAMU.
THIS IS GOING TO BE A CLASSY PLACE. SOMEWHERE FOR THE SOPHISTICATED DINER.
WHAT THE FUCK DO I CARE? IF IT'S FOOD, I CONTROL IT. I WANT MY CUT.
YOUR CUT?
YES, YOU STUPID PIECE OF PEASANT SHIT.
YOU THINK YOU CAN BUY A NICE RESTAURANT AND WE'LL ALL FORGET WHO YOU REALLY ARE?

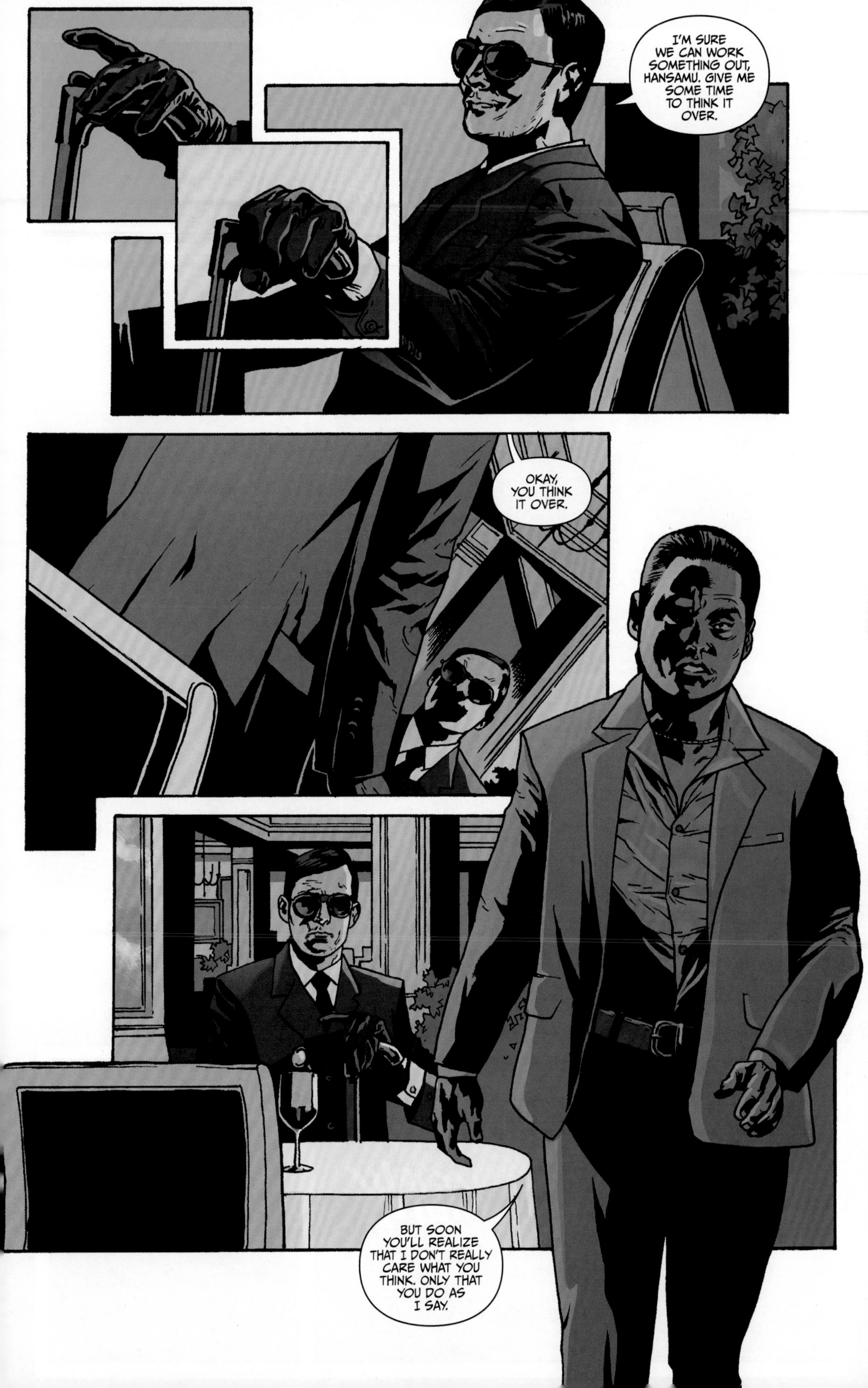
I'M SURE WE CAN WORK SOMETHING OUT, HANSAMU. GIVE ME SOME TIME TO THINK IT OVER.
OKAY, YOU THINK IT OVER.
BUT SOON YOU'LL REALIZE THAT I DON'T REALLY CARE WHAT YOU THINK. ONLY THAT YOU DO AS I SAY.

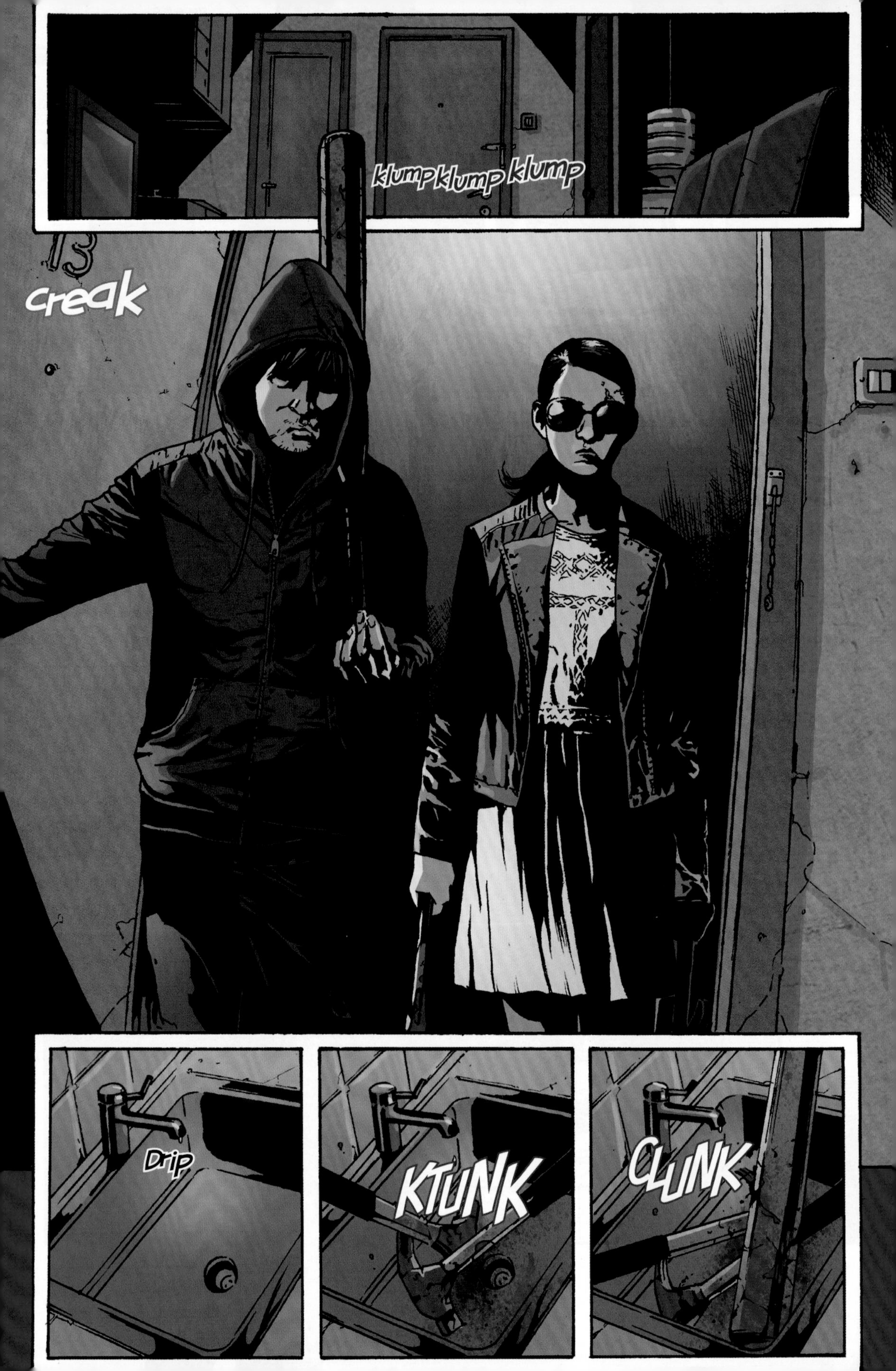
klump klump klump
creak
Drip
KTUNK
CLUNK

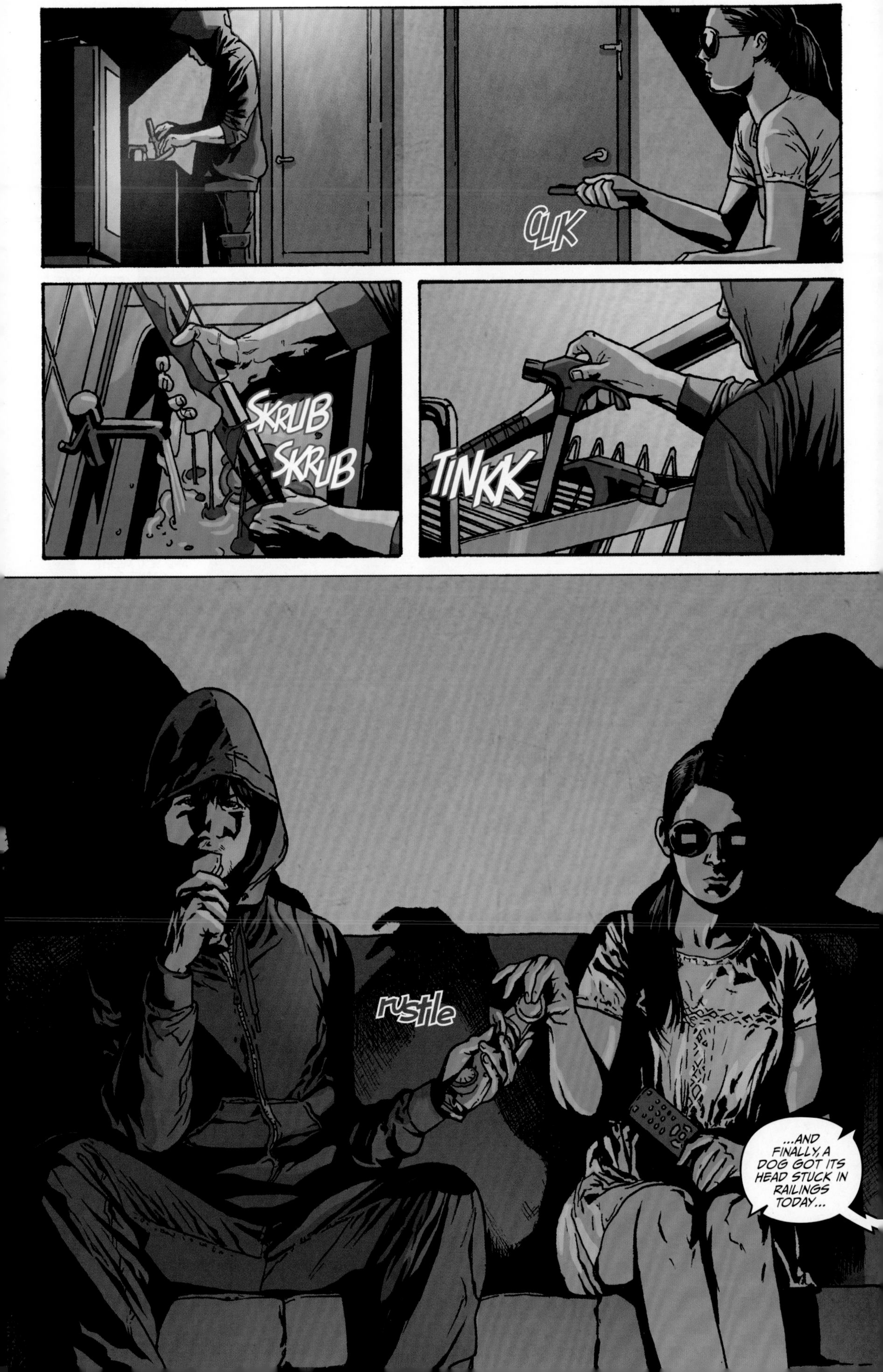
CLIK
SKRUB
SKRUB
TINKK
rustle
...AND FINALLY, A DOG GOT ITS HEAD STUCK IN RAILINGS TODAY...

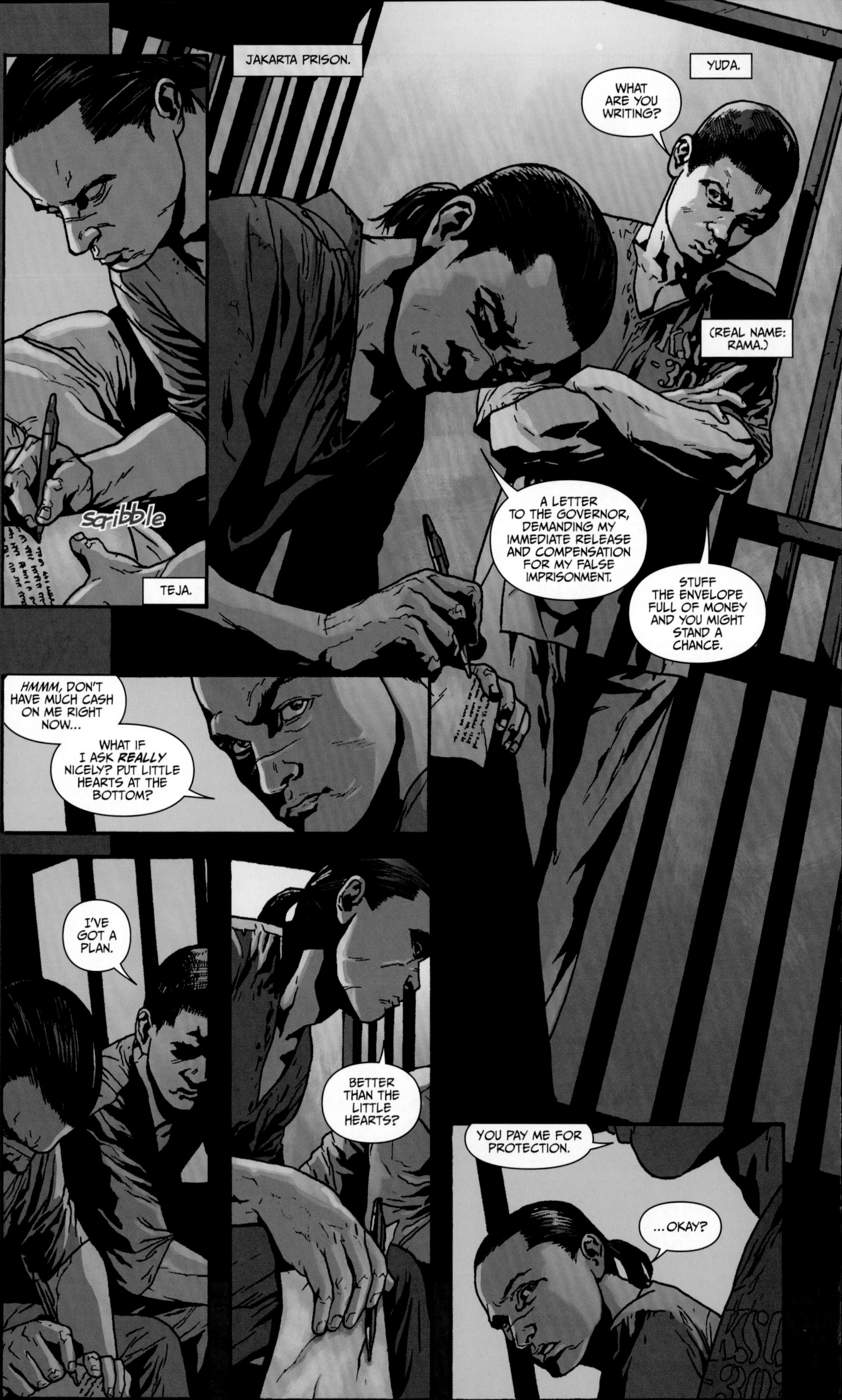
JAKARTA PRISON.
YUDA.
WHAT ARE YOU WRITING?
(REAL NAME: RAMA.)
Scribble
TEJA.
A LETTER TO THE GOVERNOR, DEMANDING MY IMMEDIATE RELEASE AND COMPENSATION FOR MY FALSE IMPRISONMENT.
STUFF THE ENVELOPE FULL OF MONEY AND YOU MIGHT STAND A CHANCE.
HMMM, DON'T HAVE MUCH CASH ON ME RIGHT NOW...
WHAT IF I ASK ***REALLY*** NICELY? PUT LITTLE HEARTS AT THE BOTTOM?
I'VE GOT A PLAN.
BETTER THAN THE LITTLE HEARTS?
YOU PAY ME FOR PROTECTION.
...OKAY?

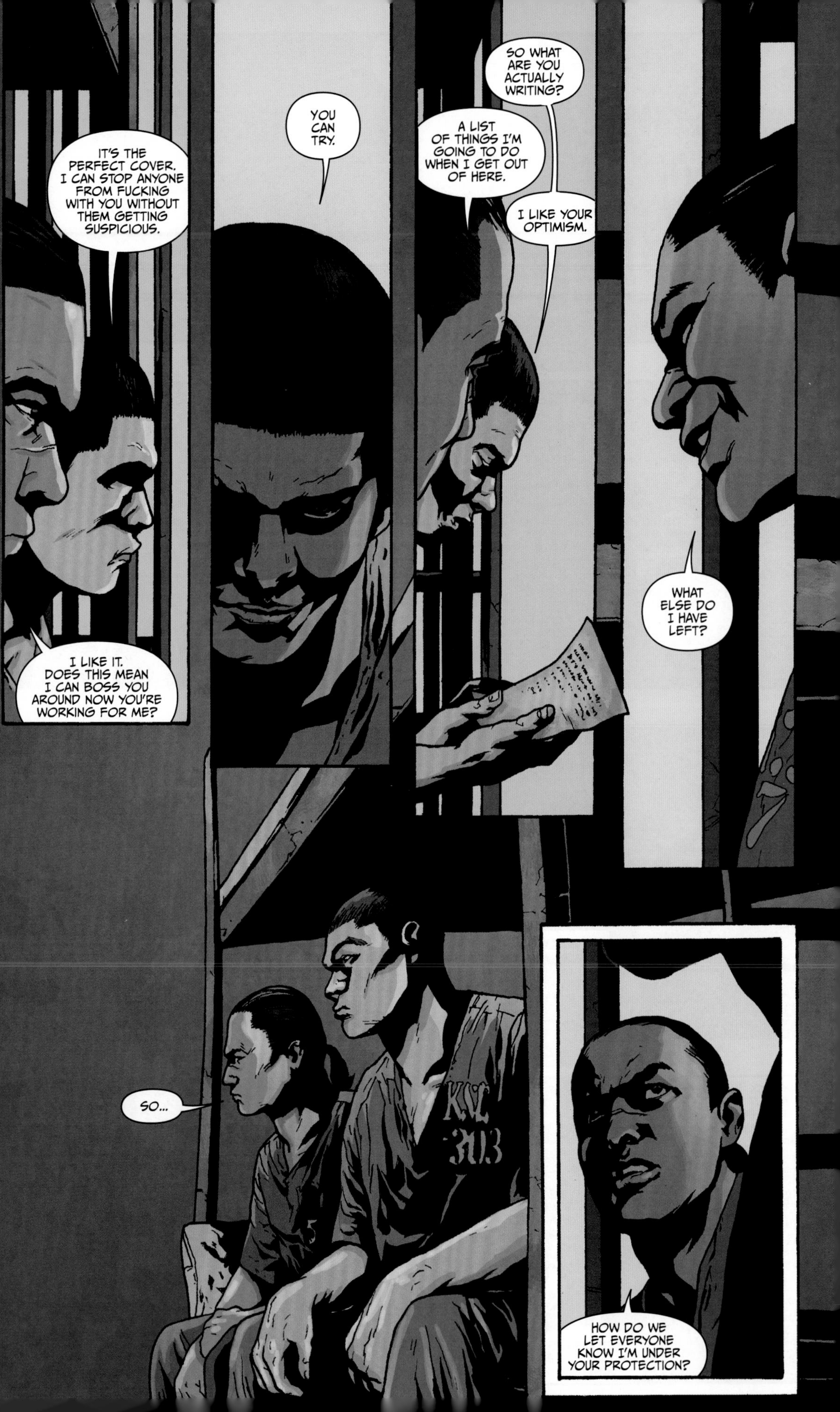
IT'S THE PERFECT COVER. I CAN STOP ANYONE FROM FUCKING WITH YOU WITHOUT THEM GETTING SUSPICIOUS.
I LIKE IT. DOES THIS MEAN I CAN BOSS YOU AROUND NOW YOU'RE WORKING FOR ME?
YOU CAN TRY.
SO WHAT ARE YOU ACTUALLY WRITING?
A LIST OF THINGS I'M GOING TO DO WHEN I GET OUT OF HERE.
I LIKE YOUR OPTIMISM.
WHAT ELSE DO I HAVE LEFT?
SO...
HOW DO WE LET EVERYONE KNOW I'M UNDER YOUR PROTECTION?

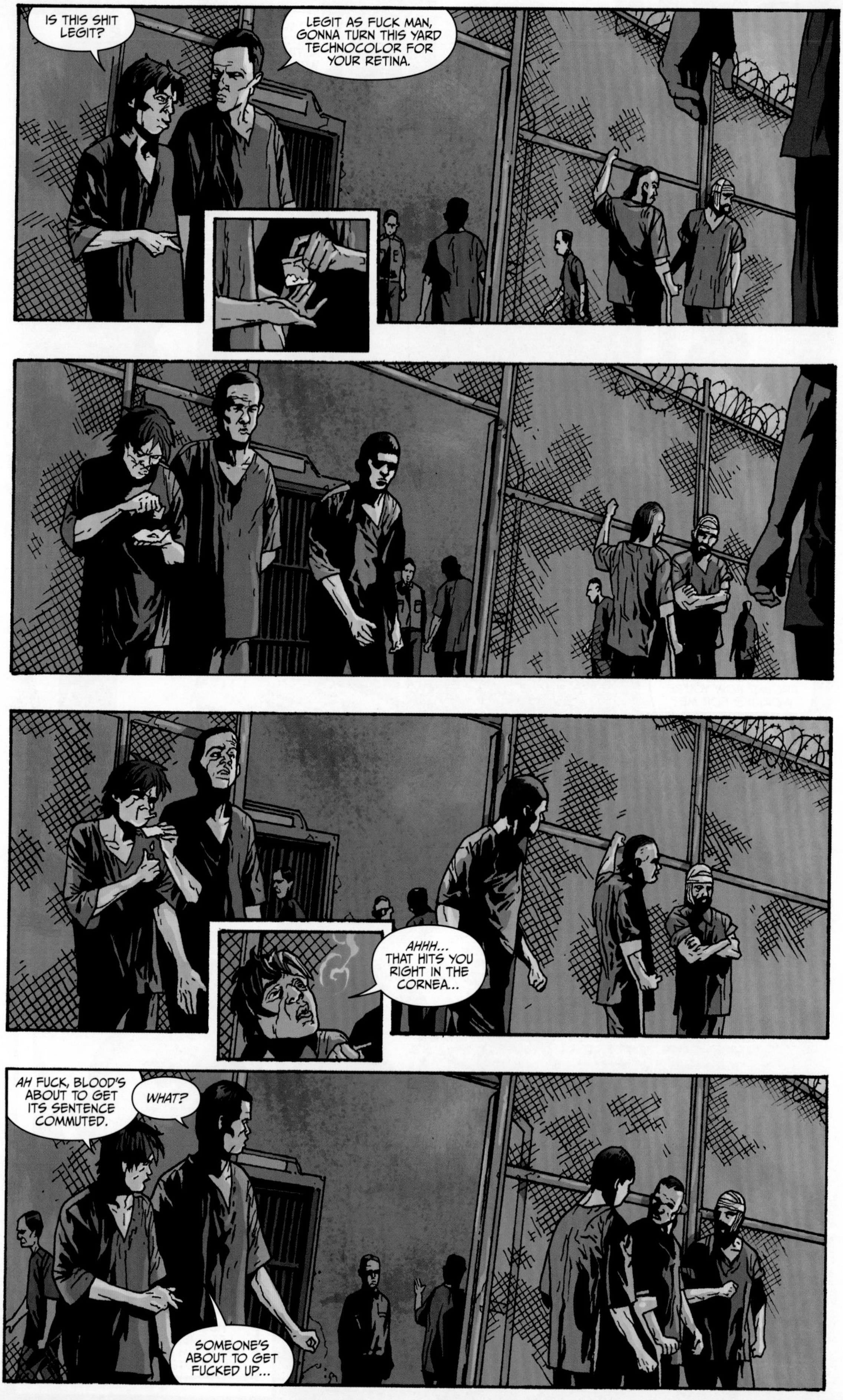
IS THIS SHIT LEGIT?
LEGIT AS FUCK MAN, GONNA TURN THIS YARD TECHNOCOLOR FOR YOUR RETINA.
AHHH... THAT HITS YOU RIGHT IN THE CORNEA...
AH FUCK, BLOOD'S ABOUT TO GET ITS SENTENCE COMMUTED.
WHAT?
SOMEONE'S ABOUT TO GET FUCKED UP...

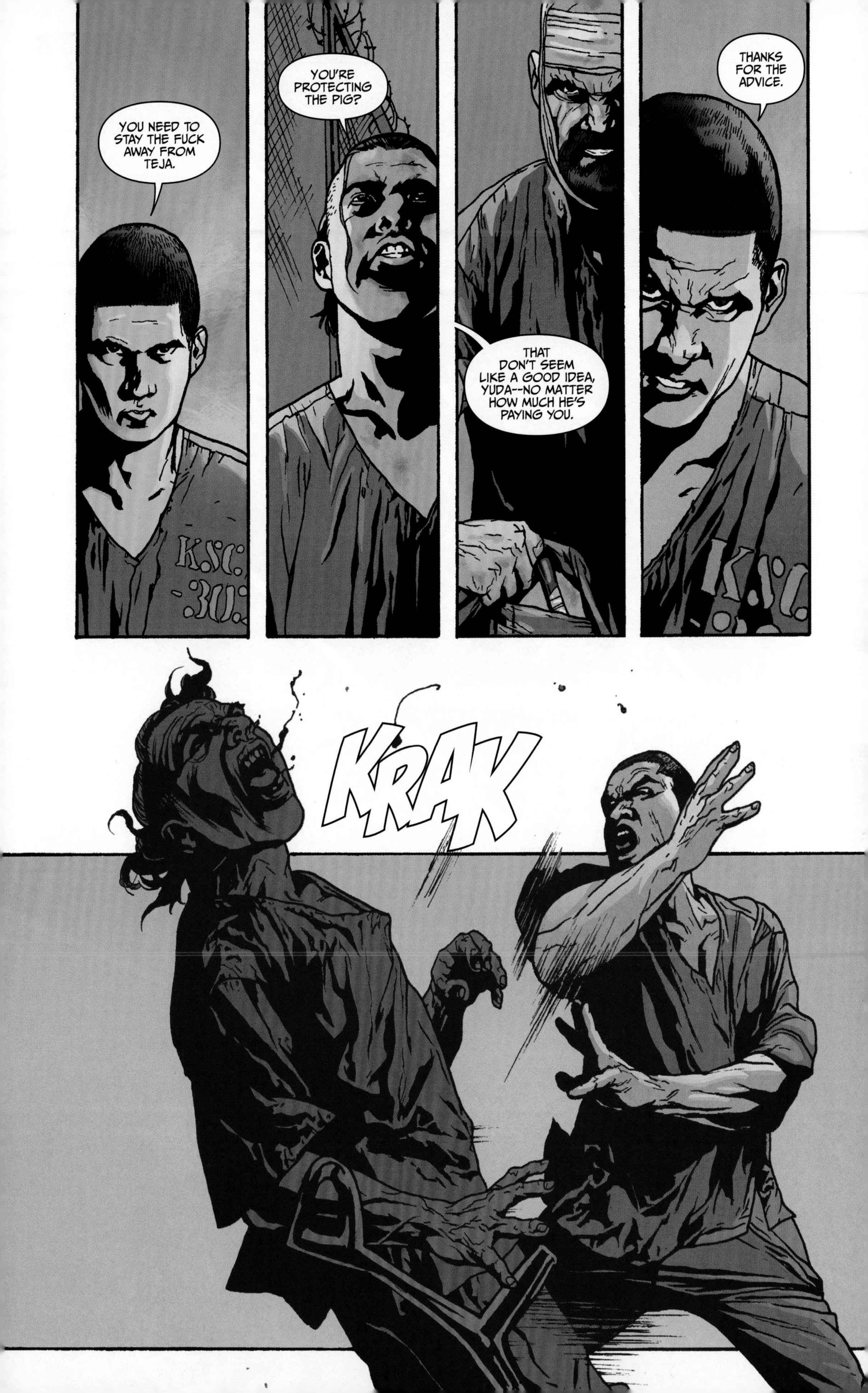
YOU NEED TO STAY THE FUCK AWAY FROM TEJA.
YOU'RE PROTECTING THE PIG?
THAT DON'T SEEM LIKE A GOOD IDEA, YUDA--NO MATTER HOW MUCH HE'S PAYING YOU.
THANKS FOR THE ADVICE.
K.S.C.
KRAK

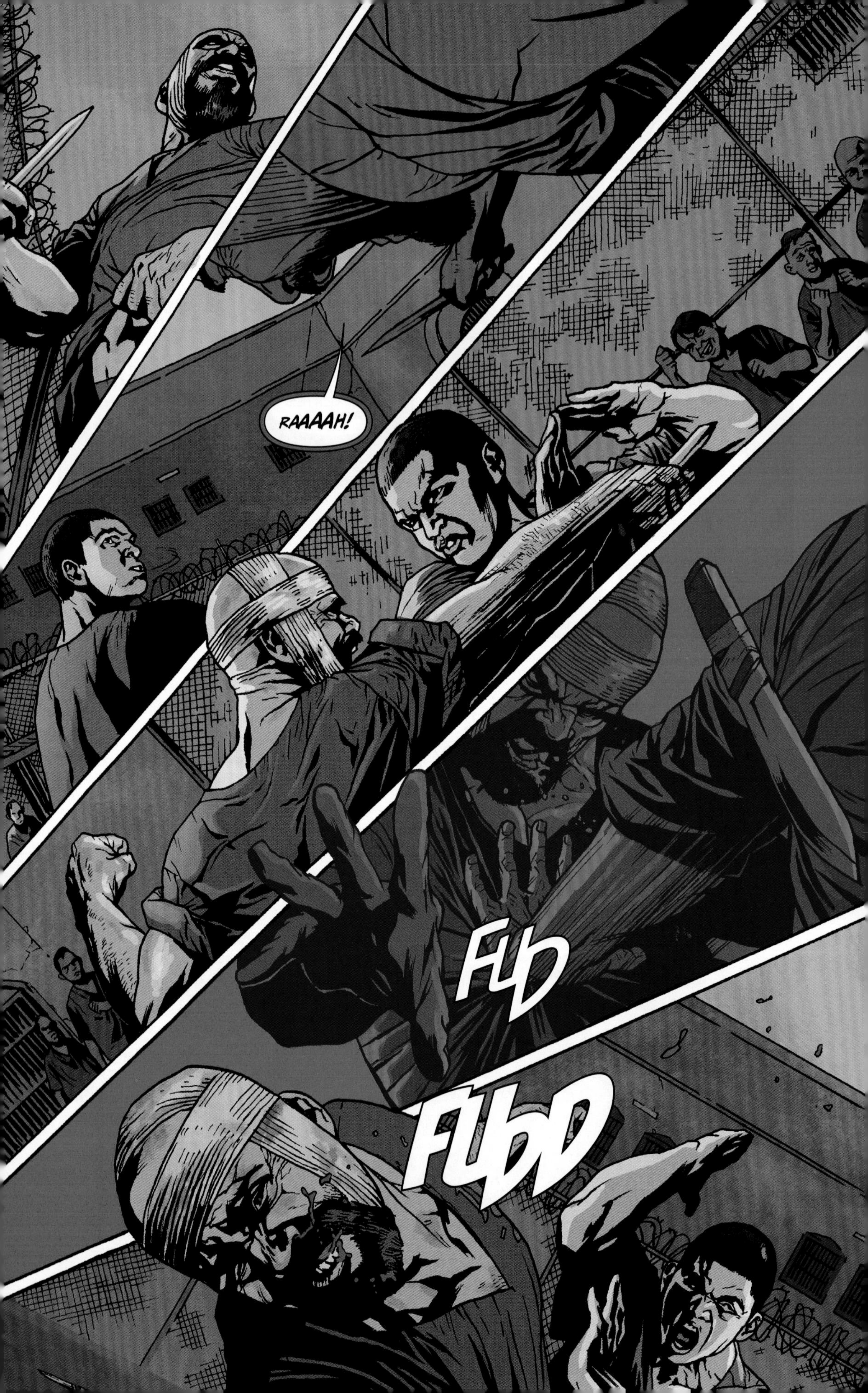
RAAAAH!
FUD
FUDD

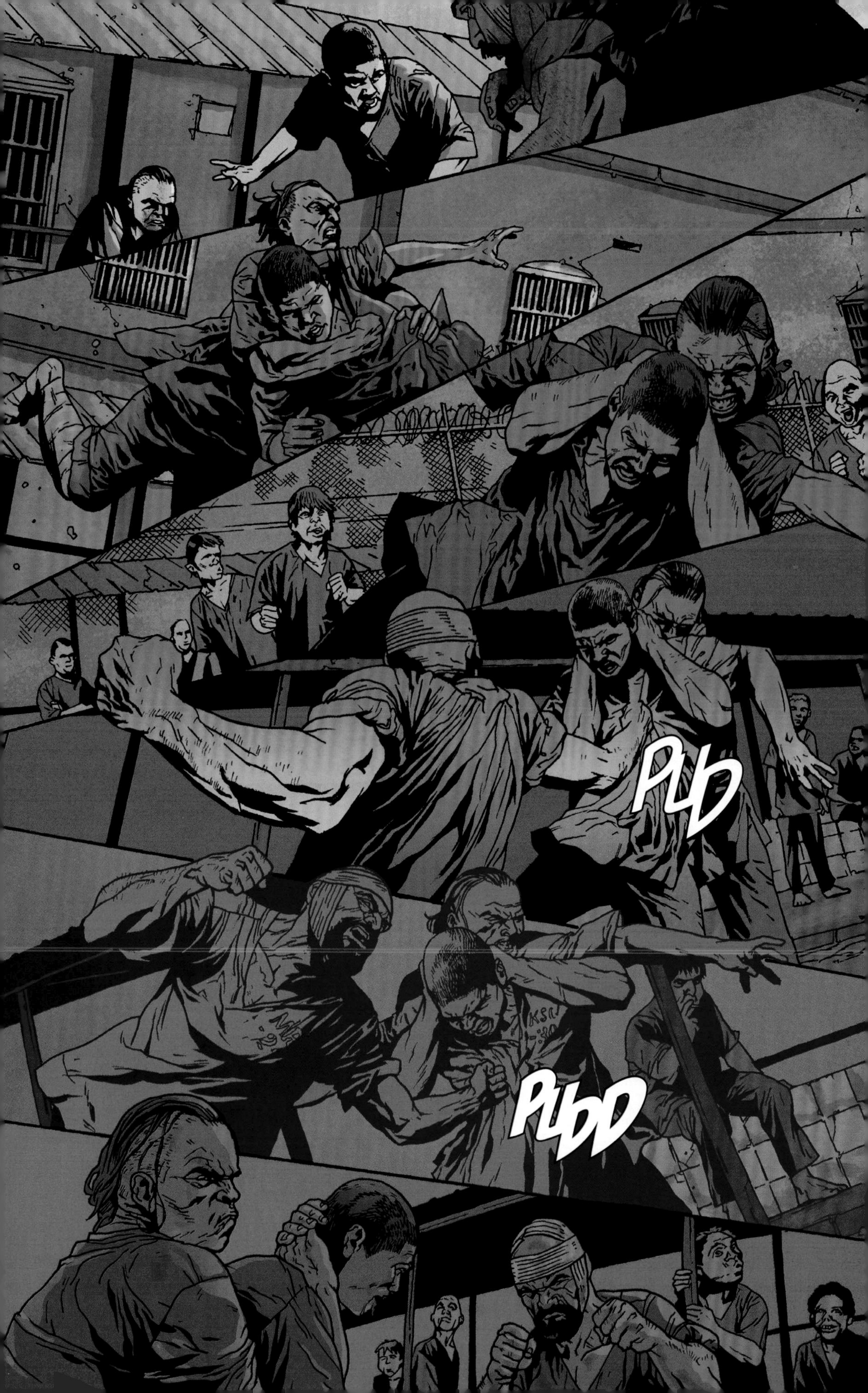
PLUD
PLUDD

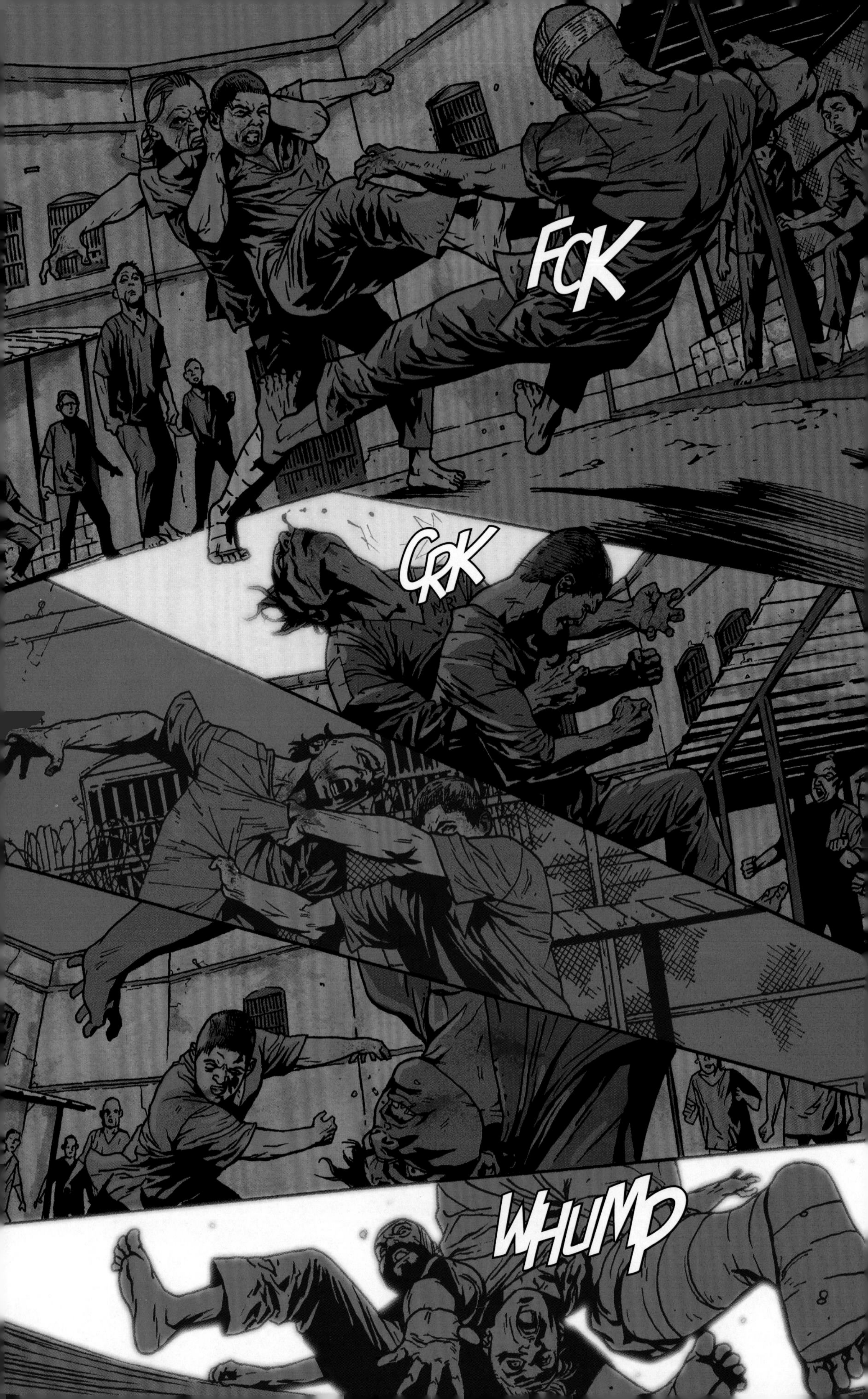

FCK
CRK
WHUMP

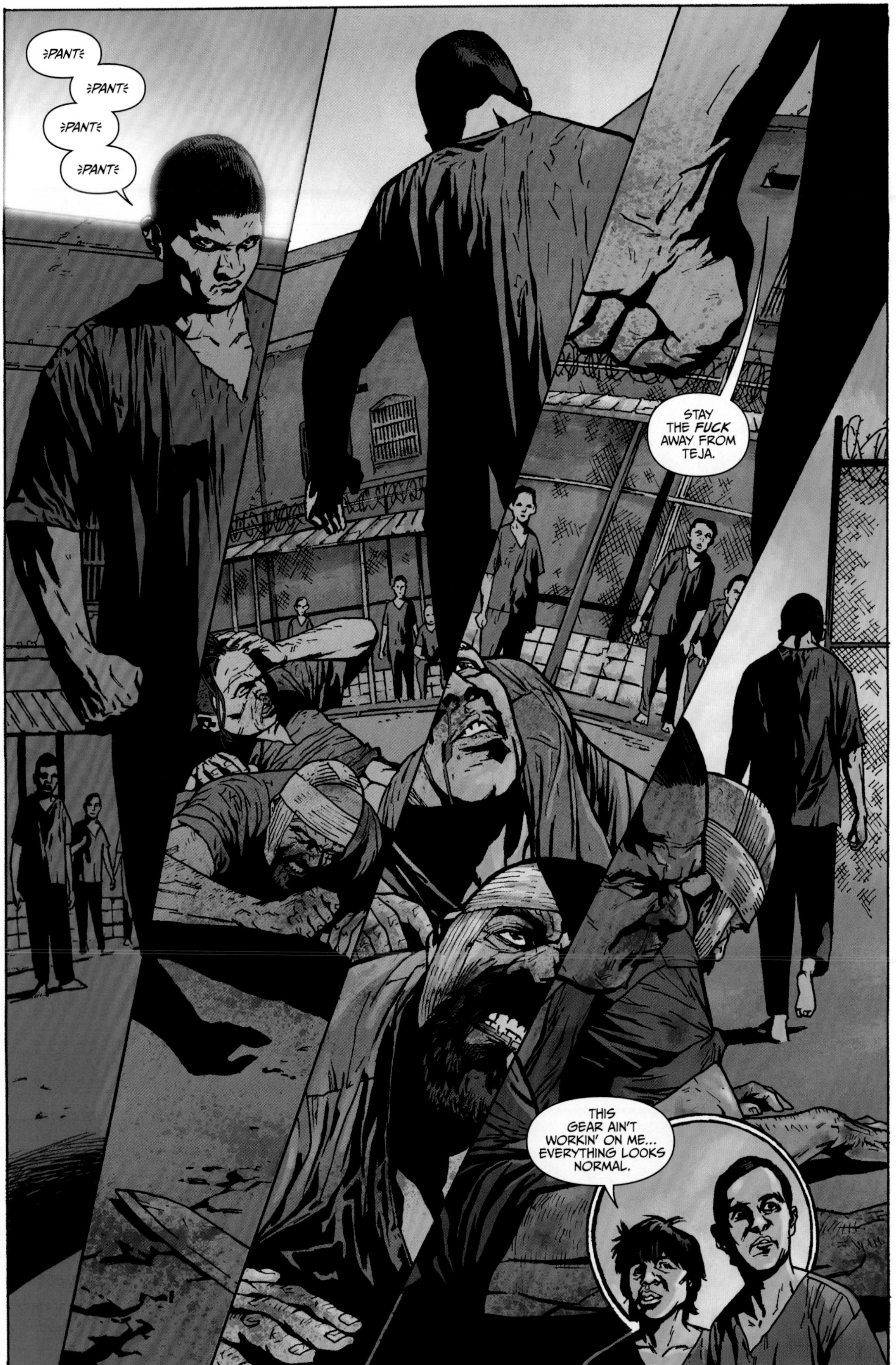
PANT
PANT
PANT
PANT
STAY THE FUCK AWAY FROM TEJA.
THIS GEAR AIN'T WORKIN' ON ME... EVERYTHING LOOKS NORMAL.

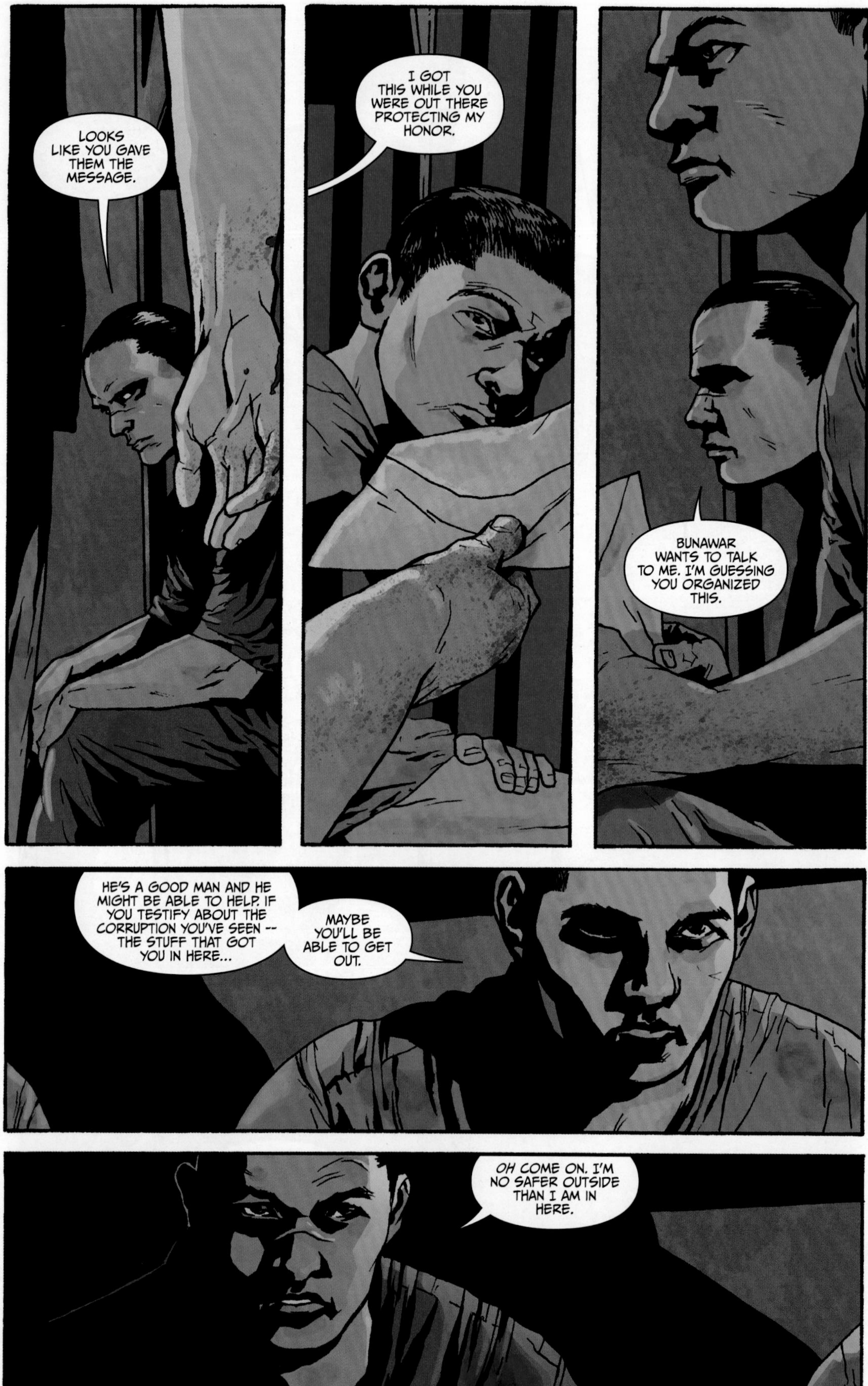
LOOKS LIKE YOU GAVE THEM THE MESSAGE.
I GOT THIS WHILE YOU WERE OUT THERE PROTECTING MY HONOR.
BUNAWAR WANTS TO TALK TO ME. I'M GUESSING YOU ORGANIZED THIS.
HE'S A GOOD MAN AND HE MIGHT BE ABLE TO HELP. IF YOU TESTIFY ABOUT THE CORRUPTION YOU'VE SEEN -- THE STUFF THAT GOT YOU IN HERE...
MAYBE YOU'LL BE ABLE TO GET OUT.
OH COME ON. I'M NO SAFER OUTSIDE THAN I AM IN HERE.

* BUNAWAR IS THE HEAD OF THE INTERNAL INVESTIGATIONS UNIT WHO RECRUITED RAMA.

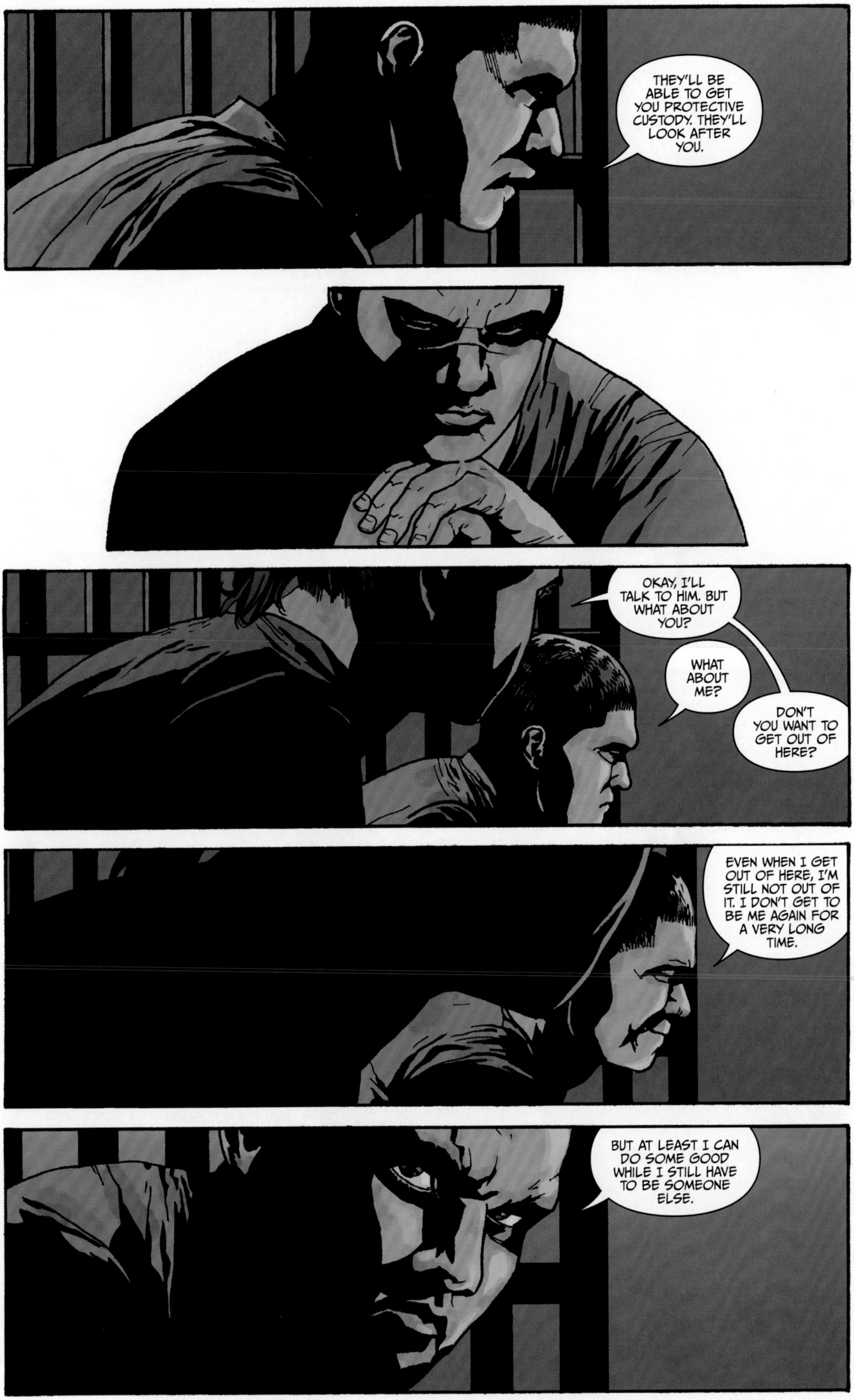
THEY'LL BE ABLE TO GET YOU PROTECTIVE CUSTODY. THEY'LL LOOK AFTER YOU.
OKAY, I'LL TALK TO HIM. BUT WHAT ABOUT YOU?
WHAT ABOUT ME?
DON'T YOU WANT TO GET OUT OF HERE?
EVEN WHEN I GET OUT OF HERE, I'M STILL NOT OUT OF IT. I DON'T GET TO BE ME AGAIN FOR A VERY LONG TIME.
BUT AT LEAST I CAN DO SOME GOOD WHILE I STILL HAVE TO BE SOMEONE ELSE.

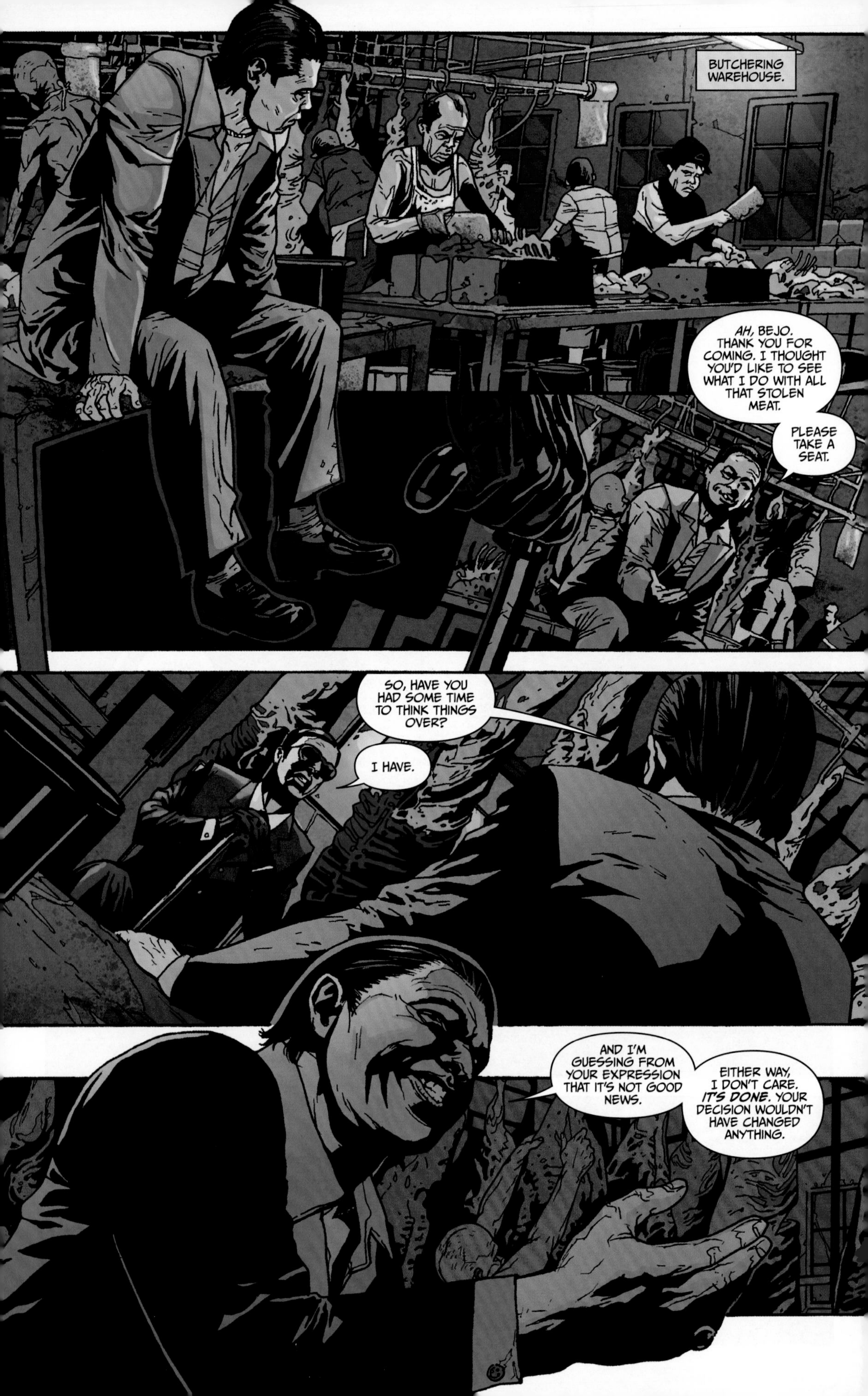
BUTCHERING WAREHOUSE.
AH, BEJO. THANK YOU FOR COMING. I THOUGHT YOU'D LIKE TO SEE WHAT I DO WITH ALL THAT STOLEN MEAT.
PLEASE TAKE A SEAT.
SO, HAVE YOU HAD SOME TIME TO THINK THINGS OVER?
I HAVE.
AND I'M GUESSING FROM YOUR EXPRESSION THAT IT'S NOT GOOD NEWS.
EITHER WAY, I DON'T CARE. *IT'S DONE.* YOUR DECISION WOULDN'T HAVE CHANGED ANYTHING.

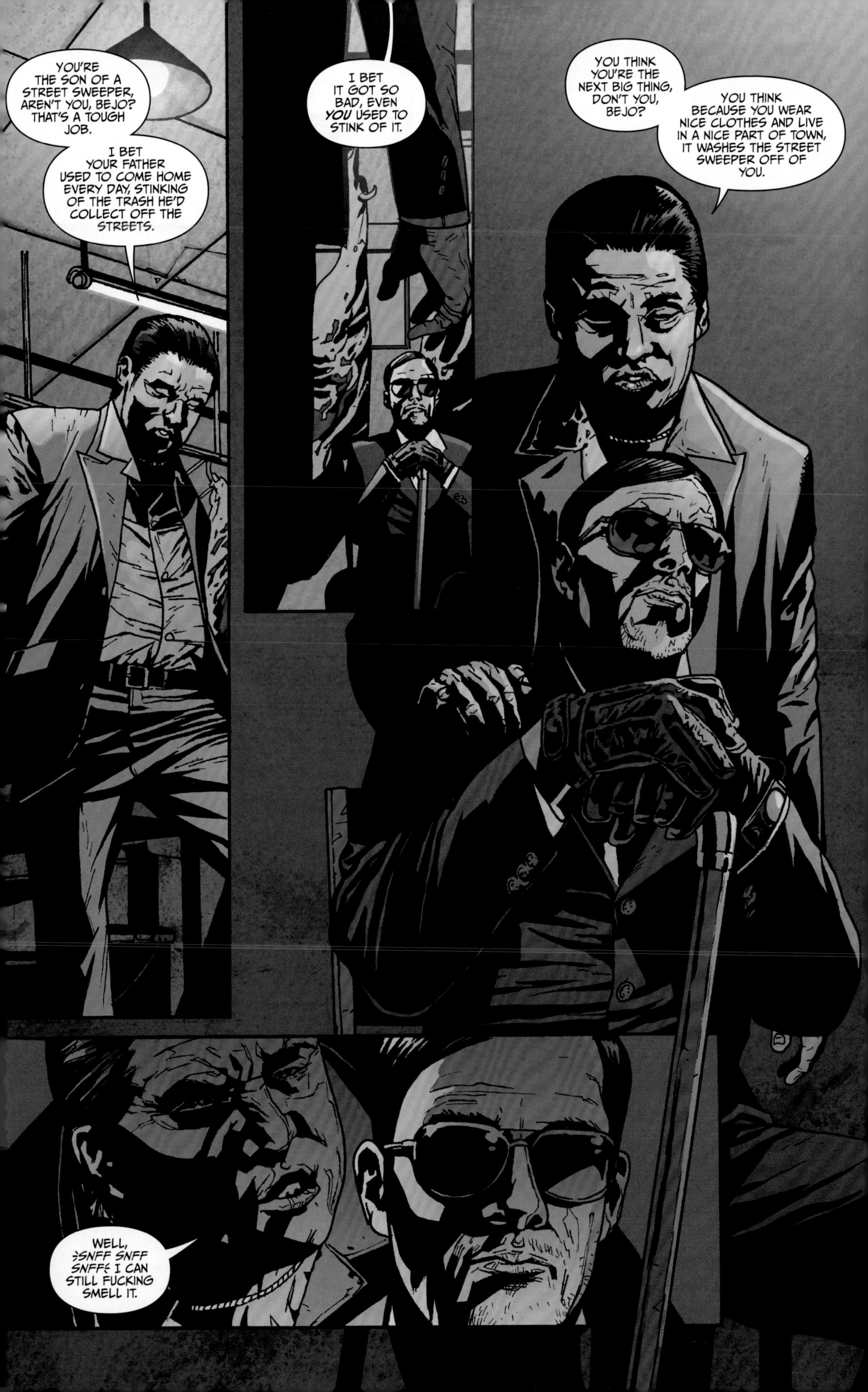
YOU'RE THE SON OF A STREET SWEEPER, AREN'T YOU, BEJO? THAT'S A TOUGH JOB.
I BET YOUR FATHER USED TO COME HOME EVERY DAY, STINKING OF THE TRASH HE'D COLLECT OFF THE STREETS.
I BET IT GOT SO BAD, EVEN *YOU* USED TO STINK OF IT.
YOU THINK YOU'RE THE NEXT BIG THING, DON'T YOU, BEJO?
YOU THINK BECAUSE YOU WEAR NICE CLOTHES AND LIVE IN A NICE PART OF TOWN, IT WASHES THE STREET SWEEPER OFF OF YOU.
WELL, ≥SNFF SNFF SNFF≤ I CAN STILL FUCKING SMELL IT.

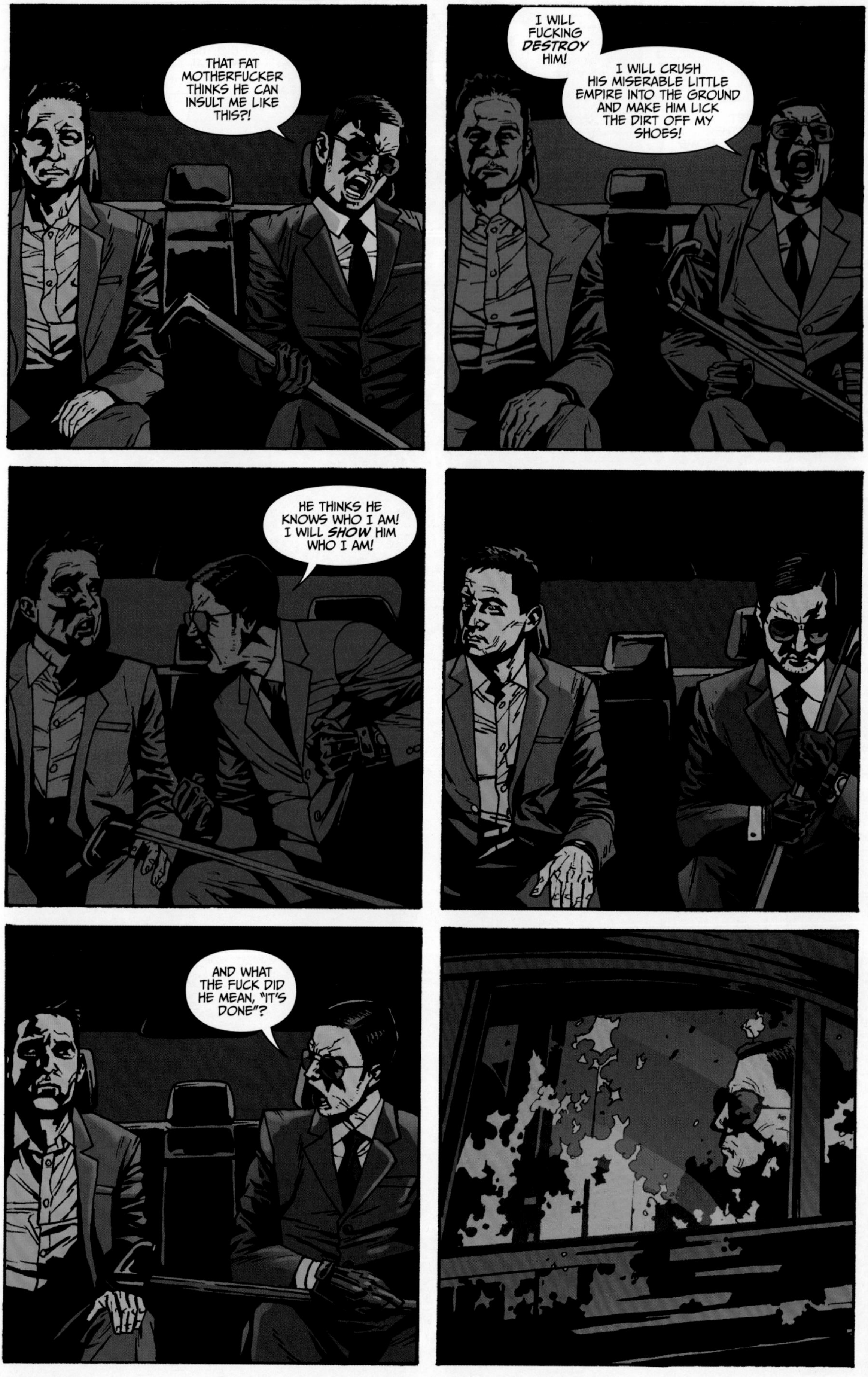
THAT FAT MOTHERFUCKER THINKS HE CAN INSULT ME LIKE THIS?!
I WILL FUCKING DESTROY HIM!
I WILL CRUSH HIS MISERABLE LITTLE EMPIRE INTO THE GROUND AND MAKE HIM LICK THE DIRT OFF MY SHOES!
HE THINKS HE KNOWS WHO I AM! I WILL SHOW HIM WHO I AM!
AND WHAT THE FUCK DID HE MEAN, "IT'S DONE"?

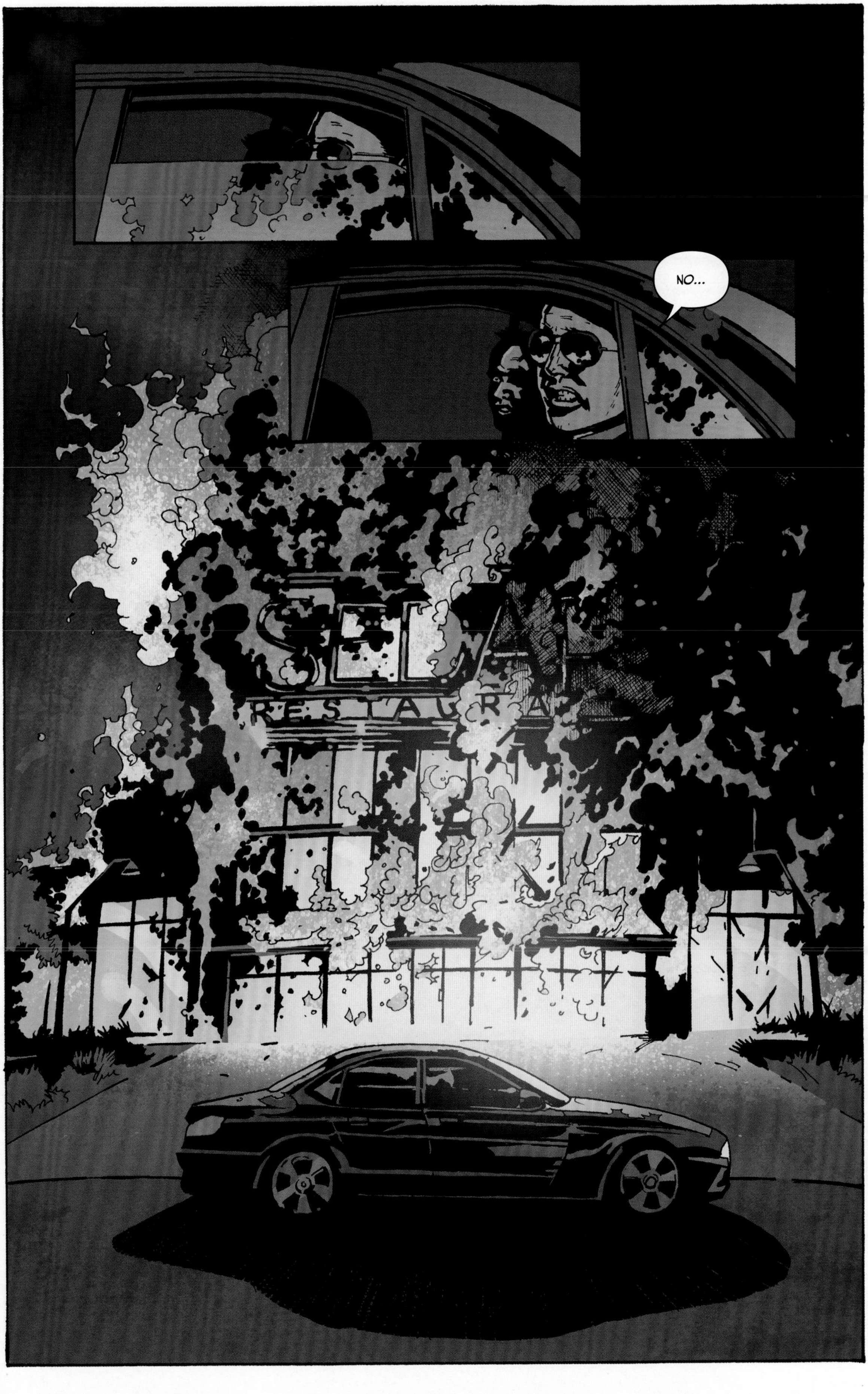
NO...

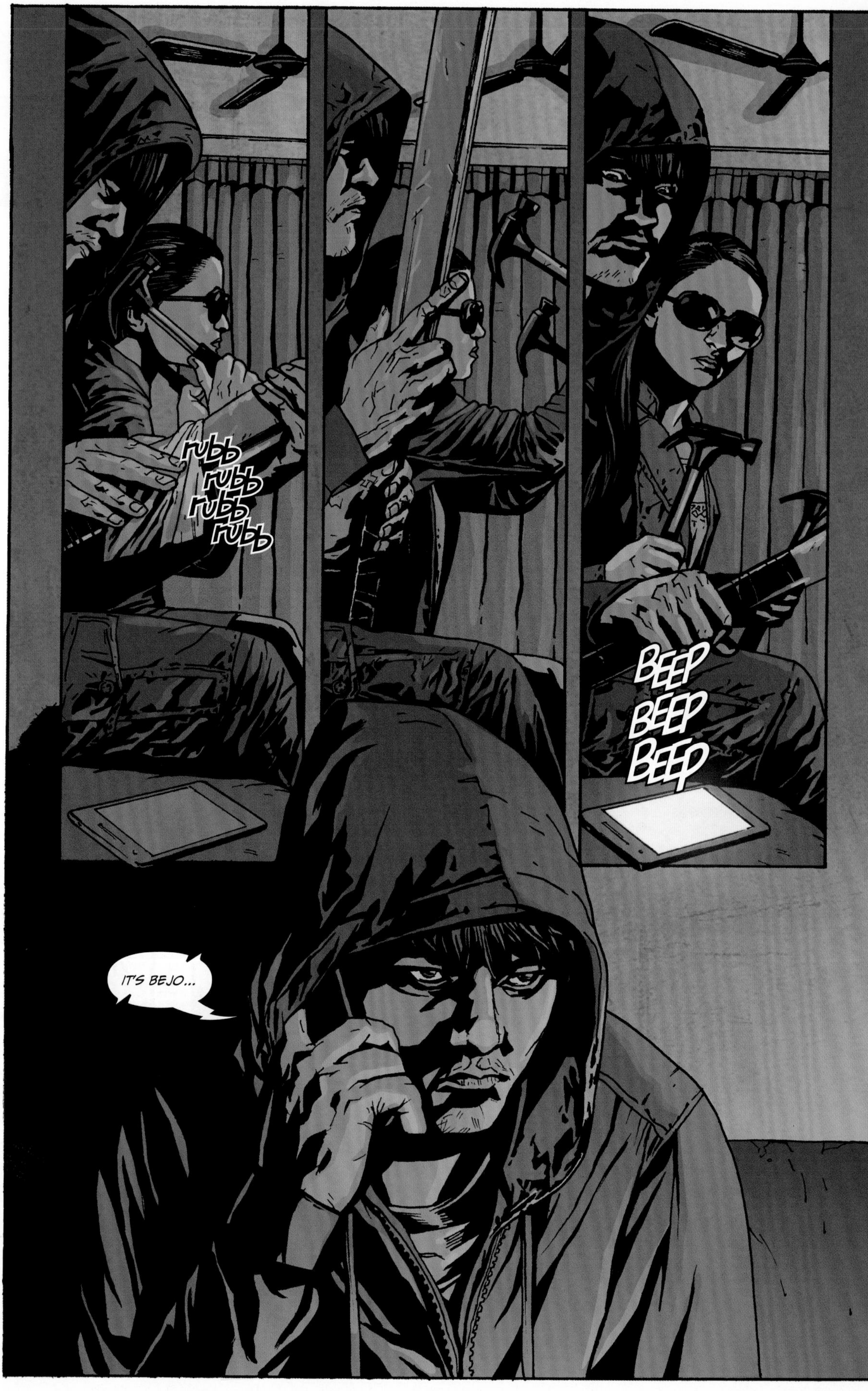
rubb rubb rubb rubb
BEEP BEEP BEEP
IT'S BEJO...

CHAPTER 3

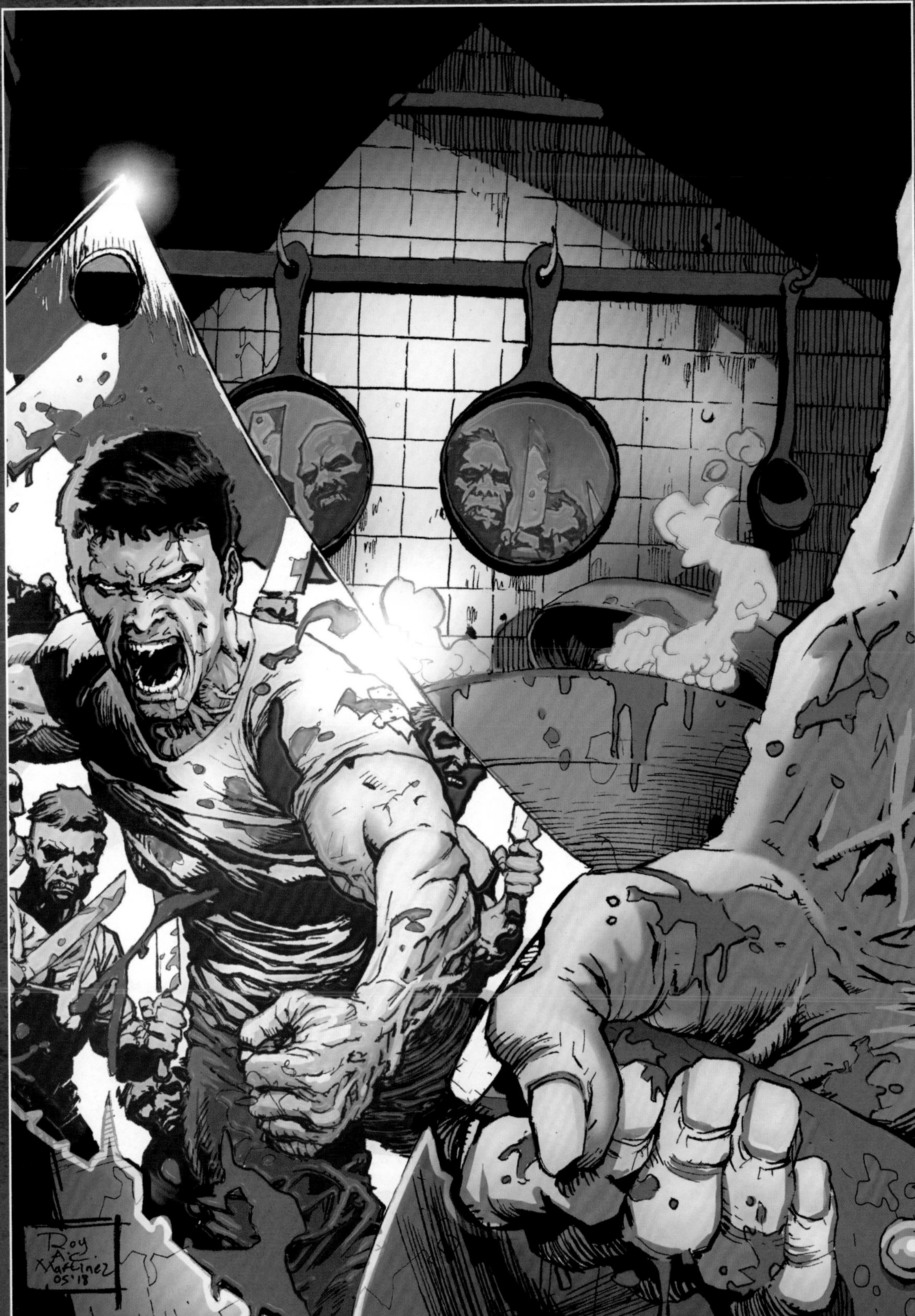

Illustration by **Roy Allan Martinez**

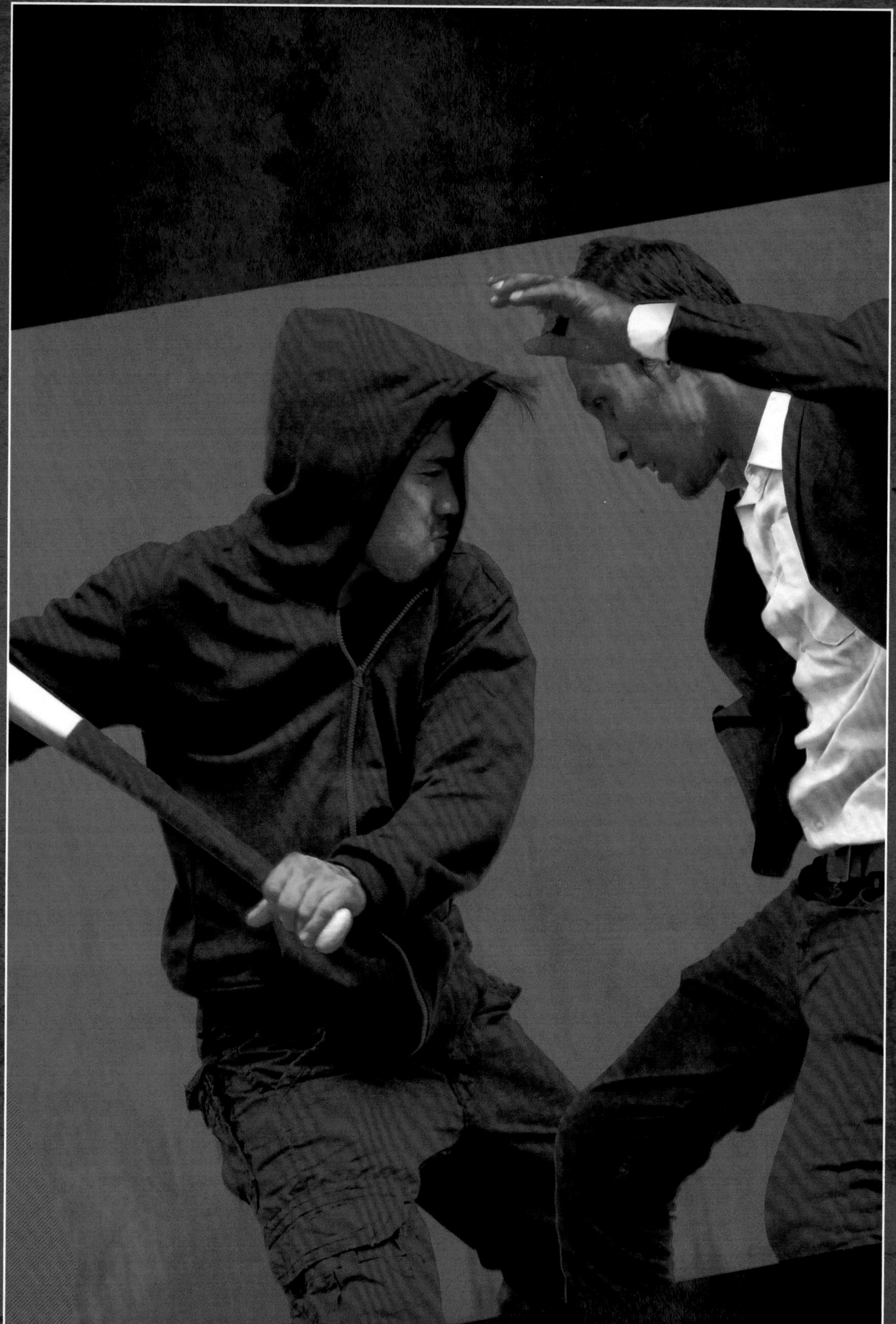

Cover 3b

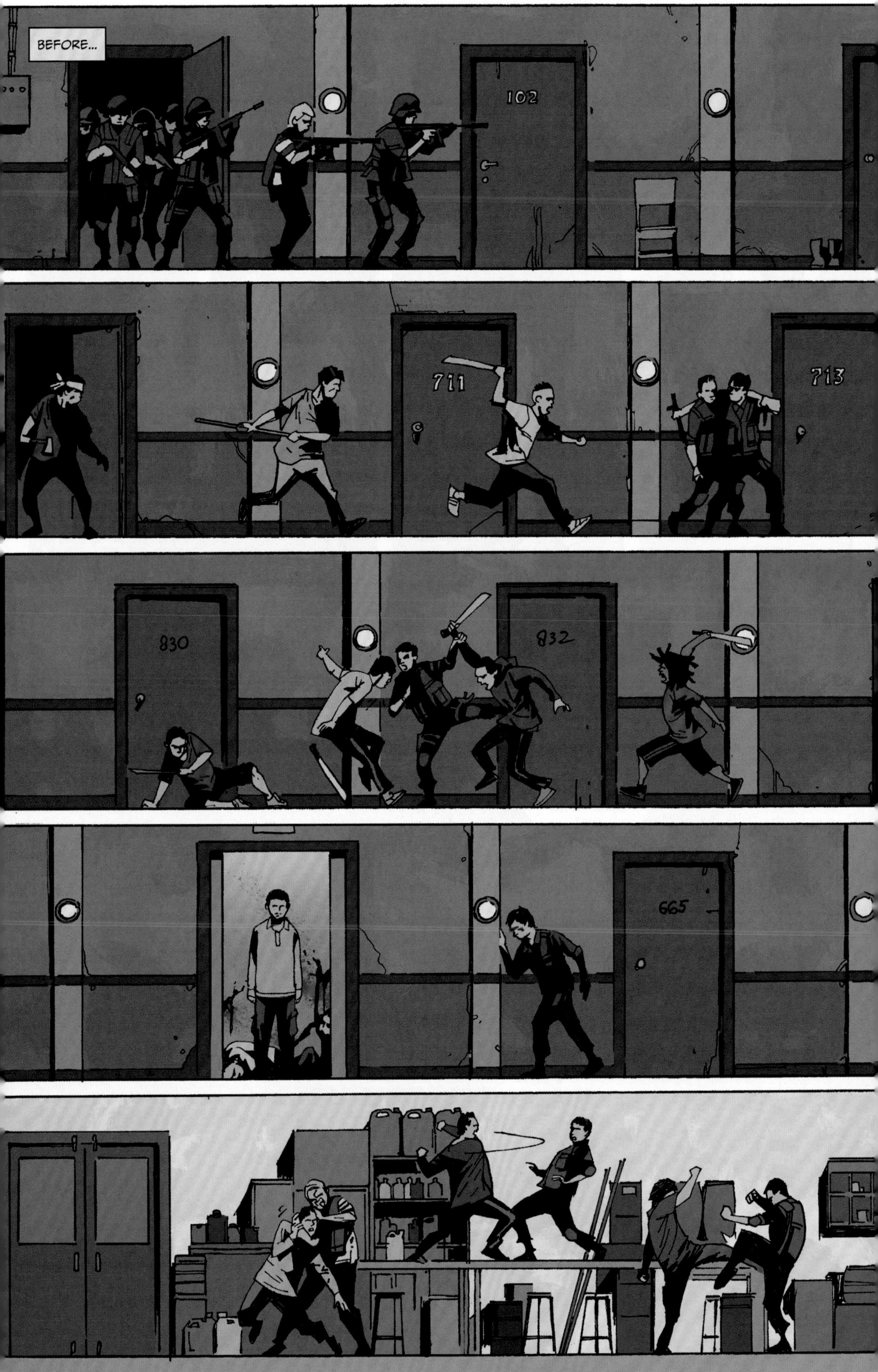
BEFORE...
102
711
713
830
832
665

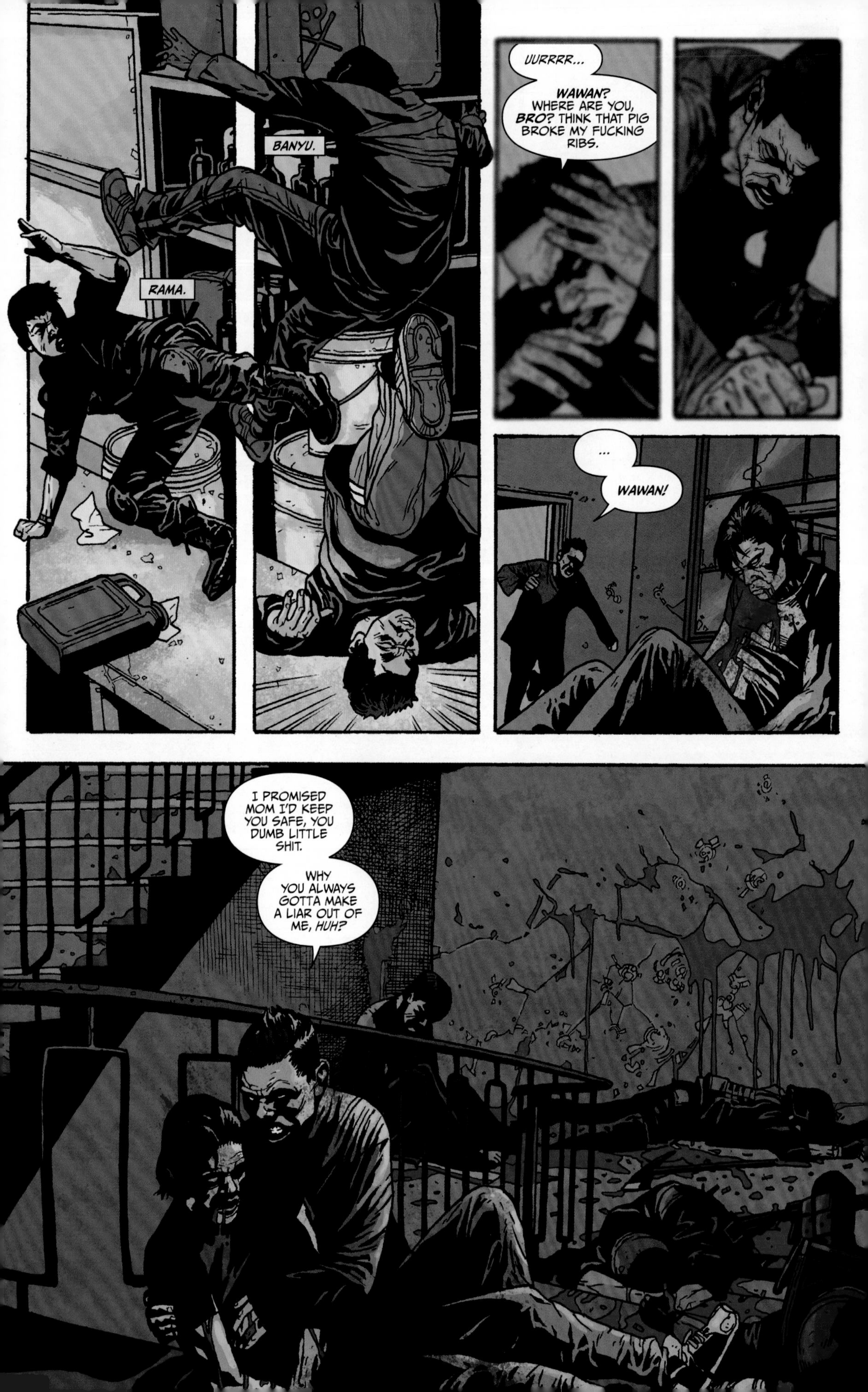
BANYU.
RAMA.
UURRRR...
WAWAN? WHERE ARE YOU, BRO? THINK THAT PIG BROKE MY FUCKING RIBS.
...
WAWAN!
I PROMISED MOM I'D KEEP YOU SAFE, YOU DUMB LITTLE SHIT.
WHY YOU ALWAYS GOTTA MAKE A LIAR OUT OF ME, HUH?

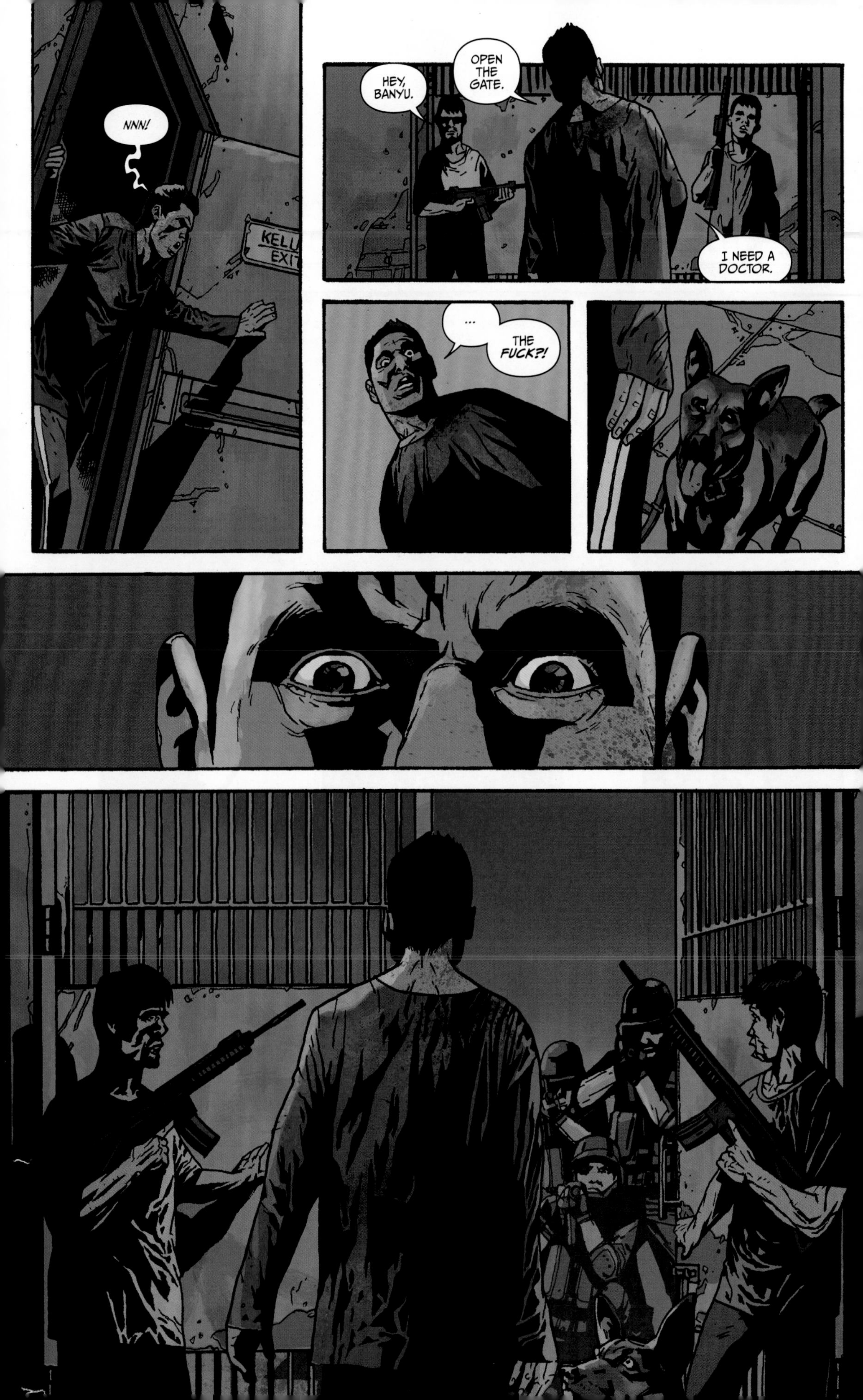
NNN!
KELL
EXIT
HEY, BANYU.
OPEN THE GATE.
I NEED A DOCTOR.
... THE FUCK?!

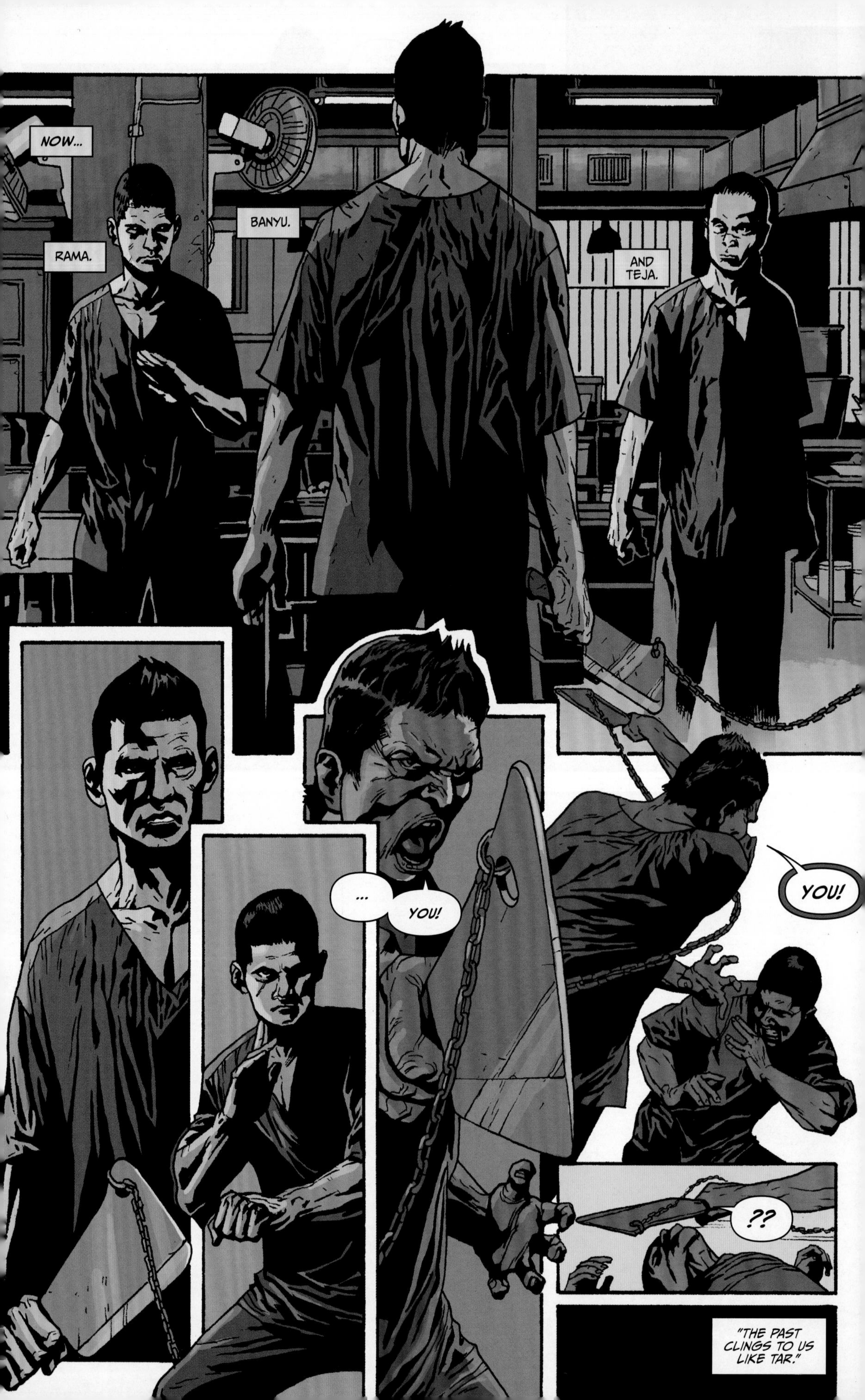
NOW...
RAMA.
BANYU.
AND TEJA.
...
YOU!
YOU!
??
"THE PAST CLINGS TO US LIKE TAR."

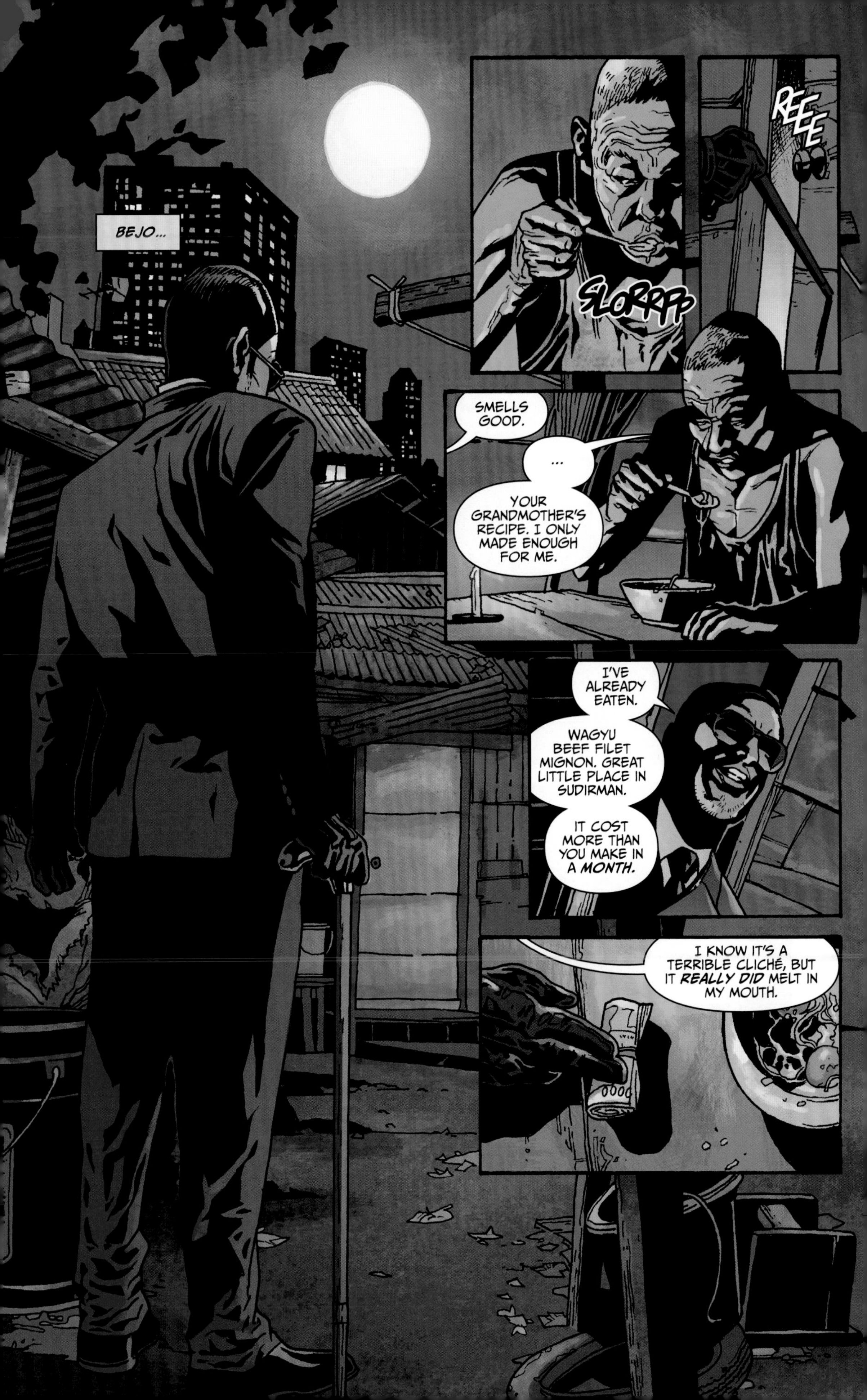
BEJO...
SLORRPP
REEEE
SMELLS GOOD.
...
YOUR GRANDMOTHER'S RECIPE. I ONLY MADE ENOUGH FOR ME.
I'VE ALREADY EATEN.
WAGYU BEEF FILET MIGNON. GREAT LITTLE PLACE IN SUDIRMAN.
IT COST MORE THAN YOU MAKE IN A *MONTH.*
I KNOW IT'S A TERRIBLE CLICHÉ, BUT IT *REALLY DID* MELT IN MY MOUTH.

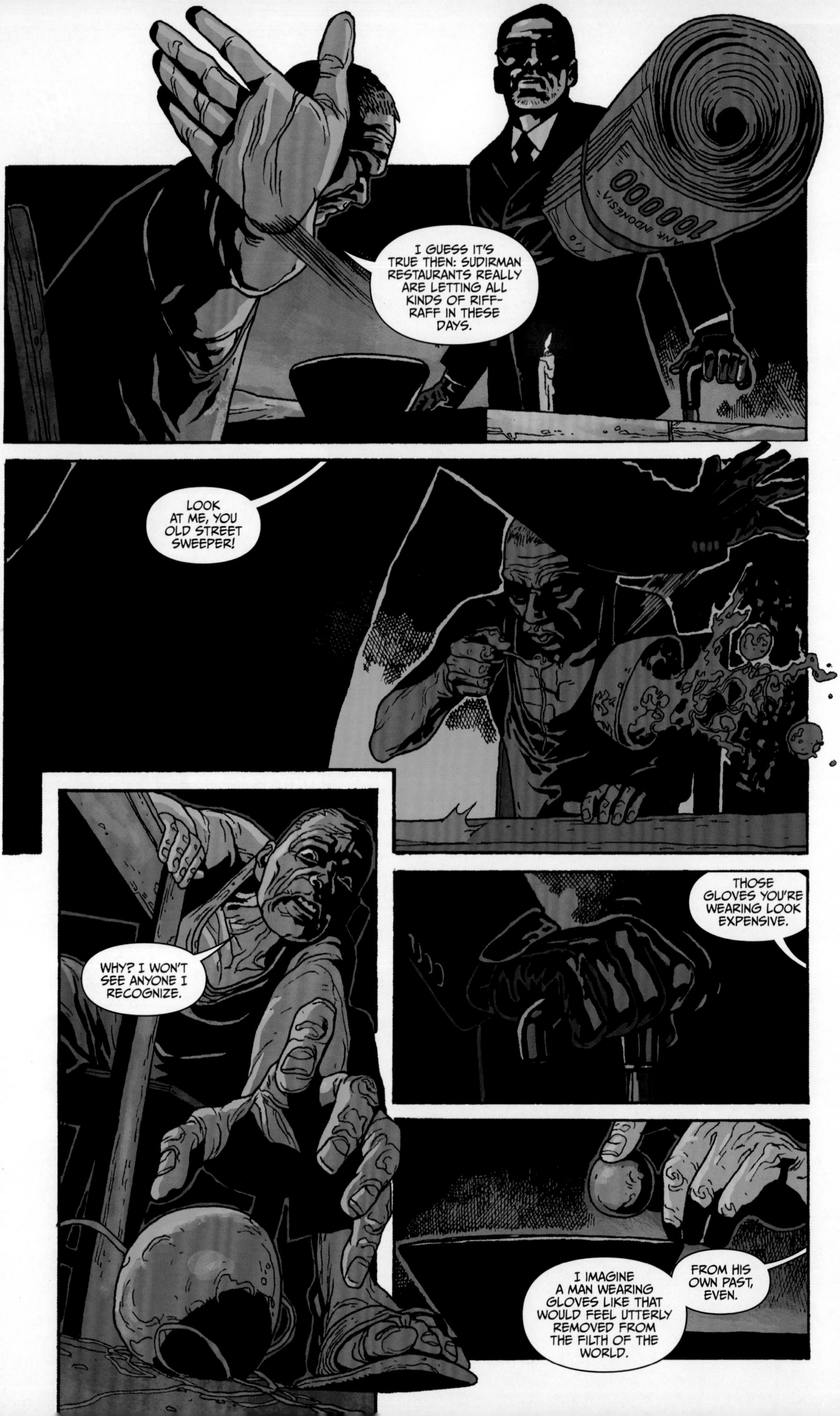
I GUESS IT'S TRUE THEN: SUDIRMAN RESTAURANTS REALLY ARE LETTING ALL KINDS OF RIFF-RAFF IN THESE DAYS.
LOOK AT ME, YOU OLD STREET SWEEPER!
WHY? I WON'T SEE ANYONE I RECOGNIZE.
THOSE GLOVES YOU'RE WEARING LOOK EXPENSIVE.
I IMAGINE A MAN WEARING GLOVES LIKE THAT WOULD FEEL UTTERLY REMOVED FROM THE FILTH OF THE WORLD.
FROM HIS OWN PAST, EVEN.

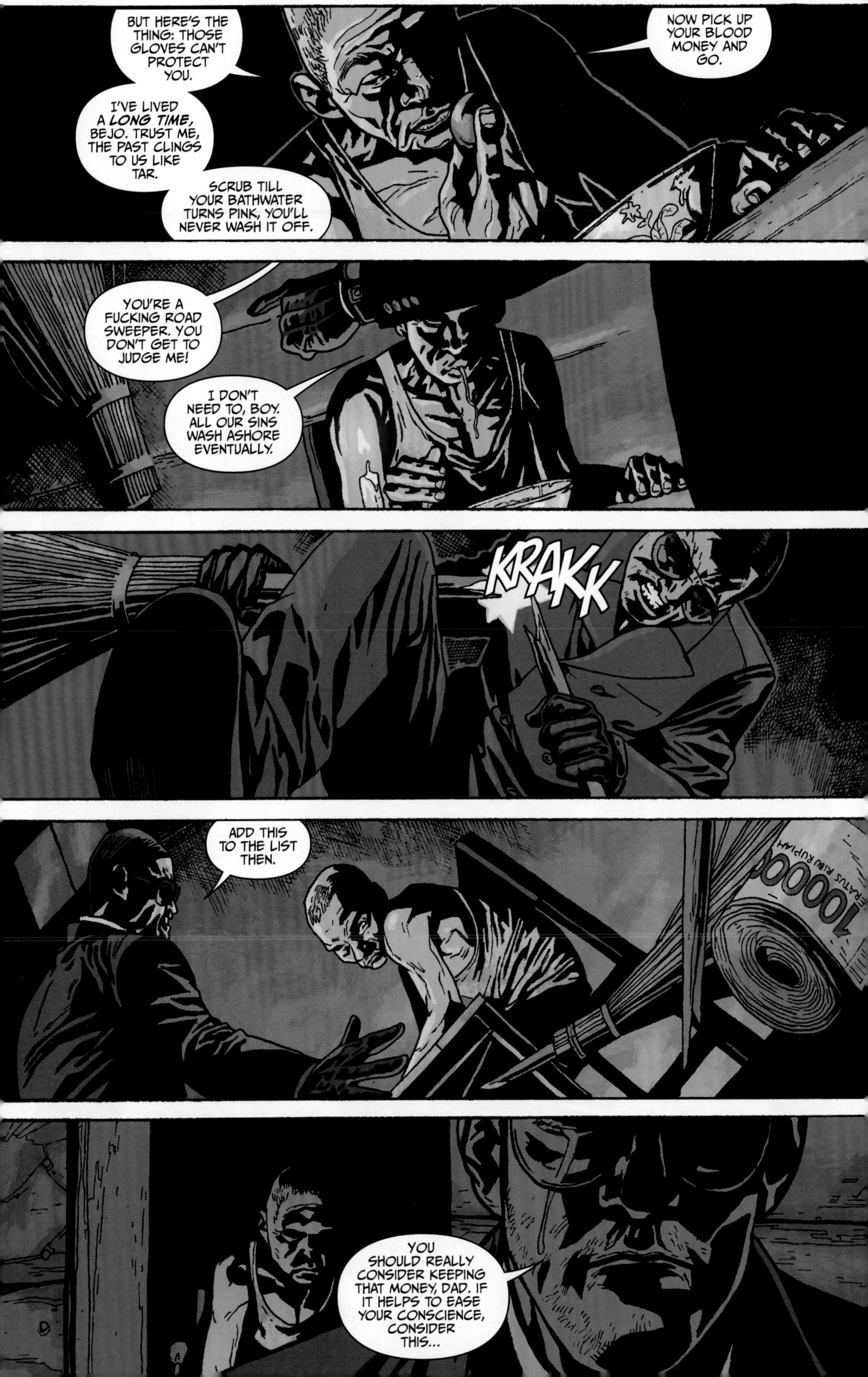
BUT HERE'S THE THING: THOSE GLOVES CAN'T PROTECT YOU.
I'VE LIVED A *LONG TIME,* BEJO. TRUST ME, THE PAST CLINGS TO US LIKE TAR.
SCRUB TILL YOUR BATHWATER TURNS PINK, YOU'LL NEVER WASH IT OFF.
NOW PICK UP YOUR BLOOD MONEY AND GO.
YOU'RE A FUCKING ROAD SWEEPER. YOU DON'T GET TO JUDGE ME!
I DON'T NEED TO, BOY. ALL OUR SINS WASH ASHORE EVENTUALLY.
KRAKK
ADD THIS TO THE LIST THEN.
YOU SHOULD REALLY CONSIDER KEEPING THAT MONEY, DAD. IF IT HELPS TO EASE YOUR CONSCIENCE, CONSIDER THIS...

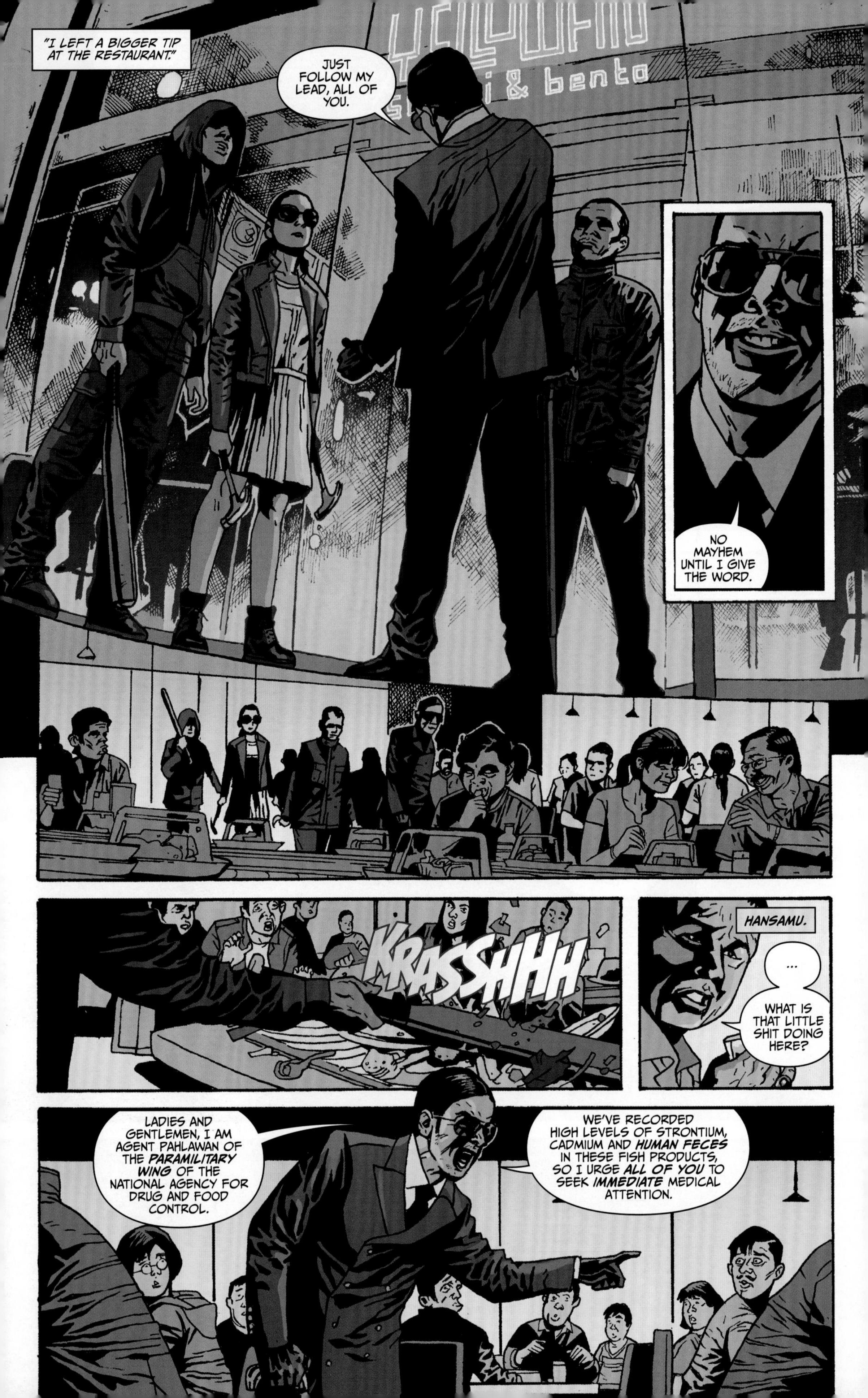
"I LEFT A BIGGER TIP AT THE RESTAURANT."
JUST FOLLOW MY LEAD, ALL OF YOU.
NO MAYHEM UNTIL I GIVE THE WORD.
KRASSHHH
HANSAMU.
...
WHAT IS THAT LITTLE SHIT DOING HERE?
LADIES AND GENTLEMEN, I AM AGENT PAHLAWAN OF THE PARAMILITARY WING OF THE NATIONAL AGENCY FOR DRUG AND FOOD CONTROL.
WE'VE RECORDED HIGH LEVELS OF STRONTIUM, CADMIUM AND HUMAN FECES IN THESE FISH PRODUCTS, SO I URGE ALL OF YOU TO SEEK IMMEDIATE MEDICAL ATTENTION.

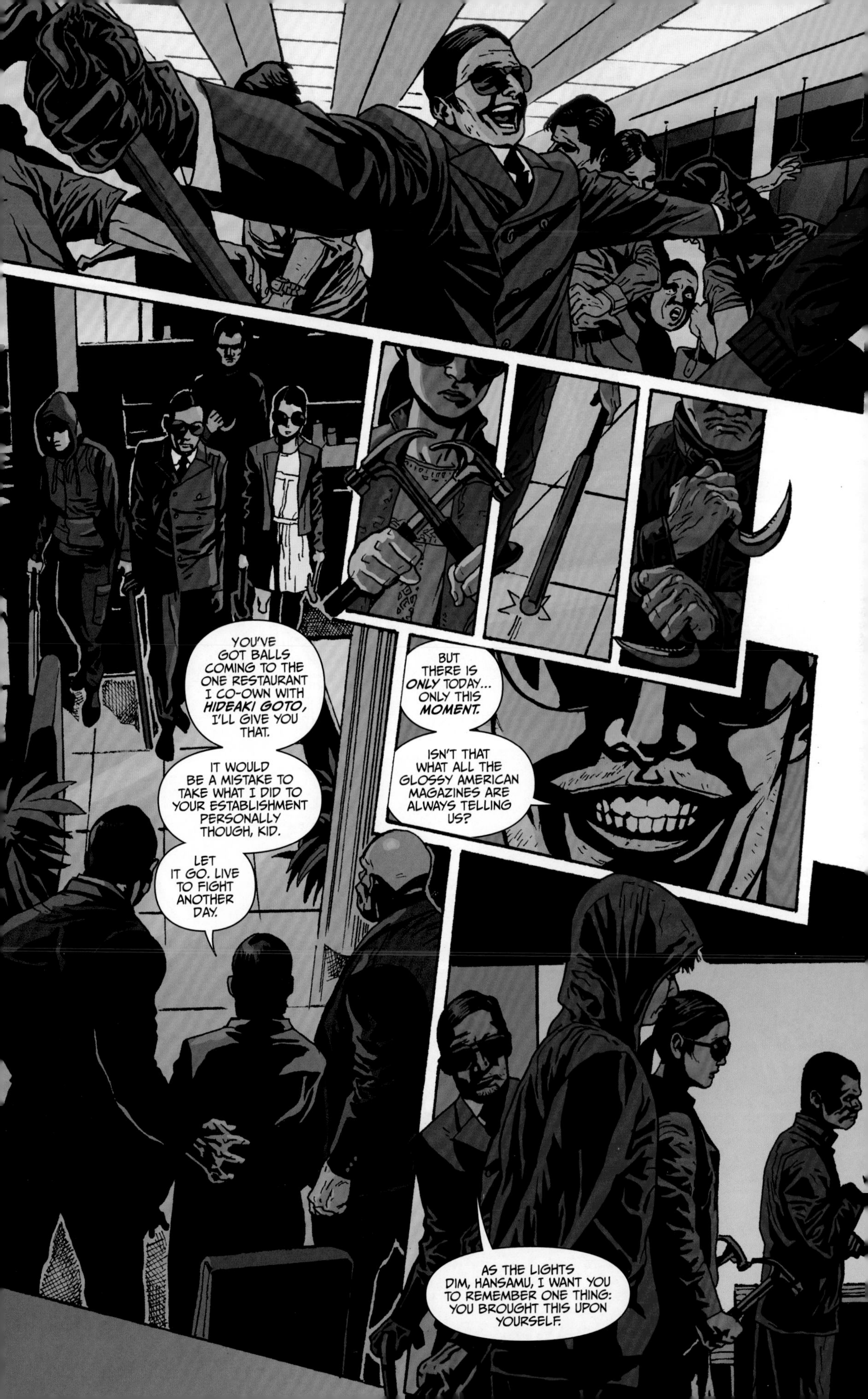
YOU'VE GOT BALLS COMING TO THE ONE RESTAURANT I CO-OWN WITH HIDEAKI GOTO, I'LL GIVE YOU THAT.
IT WOULD BE A MISTAKE TO TAKE WHAT I DID TO YOUR ESTABLISHMENT PERSONALLY THOUGH, KID.
LET IT GO. LIVE TO FIGHT ANOTHER DAY.
BUT THERE IS ONLY TODAY... ONLY THIS MOMENT.
ISN'T THAT WHAT ALL THE GLOSSY AMERICAN MAGAZINES ARE ALWAYS TELLING US?
AS THE LIGHTS DIM, HANSAMU, I WANT YOU TO REMEMBER ONE THING: YOU BROUGHT THIS UPON YOURSELF.

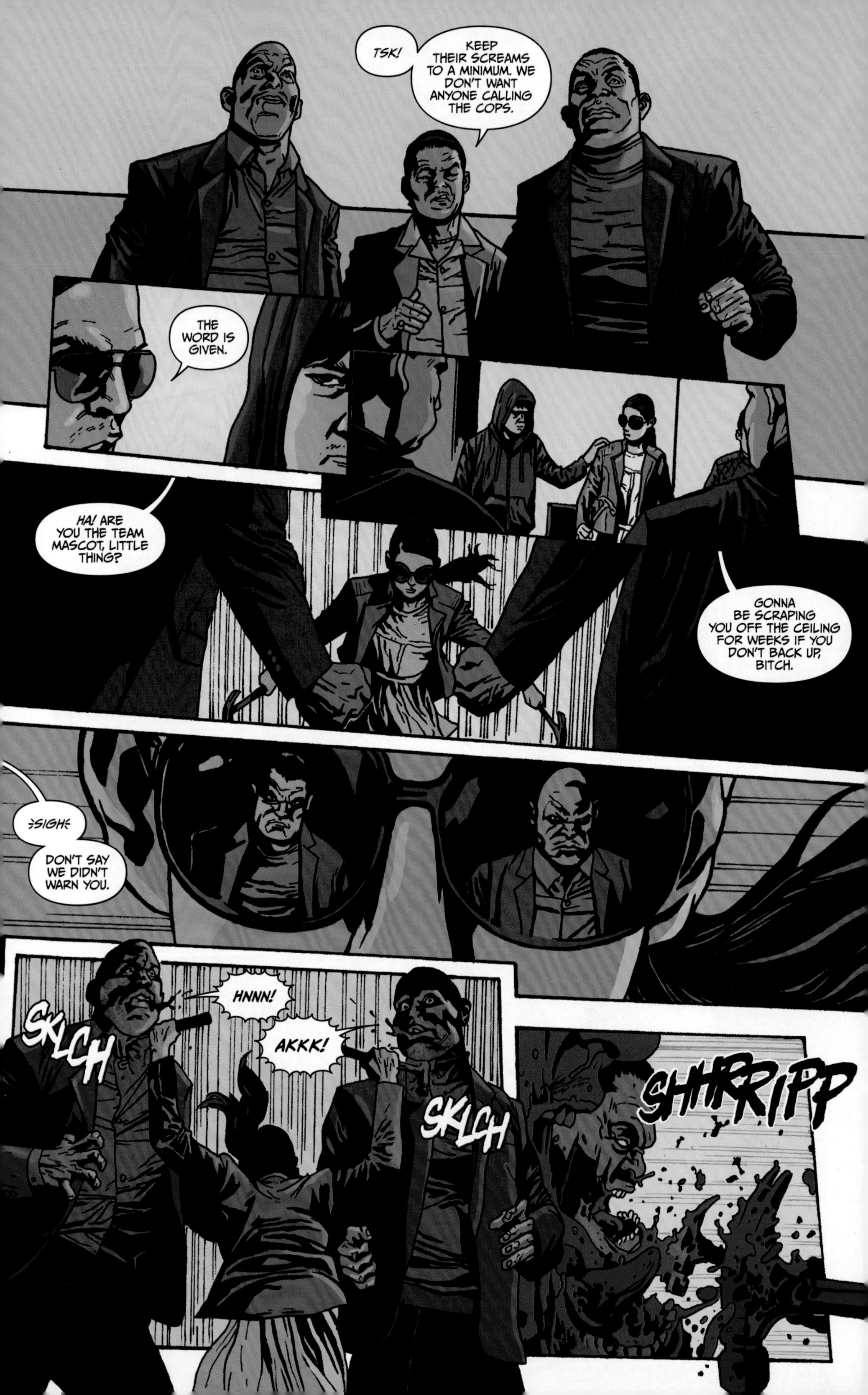
TSK!
KEEP THEIR SCREAMS TO A MINIMUM. WE DON'T WANT ANYONE CALLING THE COPS.
THE WORD IS GIVEN.
HA! ARE YOU THE TEAM MASCOT, LITTLE THING?
GONNA BE SCRAPING YOU OFF THE CEILING FOR WEEKS IF YOU DON'T BACK UP, BITCH.
SIGH
DON'T SAY WE DIDN'T WARN YOU.
SKLCH
HNNN!
AKKK!
SKLCH
SHRRIPP

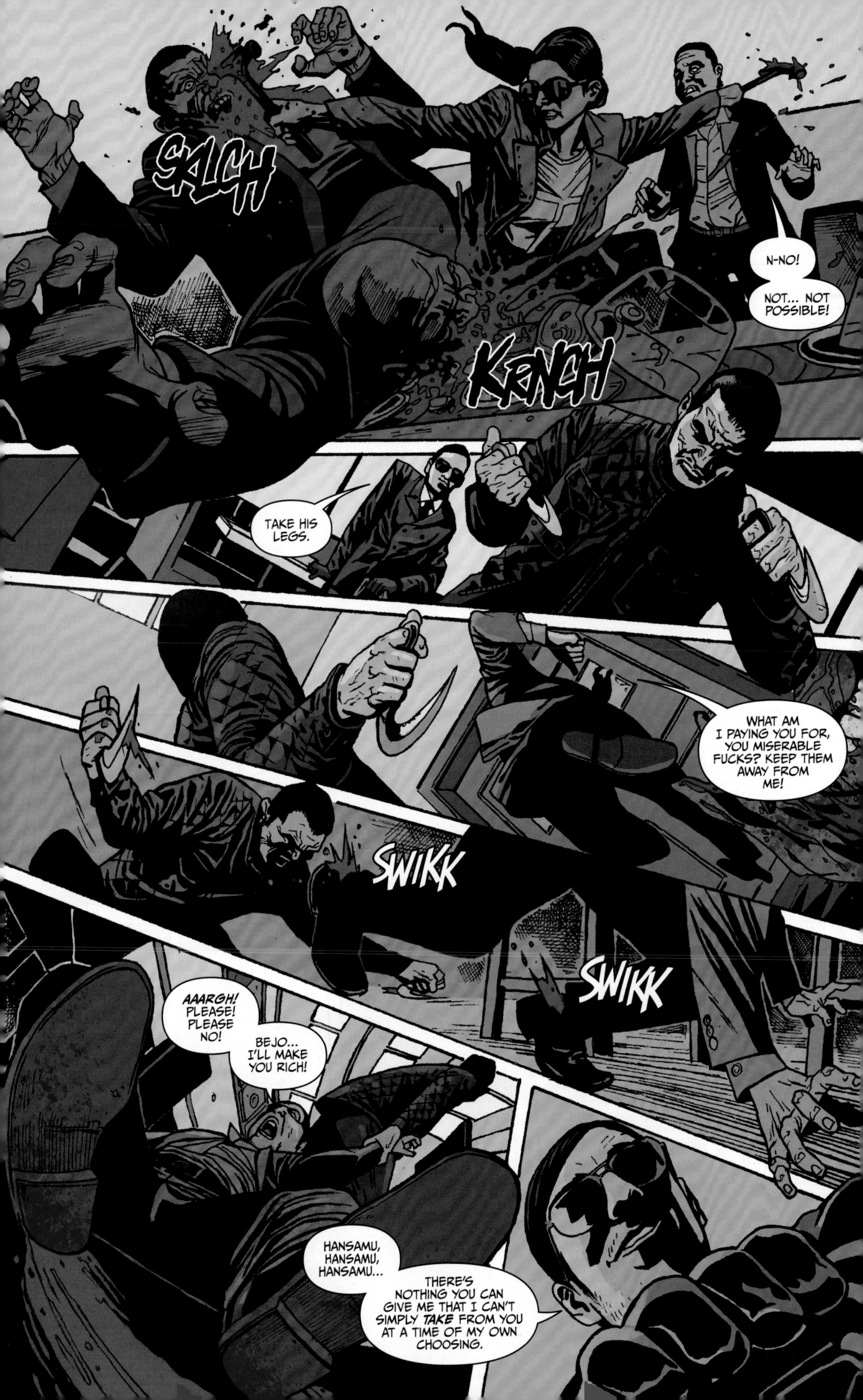
SKLCH
N-NO!
NOT... NOT POSSIBLE!
KRNCH
TAKE HIS LEGS.
WHAT AM I PAYING YOU FOR, YOU MISERABLE FUCKS? KEEP THEM AWAY FROM ME!
SWIKK
SWIKK
AAARGH! PLEASE! PLEASE NO!
BEJO... I'LL MAKE YOU RICH!
HANSAMU, HANSAMU, HANSAMU...
THERE'S NOTHING YOU CAN GIVE ME THAT I CAN'T SIMPLY TAKE FROM YOU AT A TIME OF MY OWN CHOOSING.

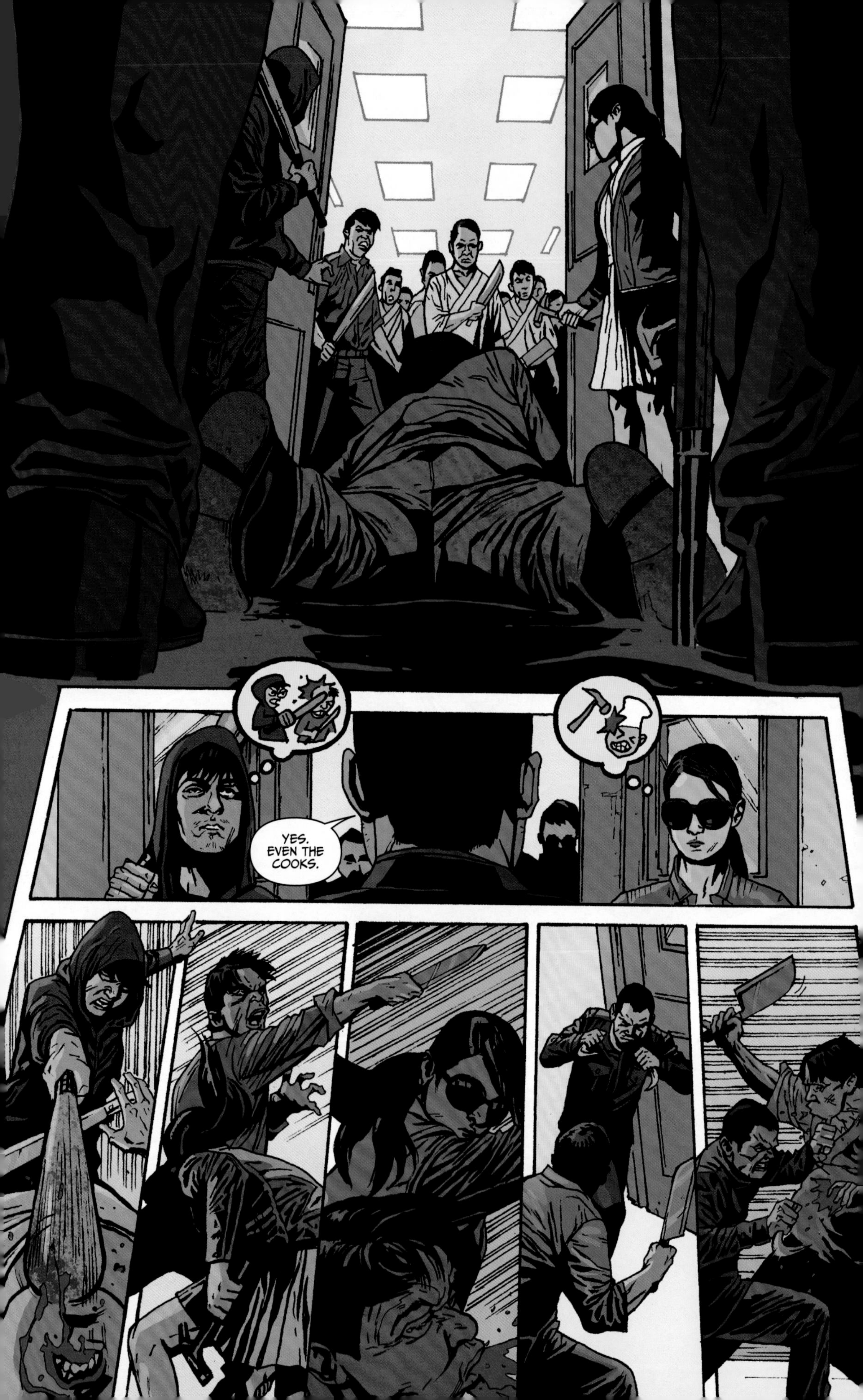
YES.
EVEN THE
COOKS.

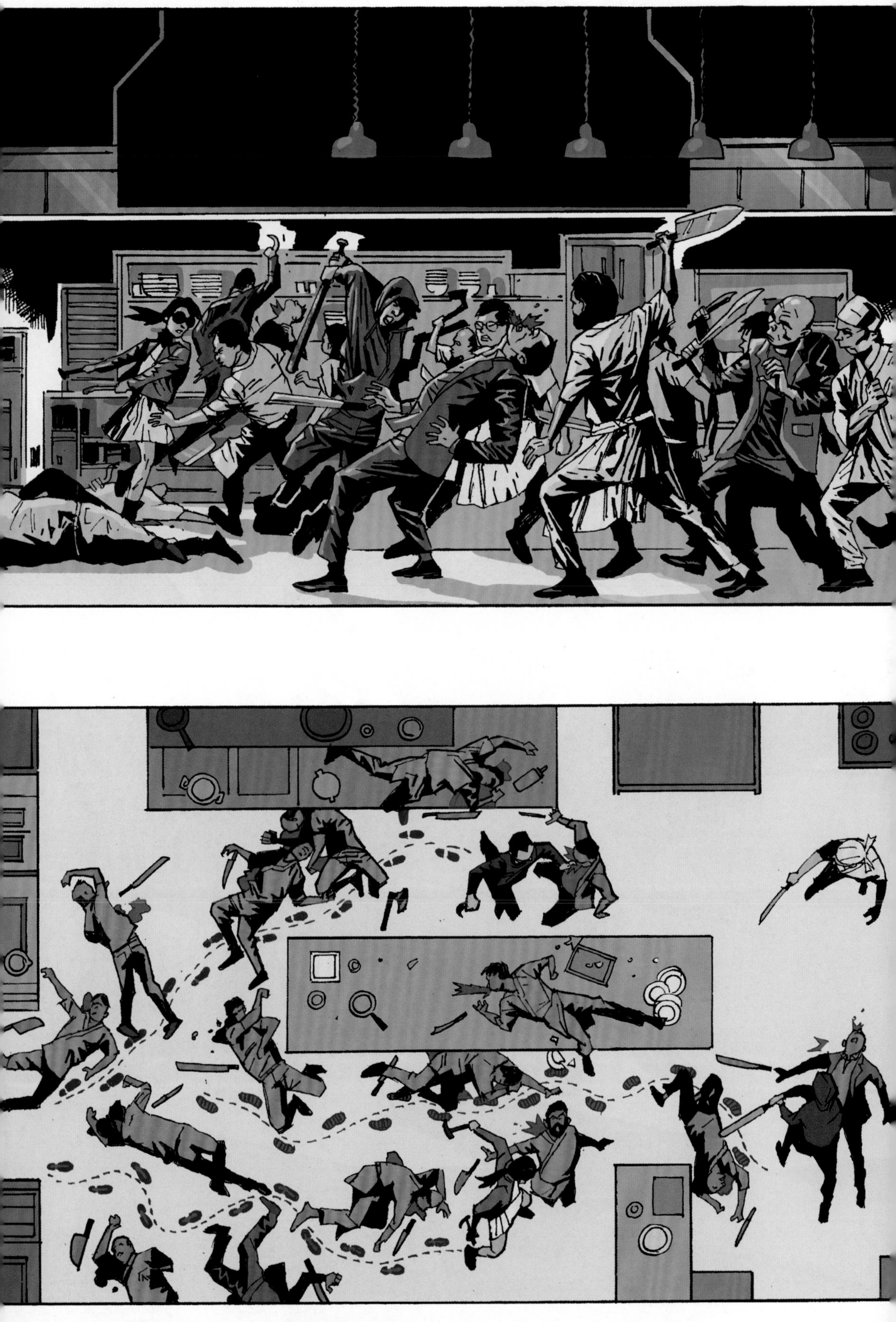

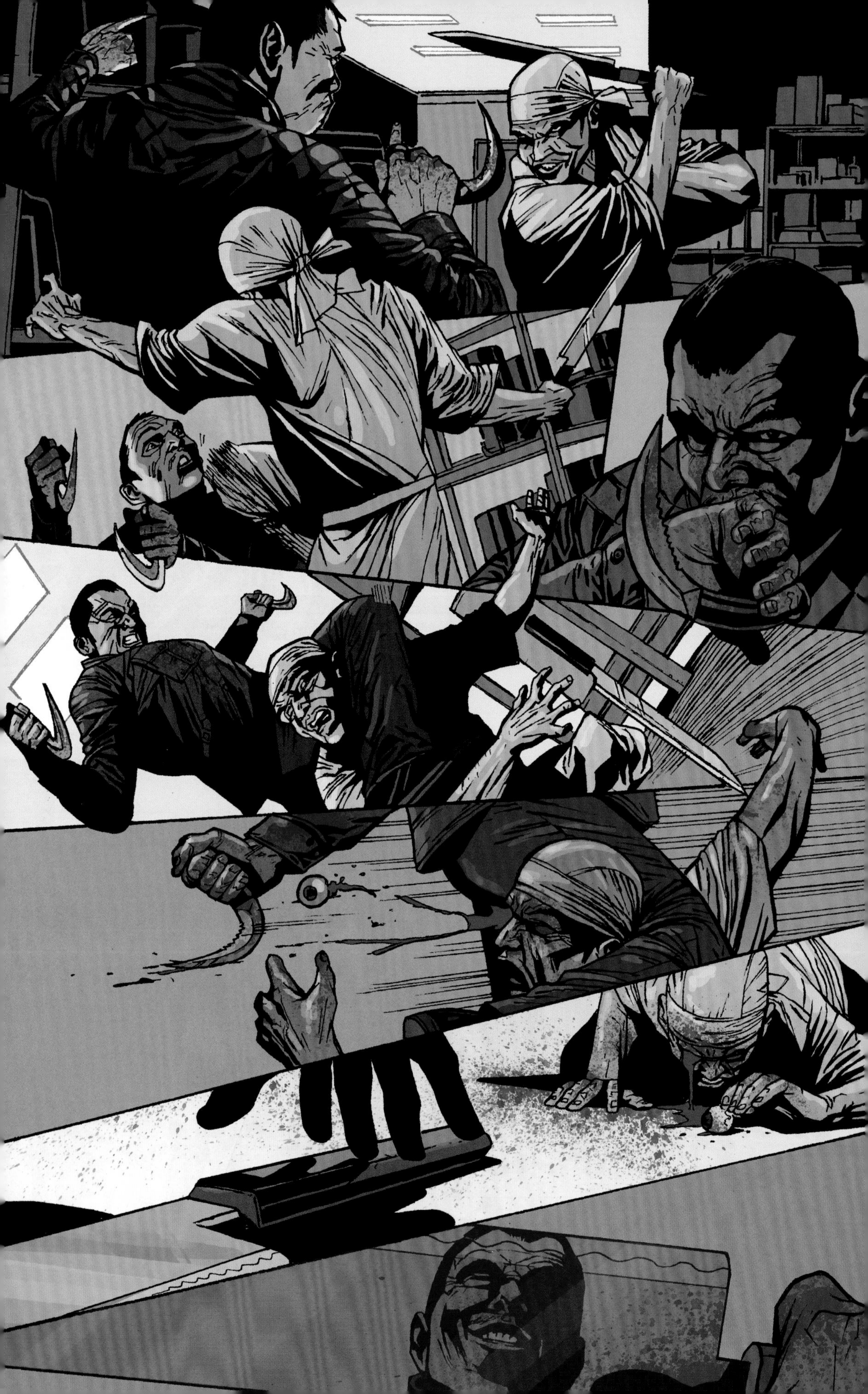

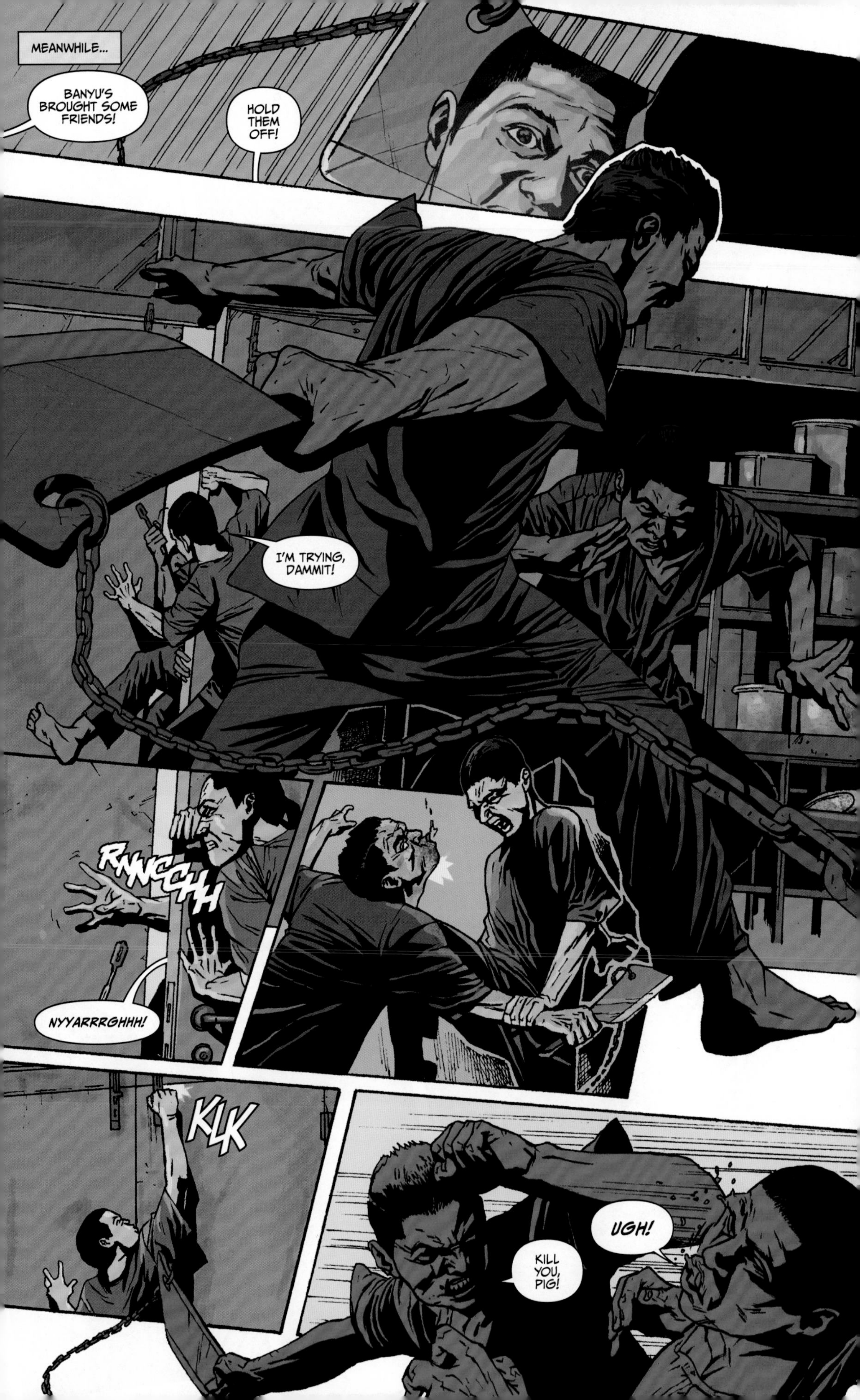
MEANWHILE...
BANYU'S BROUGHT SOME FRIENDS!
HOLD THEM OFF!
I'M TRYING, DAMMIT!
RNNCCHH
NYYARRRGHHH!
KLK
UGH!
KILL YOU, PIG!

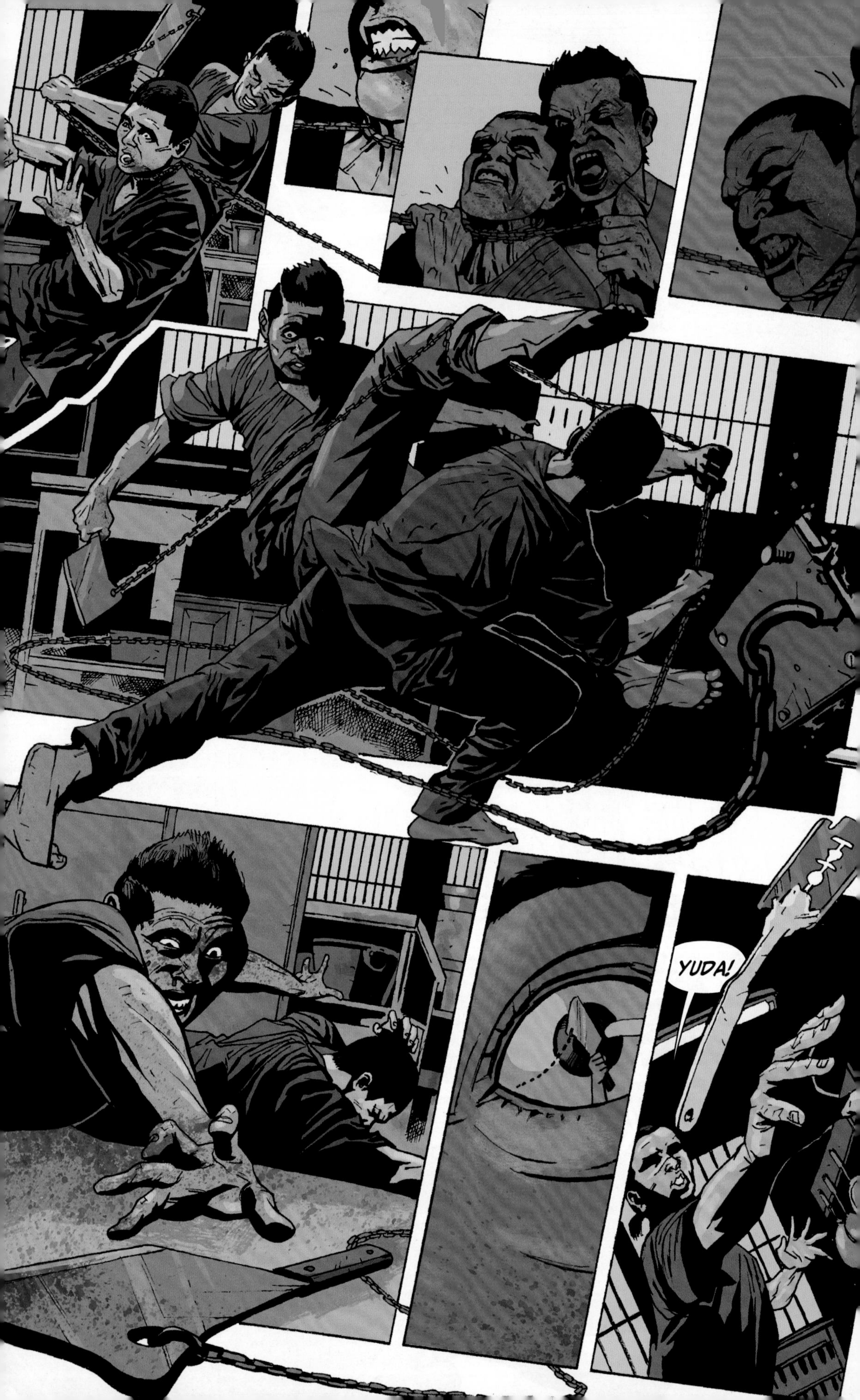
YUDA!

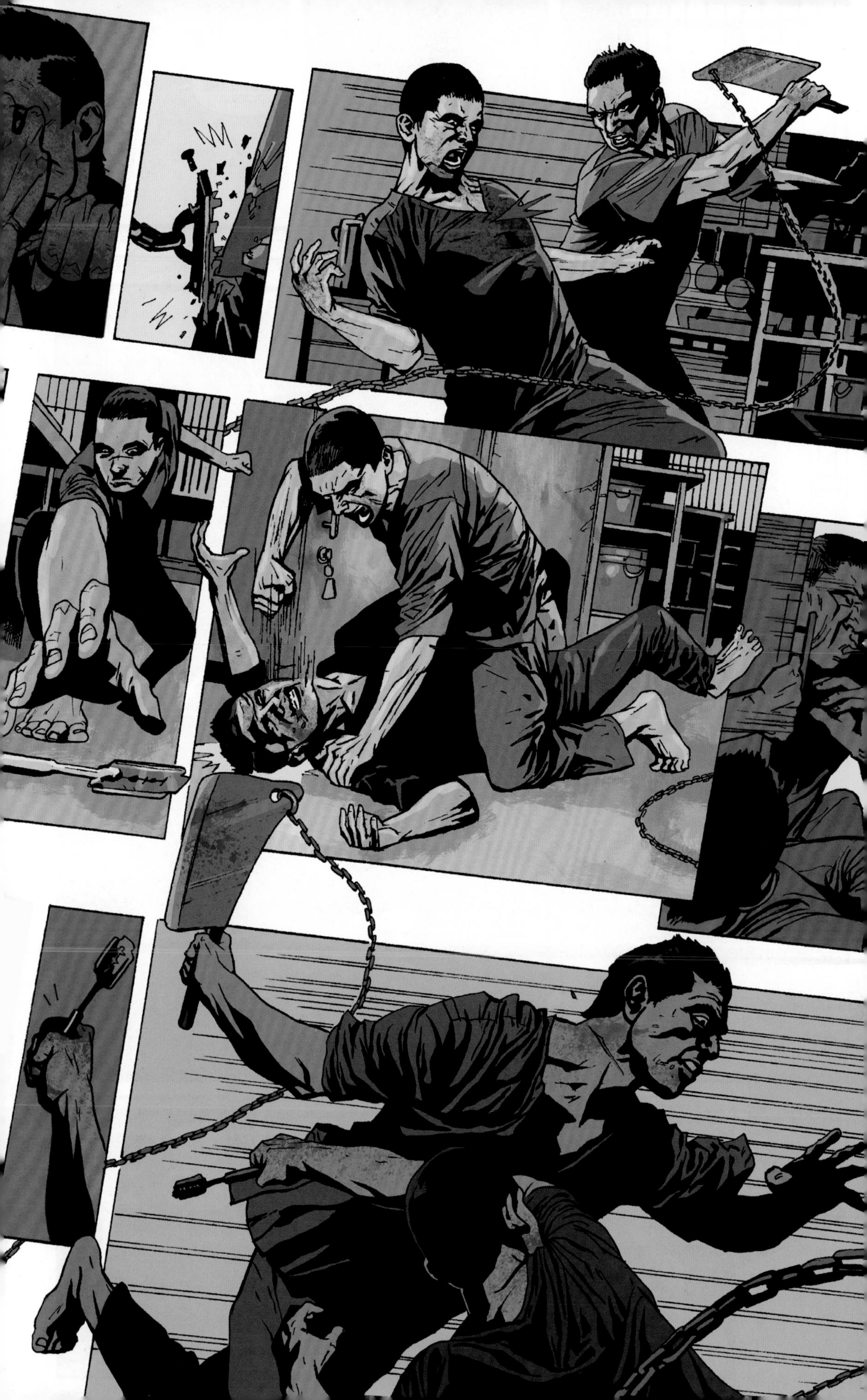

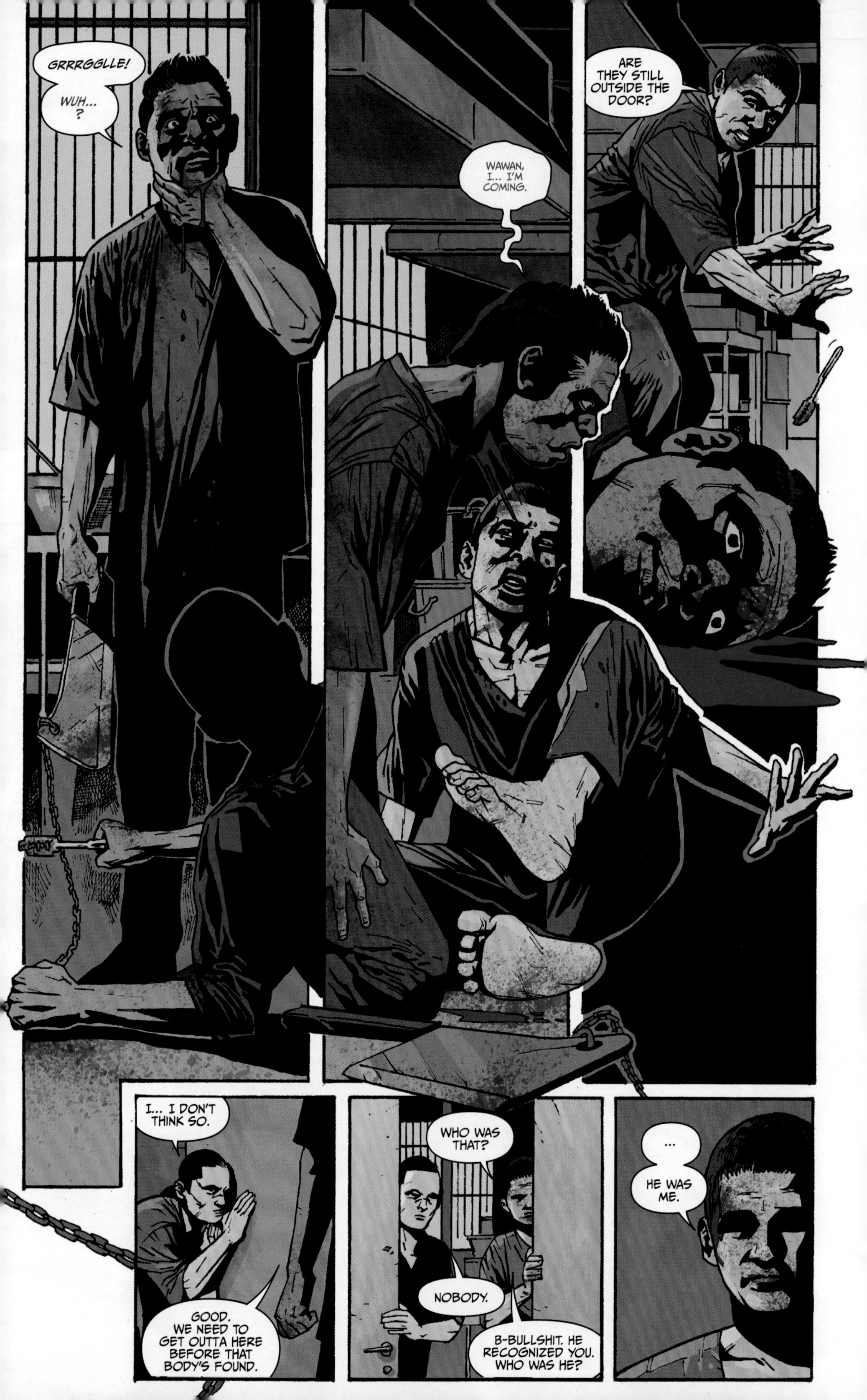
GRRRGGLLE!
WUH... ?
WAWAN, I... I'M COMING.
ARE THEY STILL OUTSIDE THE DOOR?
I... I DON'T THINK SO.
GOOD. WE NEED TO GET OUTTA HERE BEFORE THAT BODY'S FOUND.
WHO WAS THAT?
NOBODY.
B-BULLSHIT. HE RECOGNIZED YOU. WHO WAS HE?
...
HE WAS ME.

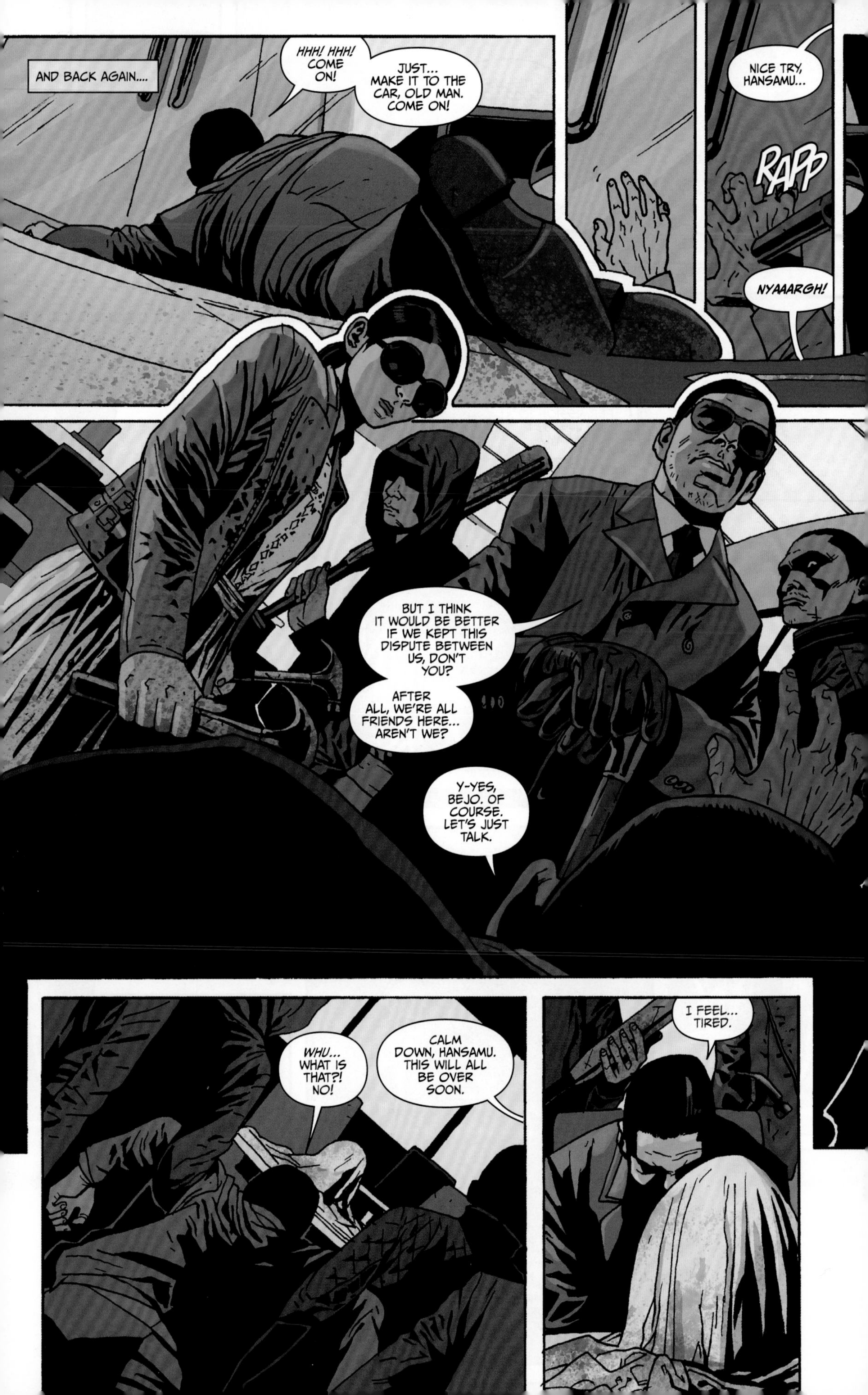
AND BACK AGAIN....
HHH! HHH! COME ON!
JUST... MAKE IT TO THE CAR, OLD MAN. COME ON!
NICE TRY, HANSAMU...
RAPP
NYAAARGH!
BUT I THINK IT WOULD BE BETTER IF WE KEPT THIS DISPUTE BETWEEN US, DON'T YOU?
AFTER ALL, WE'RE ALL FRIENDS HERE... AREN'T WE?
Y-YES, BEJO. OF COURSE. LET'S JUST TALK.
WHU... WHAT IS THAT?! NO!
CALM DOWN, HANSAMU. THIS WILL ALL BE OVER SOON.
I FEEL... TIRED.

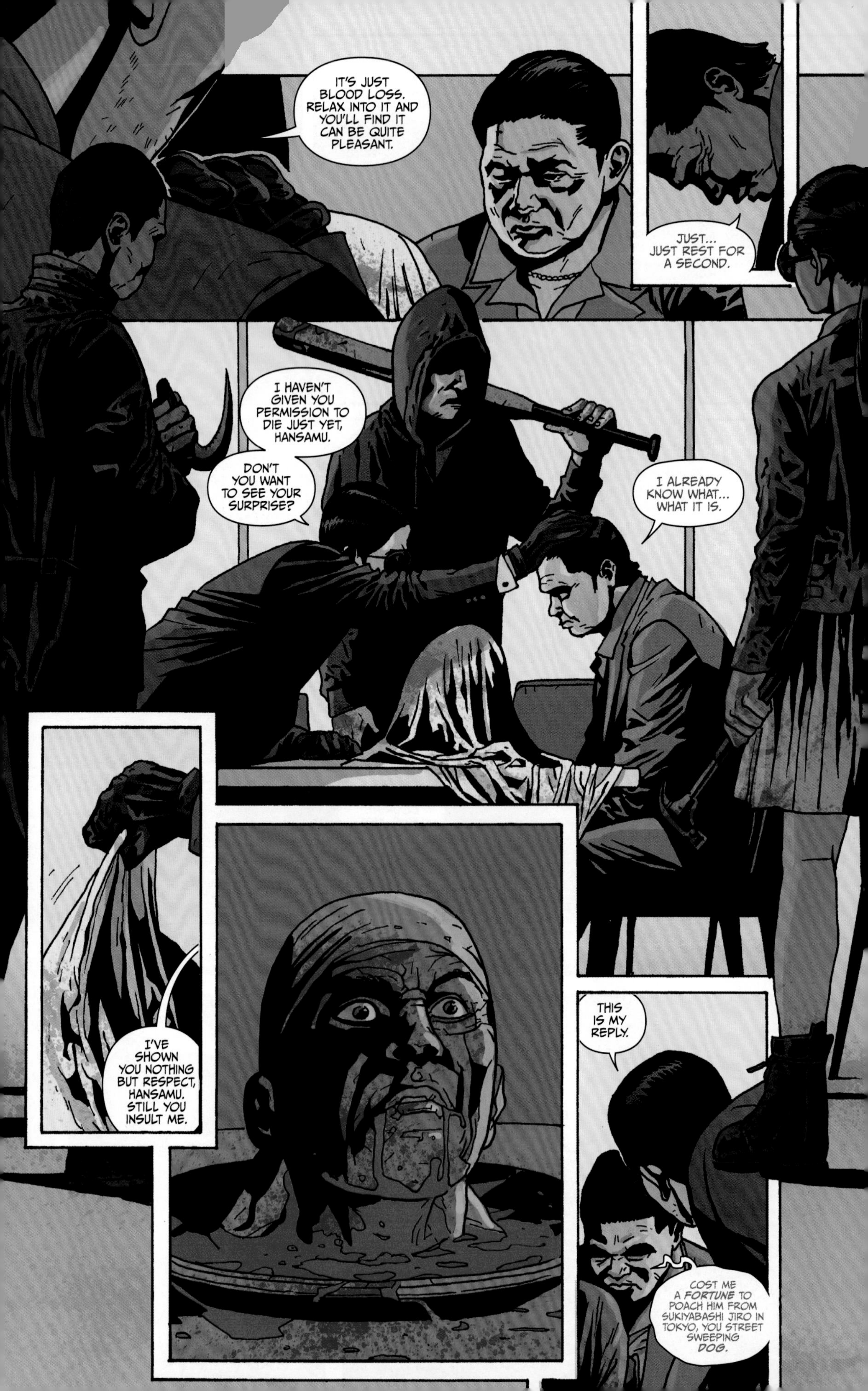
IT'S JUST BLOOD LOSS. RELAX INTO IT AND YOU'LL FIND IT CAN BE QUITE PLEASANT.
JUST... JUST REST FOR A SECOND.
I HAVEN'T GIVEN YOU PERMISSION TO DIE JUST YET, HANSAMU.
DON'T YOU WANT TO SEE YOUR SURPRISE?
I ALREADY KNOW WHAT... WHAT IT IS.
I'VE SHOWN YOU NOTHING BUT RESPECT, HANSAMU. STILL YOU INSULT ME.
THIS IS MY REPLY.
COST ME A FORTUNE TO POACH HIM FROM SUKIYABASHI JIRO IN TOKYO, YOU STREET SWEEPING DOG.

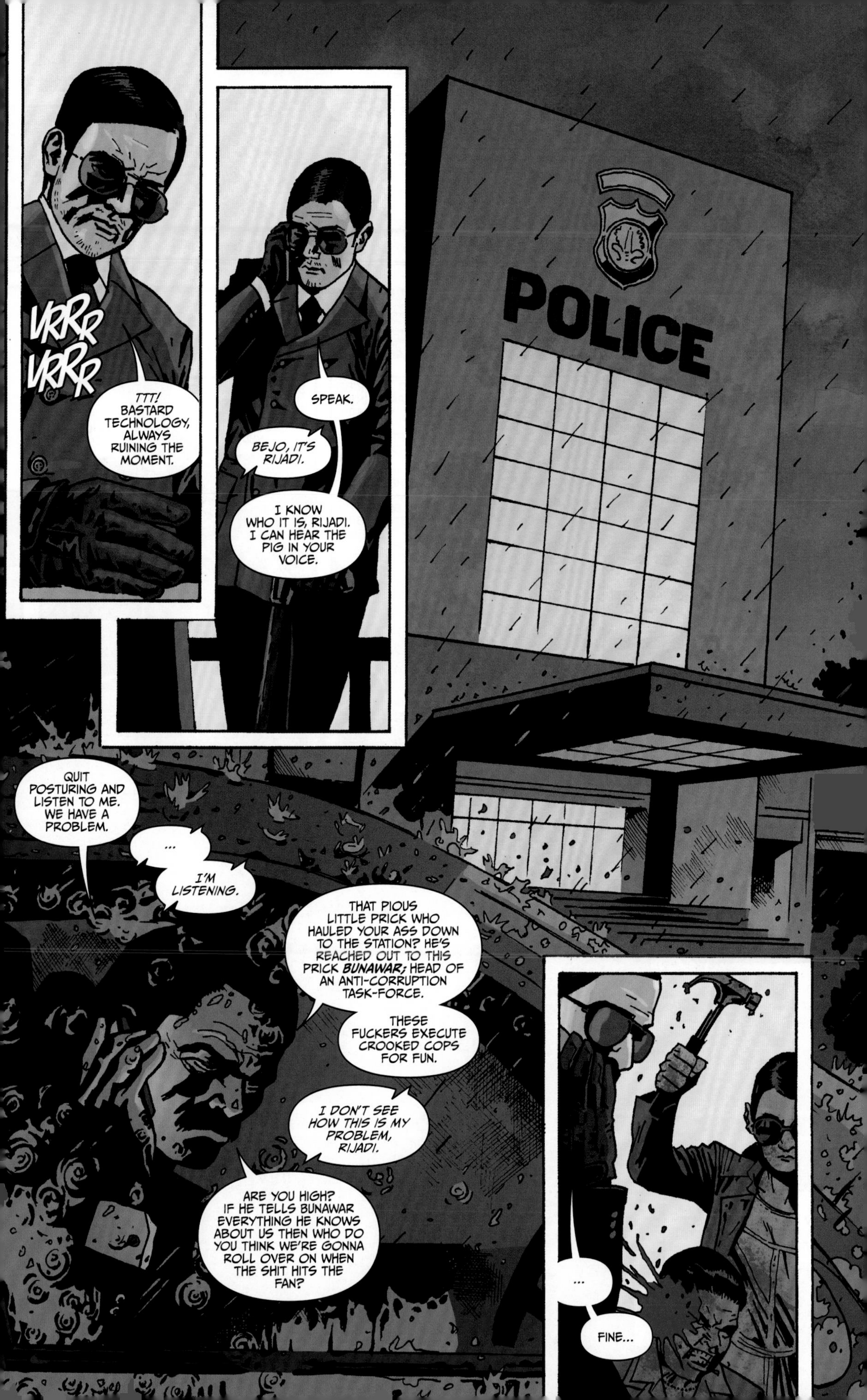
VRRR VRRR
TTT! BASTARD TECHNOLOGY, ALWAYS RUINING THE MOMENT.
SPEAK.
BEJO, IT'S RIJADI.
I KNOW WHO IT IS, RIJADI. I CAN HEAR THE PIG IN YOUR VOICE.
POLICE
QUIT POSTURING AND LISTEN TO ME. WE HAVE A PROBLEM.
...
I'M LISTENING.
THAT PIOUS LITTLE PRICK WHO HAULED YOUR ASS DOWN TO THE STATION? HE'S REACHED OUT TO THIS PRICK BUNAWAR; HEAD OF AN ANTI-CORRUPTION TASK-FORCE.
THESE FUCKERS EXECUTE CROOKED COPS FOR FUN.
I DON'T SEE HOW THIS IS MY PROBLEM, RIJADI.
ARE YOU HIGH? IF HE TELLS BUNAWAR EVERYTHING HE KNOWS ABOUT US THEN WHO DO YOU THINK WE'RE GONNA ROLL OVER ON WHEN THE SHIT HITS THE FAN?
...
FINE...

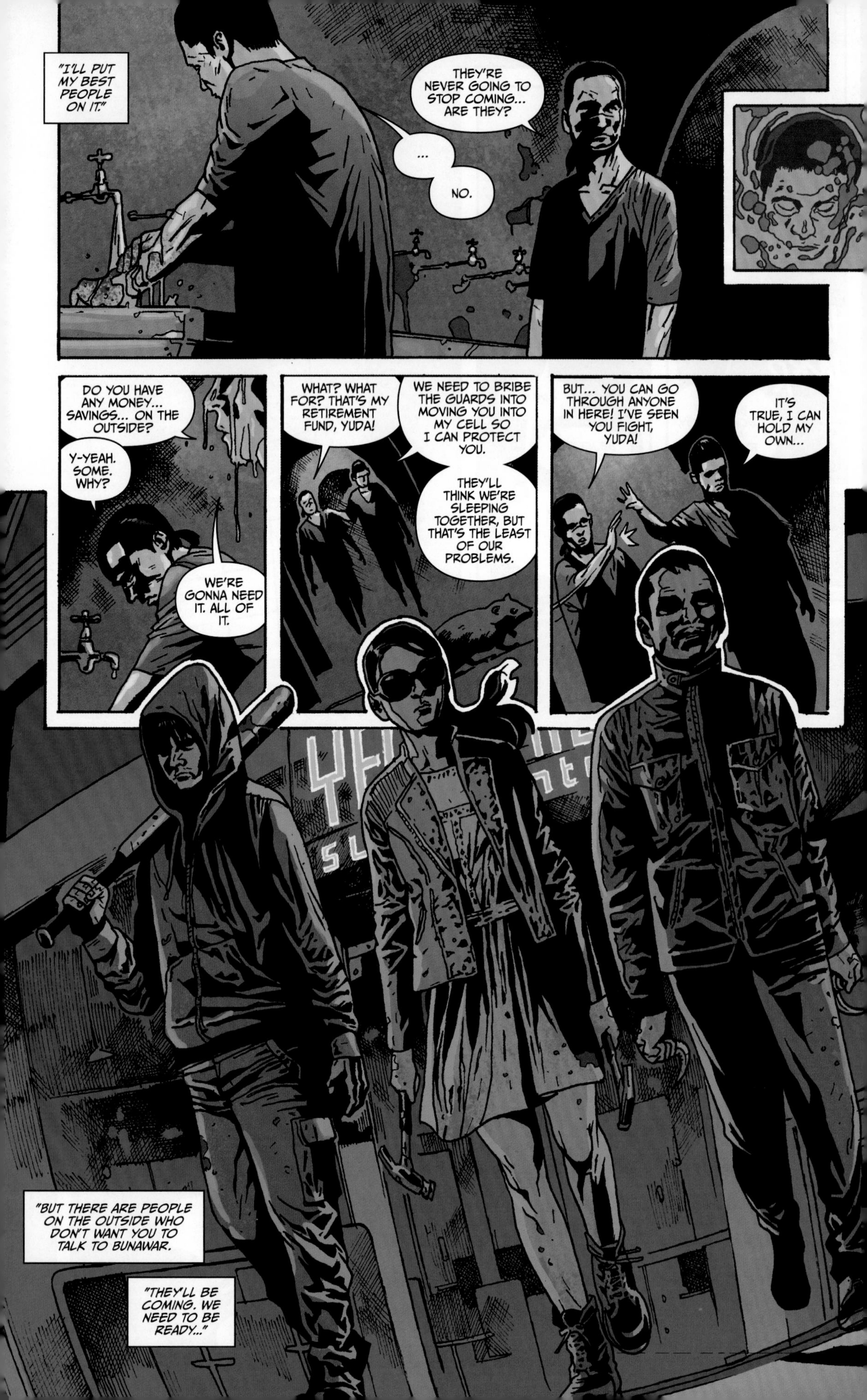
"I'LL PUT MY BEST PEOPLE ON IT."
THEY'RE NEVER GOING TO STOP COMING... ARE THEY?
...
NO.
DO YOU HAVE ANY MONEY... SAVINGS... ON THE OUTSIDE?
Y-YEAH. SOME. WHY?
WE'RE GONNA NEED IT. ALL OF IT.
WHAT? WHAT FOR? THAT'S MY RETIREMENT FUND, YUDA!
WE NEED TO BRIBE THE GUARDS INTO MOVING YOU INTO MY CELL SO I CAN PROTECT YOU.
THEY'LL THINK WE'RE SLEEPING TOGETHER, BUT THAT'S THE LEAST OF OUR PROBLEMS.
BUT... YOU CAN GO THROUGH ANYONE IN HERE! I'VE SEEN YOU FIGHT, YUDA!
IT'S TRUE, I CAN HOLD MY OWN...
"BUT THERE ARE PEOPLE ON THE OUTSIDE WHO DON'T WANT YOU TO TALK TO BUNAWAR.
"THEY'LL BE COMING. WE NEED TO BE READY..."

CHAPTER 4

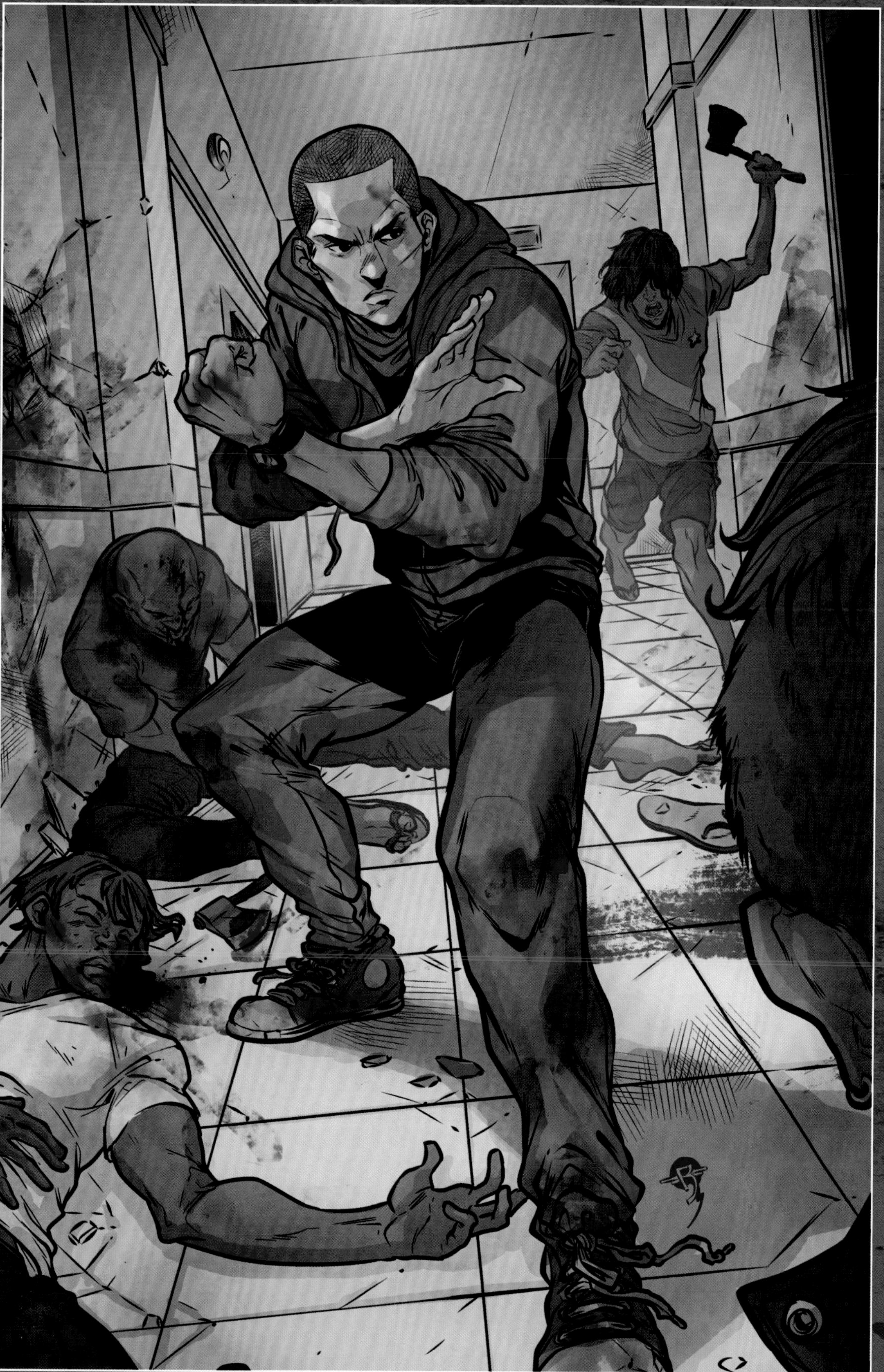

Illustration by **Rhoald Marcellius**

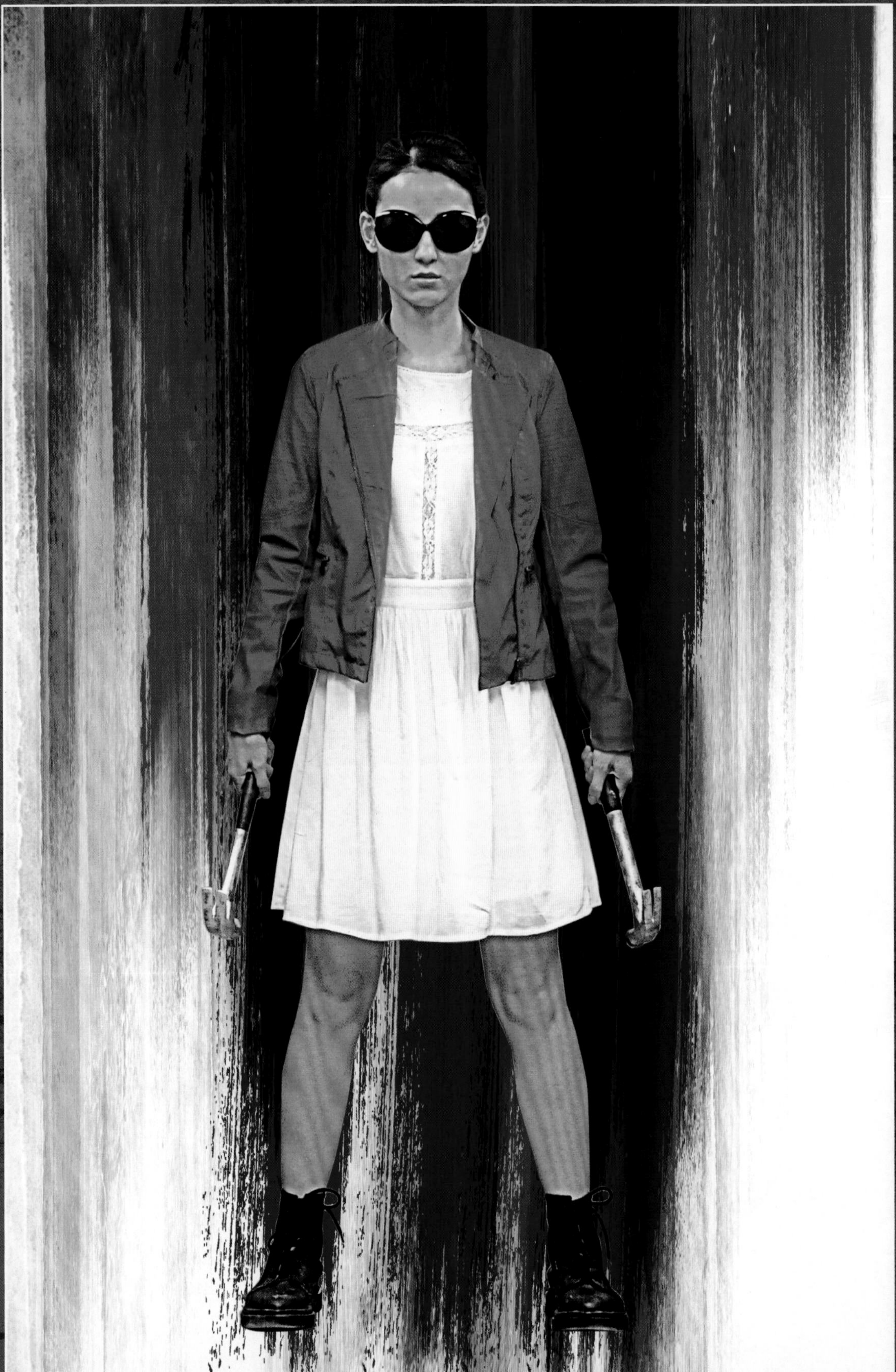

Cover 4b

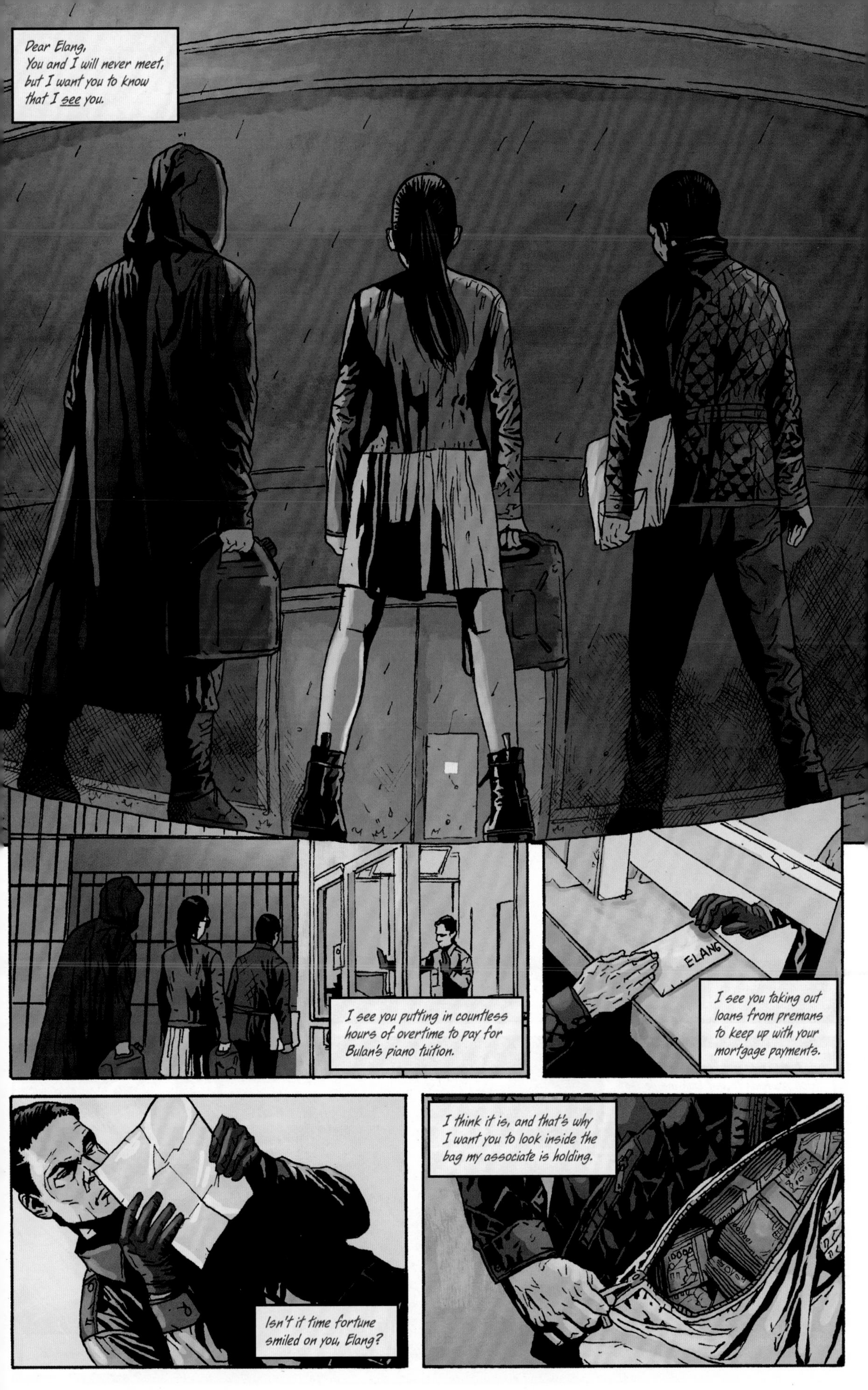
Dear Elang,
You and I will never meet, but I want you to know that I see you.
I see you putting in countless hours of overtime to pay for Bulan's piano tuition.
ELANG
I see you taking out loans from premans to keep up with your mortgage payments.
Isn't it time fortune smiled on you, Elang?
I think it is, and that's why I want you to look inside the bag my associate is holding.

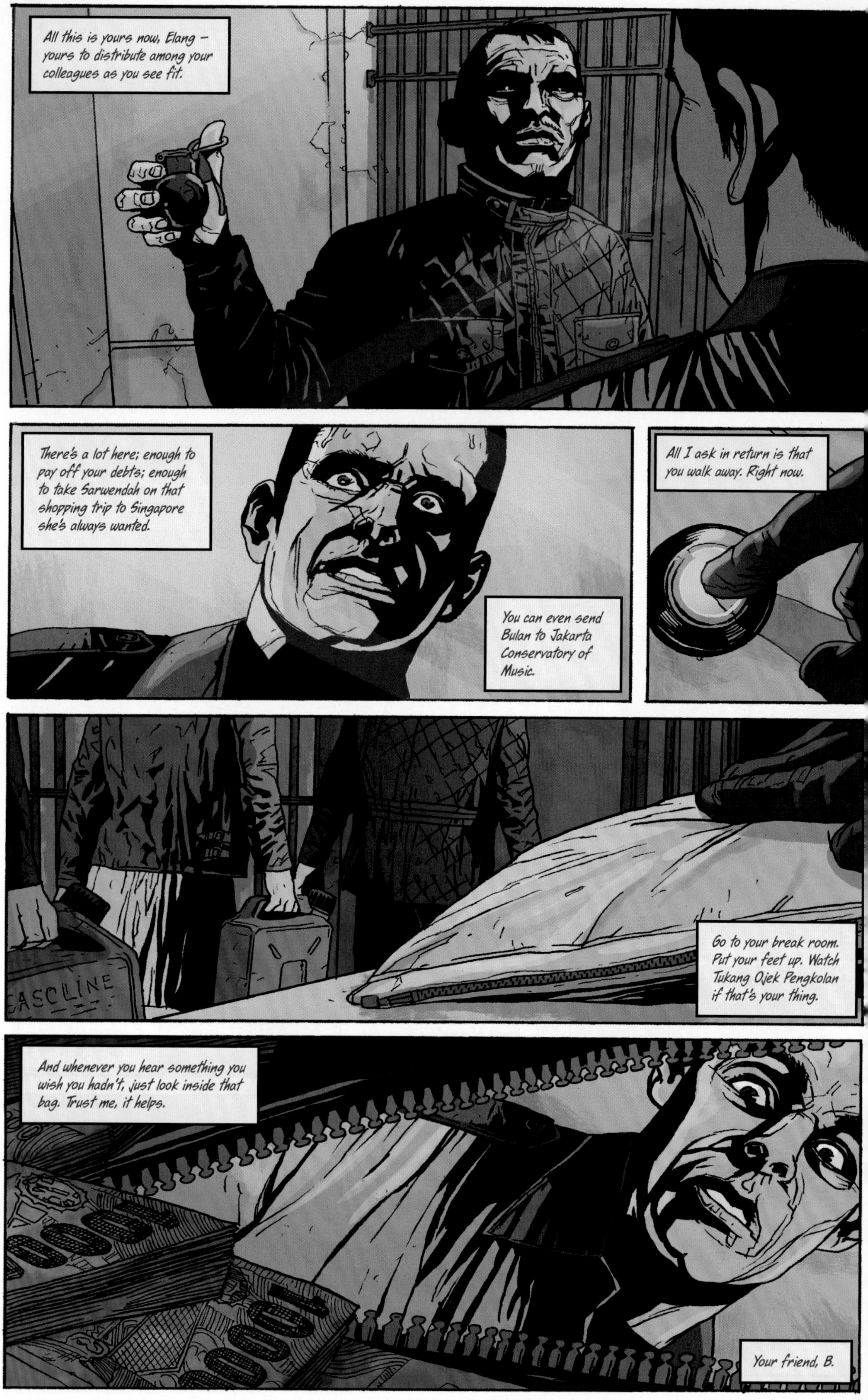
All this is yours now, Elang – yours to distribute among your colleagues as you see fit.
There's a lot here; enough to pay off your debts; enough to take Sarwendah on that shopping trip to Singapore she's always wanted.
You can even send Bulan to Jakarta Conservatory of Music.
All I ask in return is that you walk away. Right now.
GASOLINE
Go to your break room. Put your feet up. Watch Tukang Ojek Pengkolan if that's your thing.
And whenever you hear something you wish you hadn't, just look inside that bag. Trust me, it helps.
Your friend, B.

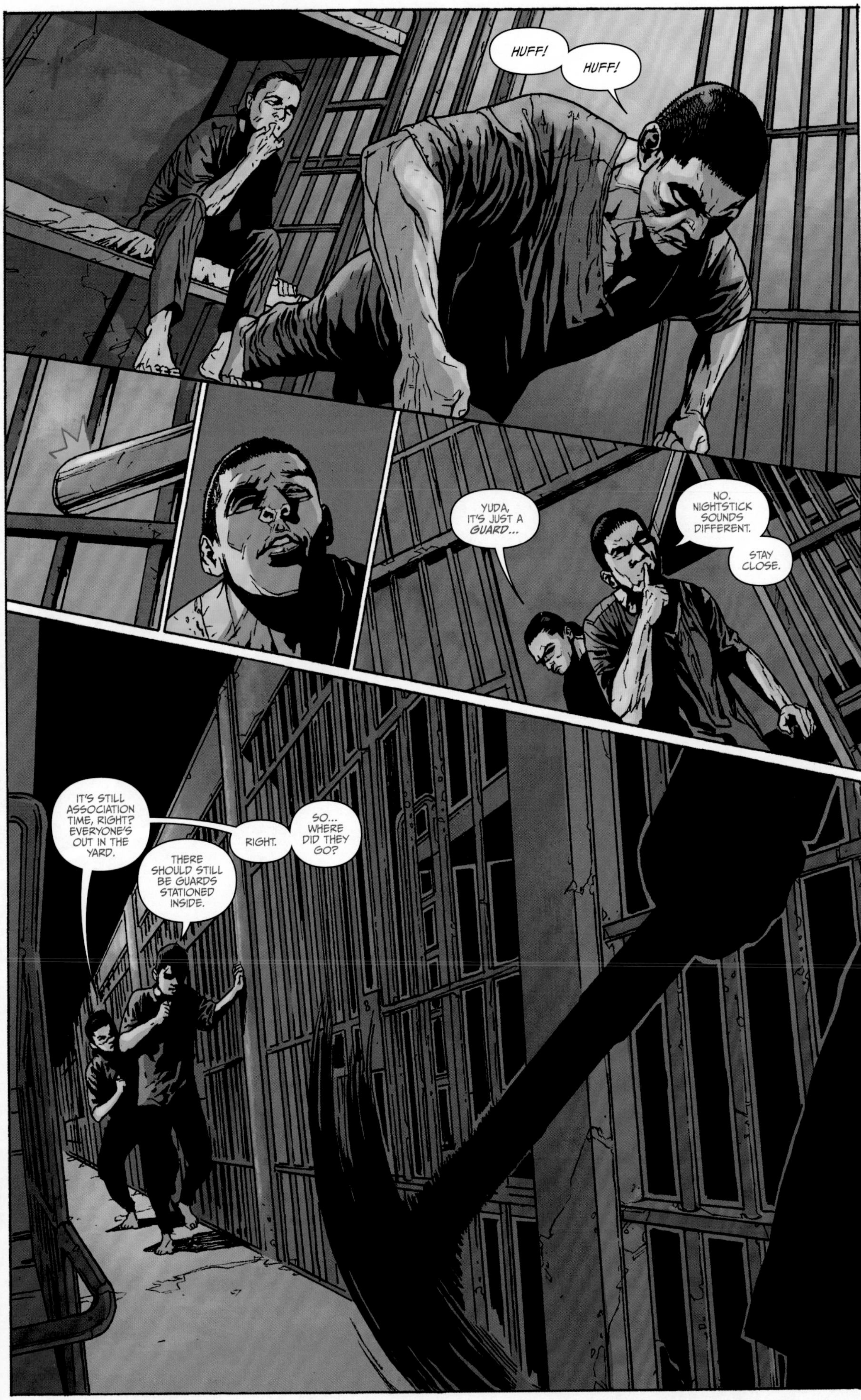
HUFF!
HUFF!
YUDA, IT'S JUST A GUARD...
NO. NIGHTSTICK SOUNDS DIFFERENT.
STAY CLOSE.
IT'S STILL ASSOCIATION TIME, RIGHT? EVERYONE'S OUT IN THE YARD.
RIGHT.
SO... WHERE DID THEY GO?
THERE SHOULD STILL BE GUARDS STATIONED INSIDE.

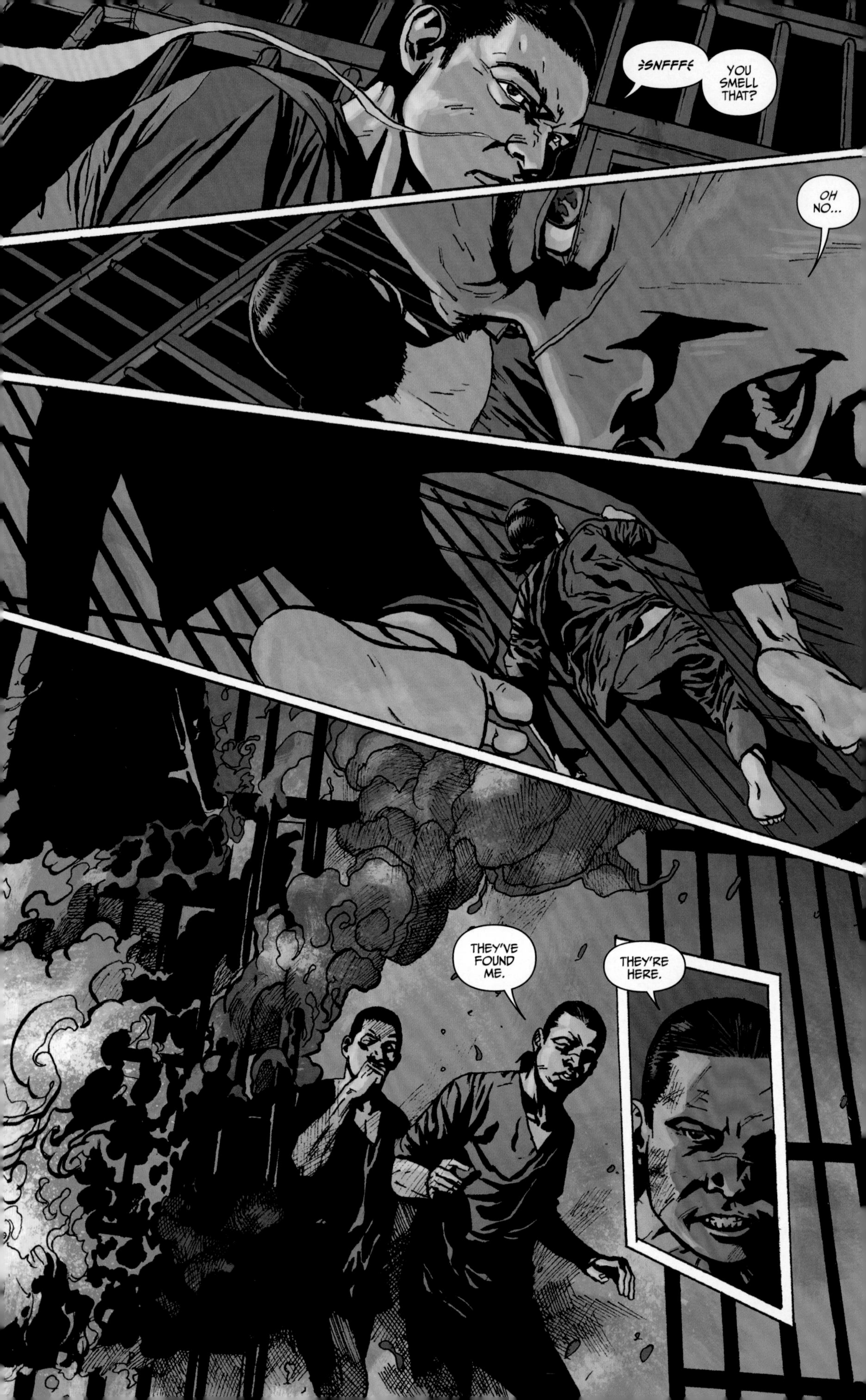

>SNFFF<
YOU SMELL THAT?
OH NO...
THEY'VE FOUND ME.
THEY'RE HERE.

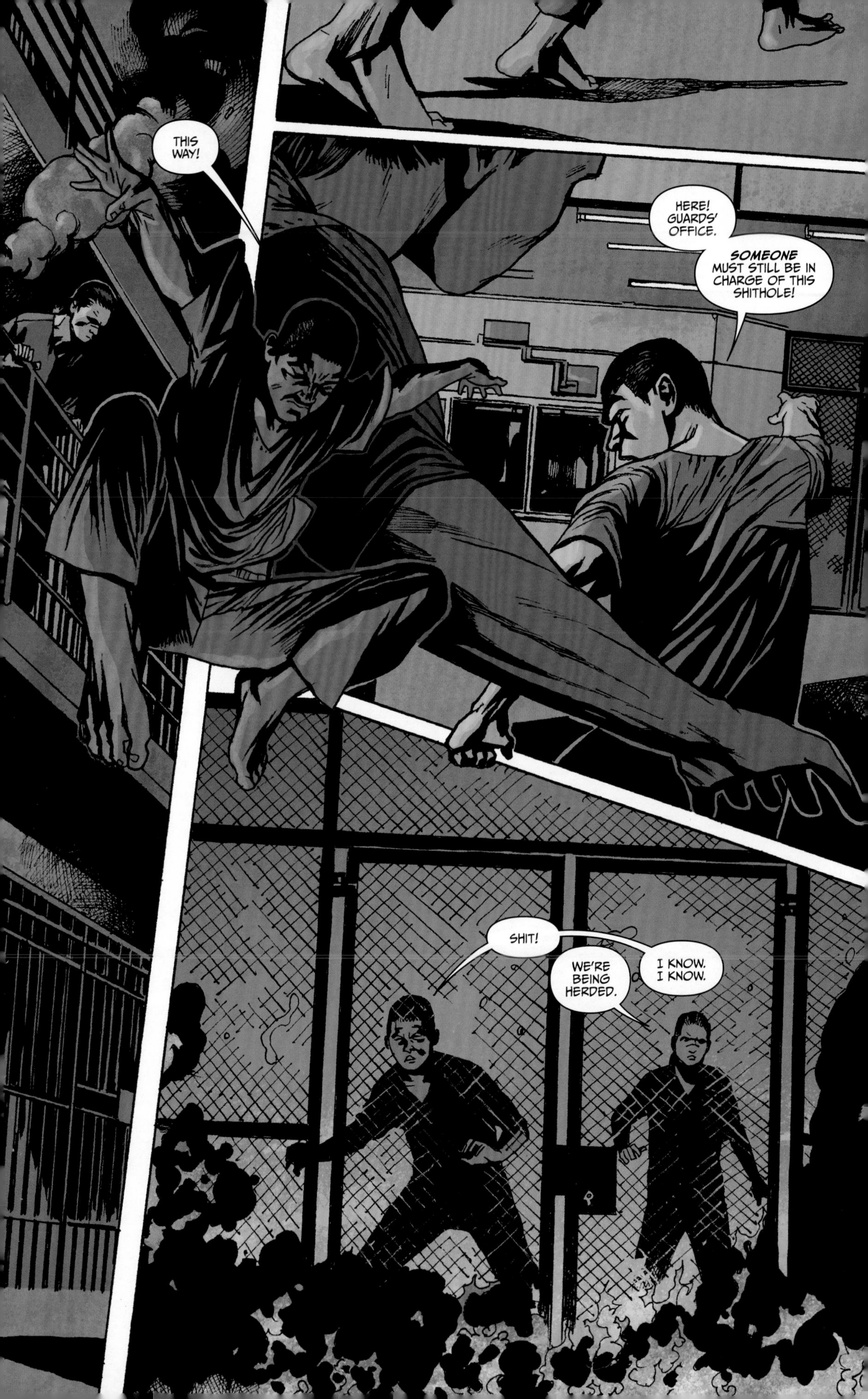
THIS WAY!
HERE! GUARDS' OFFICE.
SOMEONE MUST STILL BE IN CHARGE OF THIS SHITHOLE!
SHIT!
WE'RE BEING HERDED.
I KNOW. I KNOW.

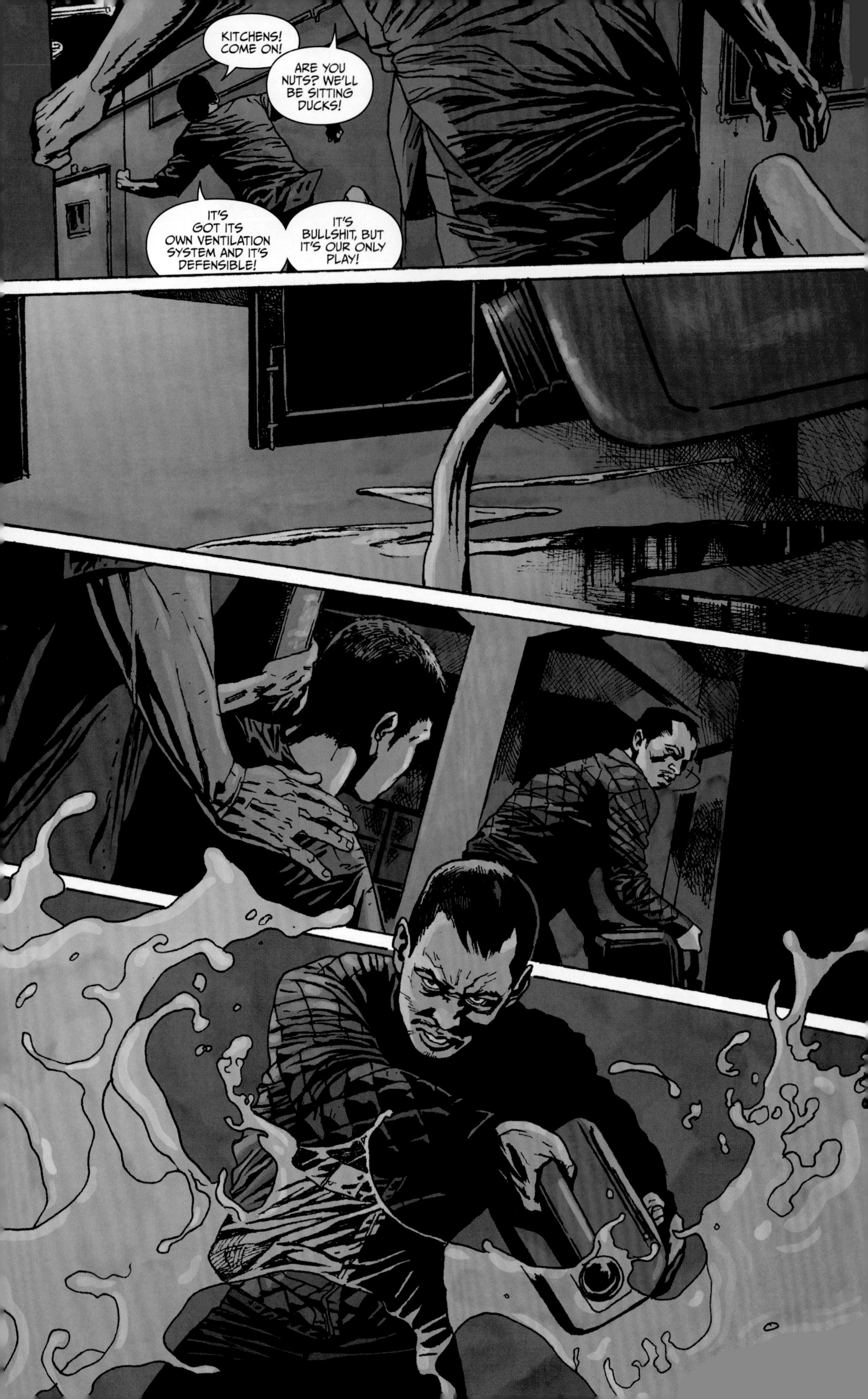
KITCHENS! COME ON!
ARE YOU NUTS? WE'LL BE SITTING DUCKS!
IT'S GOT ITS OWN VENTILATION SYSTEM AND IT'S DEFENSIBLE!
IT'S BULLSHIT, BUT IT'S OUR ONLY PLAY!

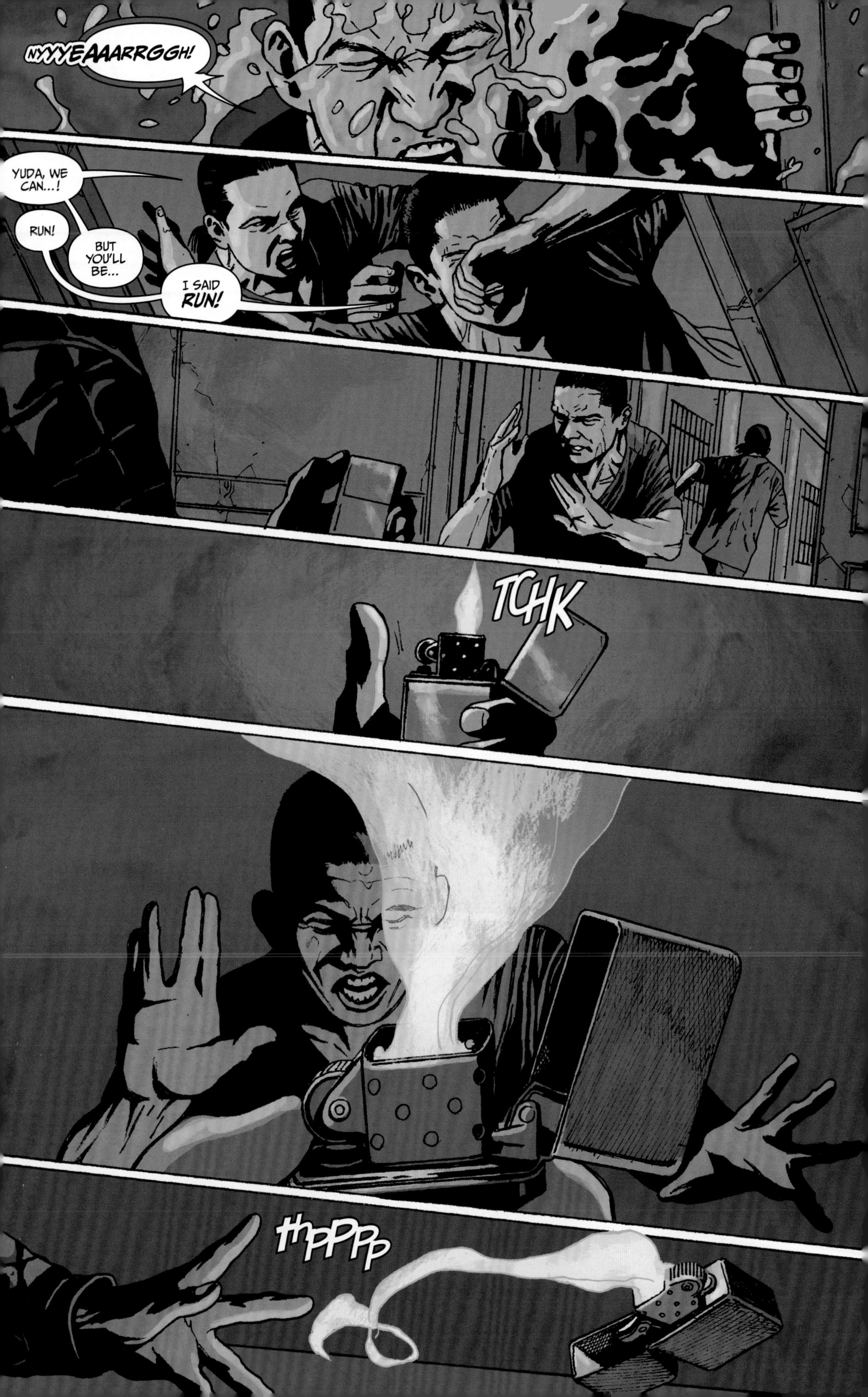
NYYYEAAARRGGH!
YUDA, WE CAN...!
RUN!
BUT YOU'LL BE...
I SAID RUN!
TCHK
thPPPp

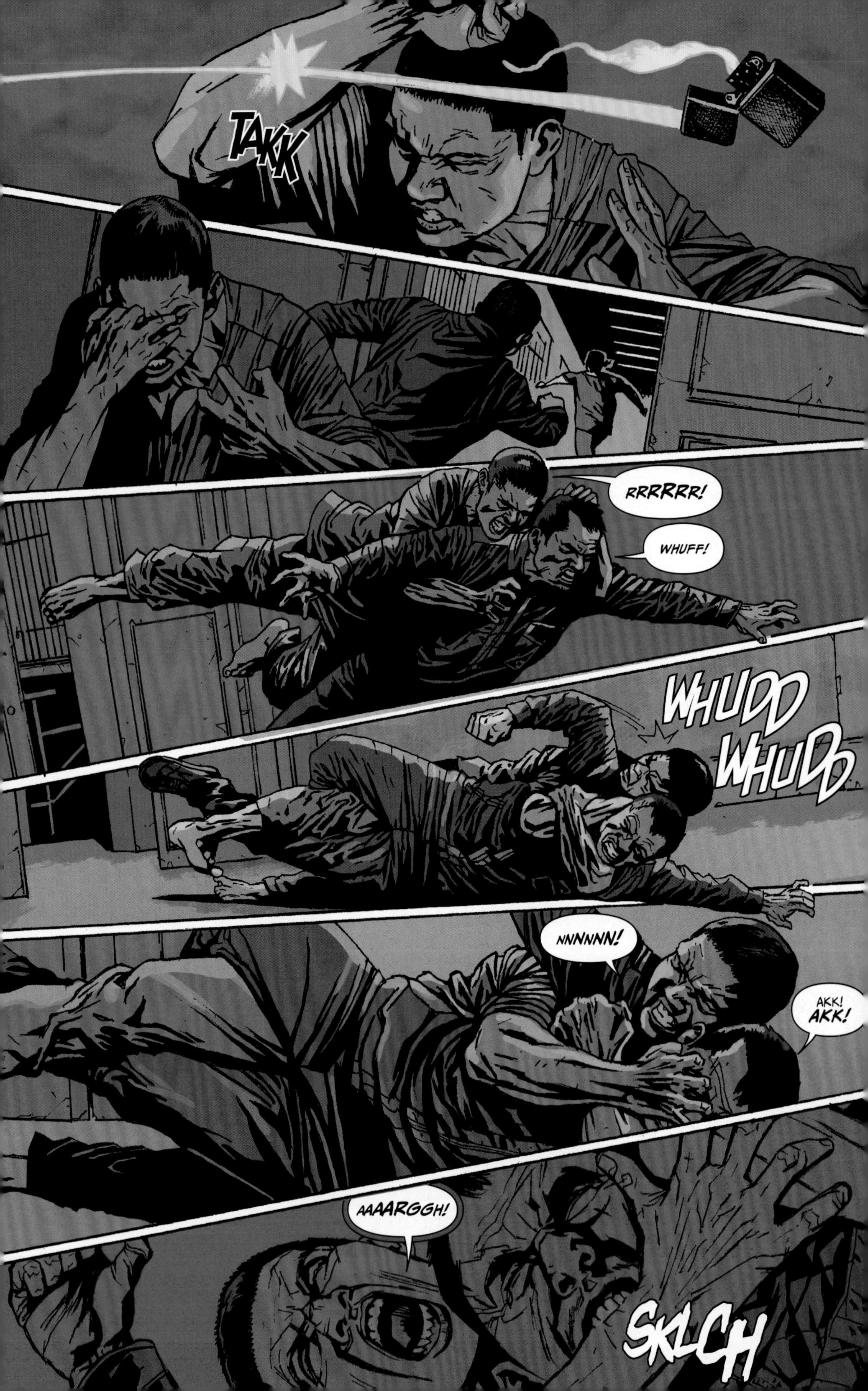
TAKK
RRRRRR!
WHUFF!
WHUDD
WHUDD
NNNNNN!
AKK!
AKK!
AAAARGGH!
SKLCH

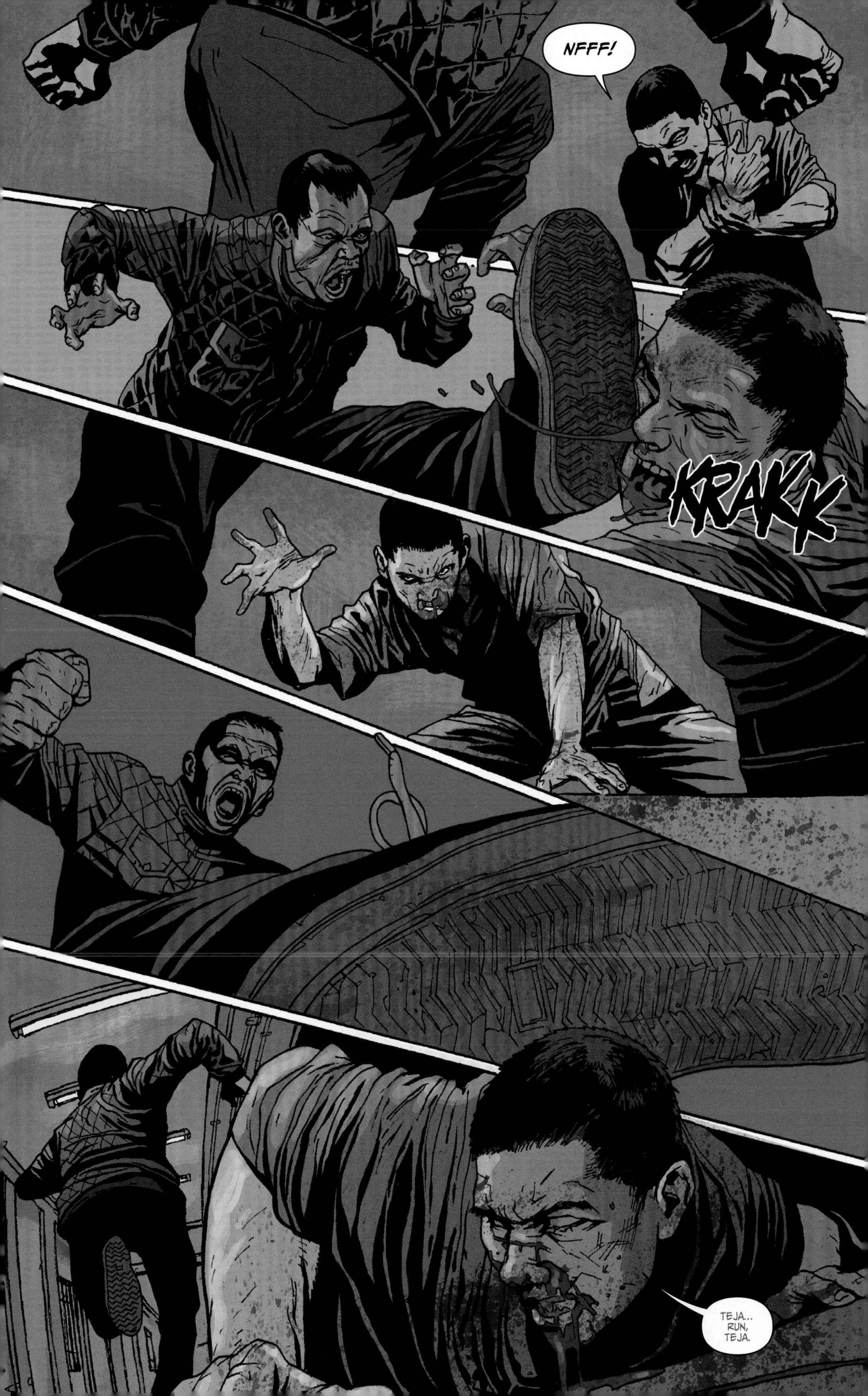
NFFF!
KRAKK
TEJA... RUN, TEJA.

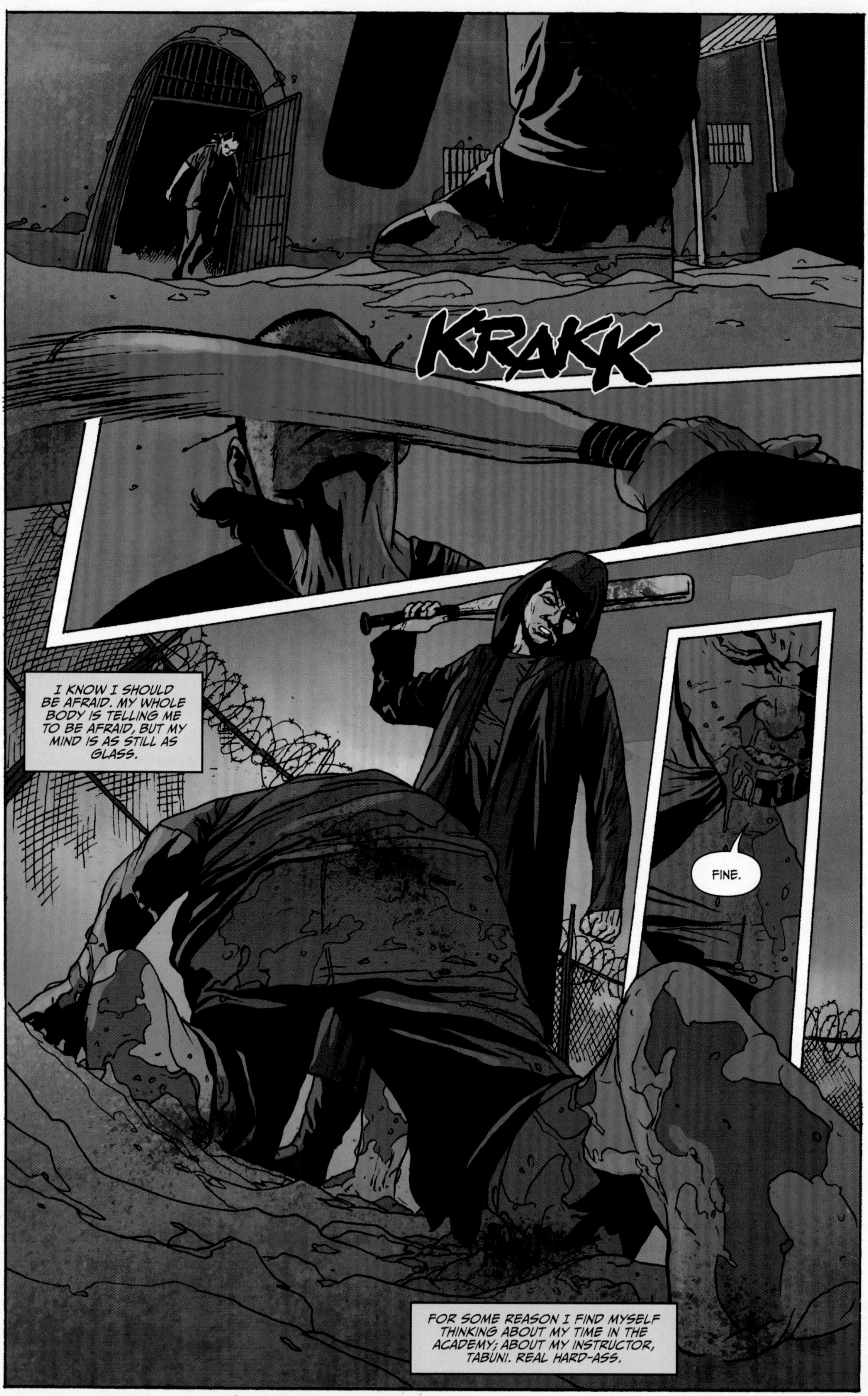
KRAKK
I KNOW I SHOULD BE AFRAID. MY WHOLE BODY IS TELLING ME TO BE AFRAID, BUT MY MIND IS AS STILL AS GLASS.
FINE.
FOR SOME REASON I FIND MYSELF THINKING ABOUT MY TIME IN THE ACADEMY; ABOUT MY INSTRUCTOR, TABUNI. REAL HARD-ASS.

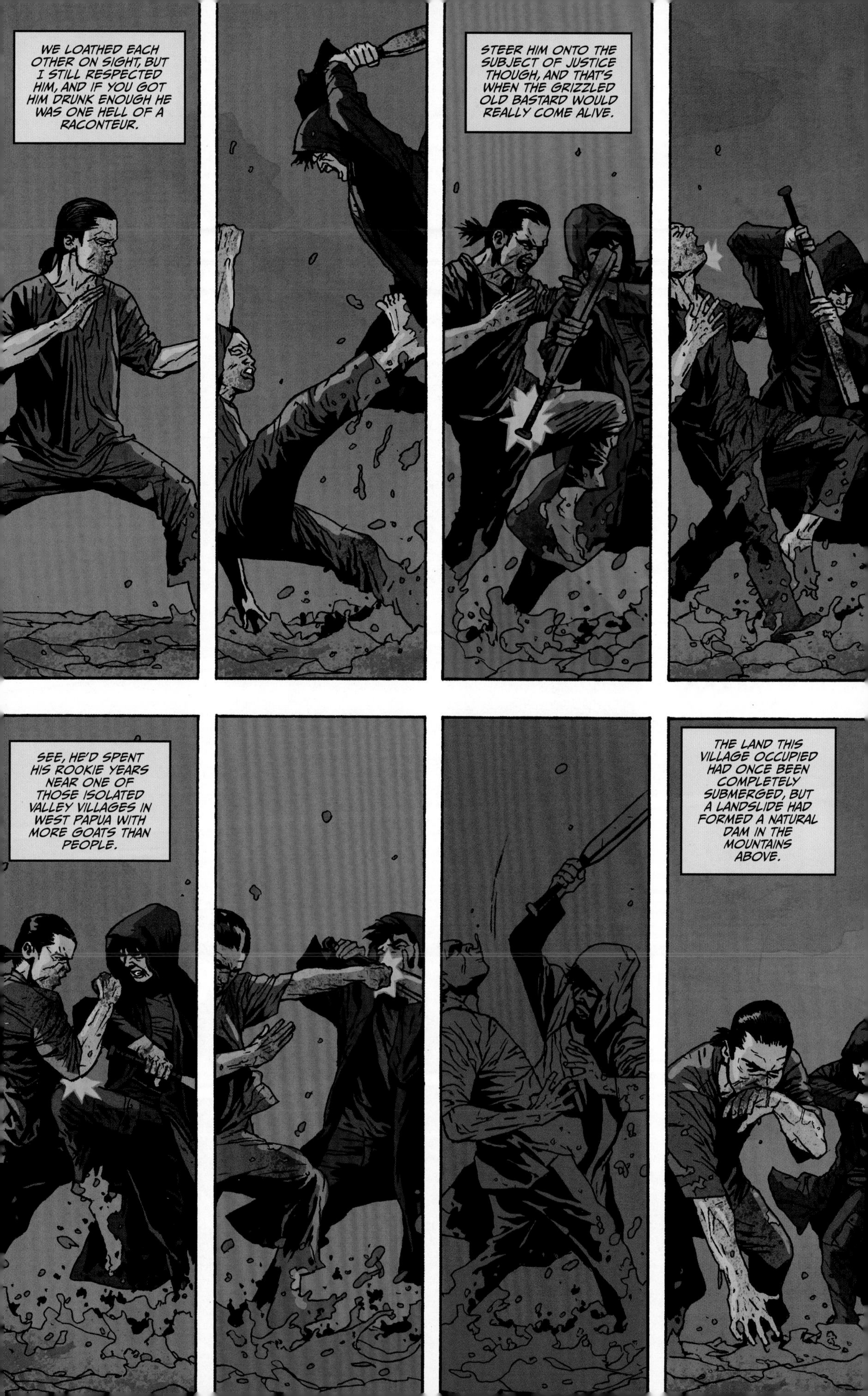
WE LOATHED EACH OTHER ON SIGHT, BUT I STILL RESPECTED HIM, AND IF YOU GOT HIM DRUNK ENOUGH HE WAS ONE HELL OF A RACONTEUR.
STEER HIM ONTO THE SUBJECT OF JUSTICE THOUGH, AND THAT'S WHEN THE GRIZZLED OLD BASTARD WOULD REALLY COME ALIVE.
SEE, HE'D SPENT HIS ROOKIE YEARS NEAR ONE OF THOSE ISOLATED VALLEY VILLAGES IN WEST PAPUA WITH MORE GOATS THAN PEOPLE.
THE LAND THIS VILLAGE OCCUPIED HAD ONCE BEEN COMPLETELY SUBMERGED, BUT A LANDSLIDE HAD FORMED A NATURAL DAM IN THE MOUNTAINS ABOVE.

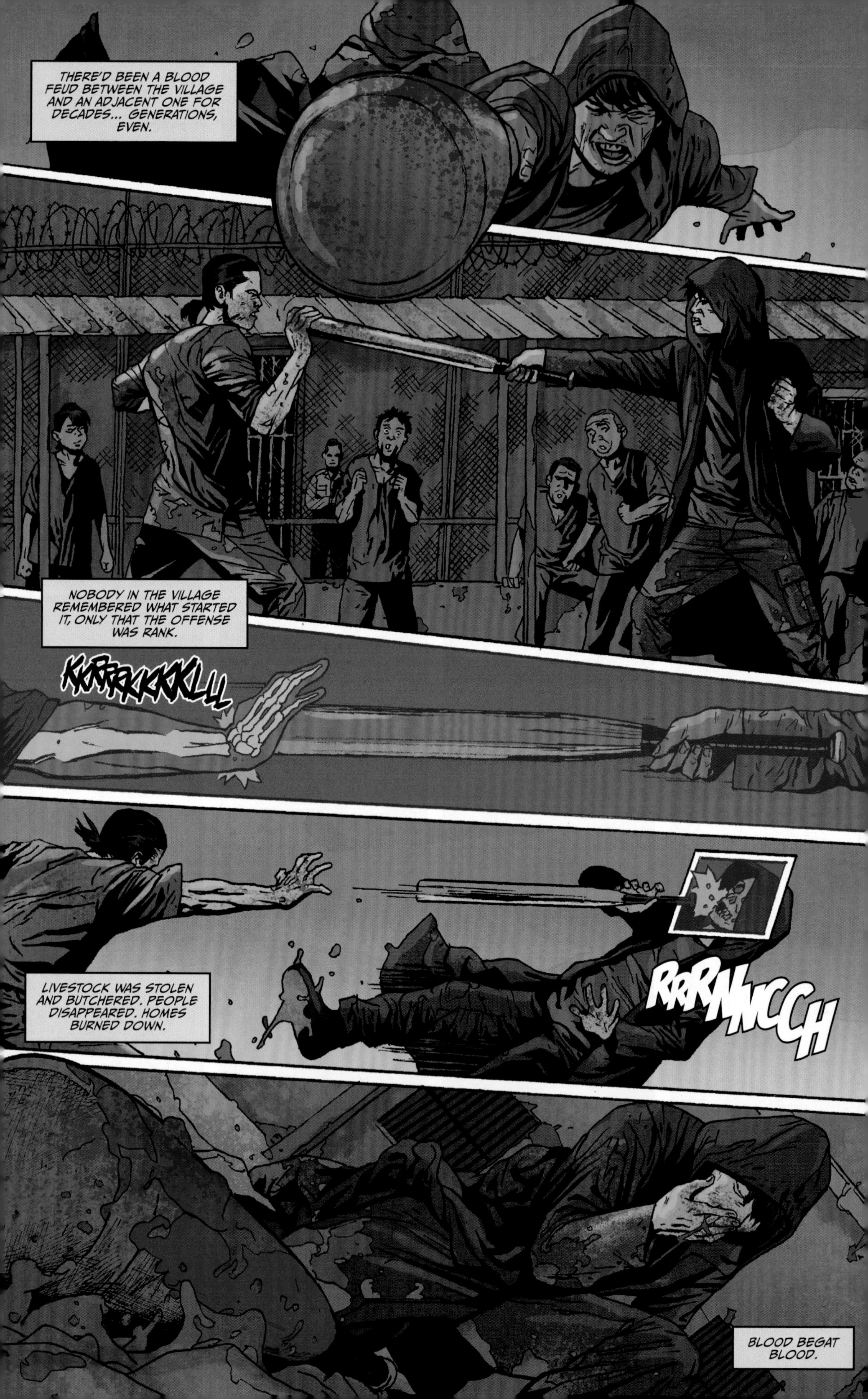
THERE'D BEEN A BLOOD FEUD BETWEEN THE VILLAGE AND AN ADJACENT ONE FOR DECADES... GENERATIONS, EVEN.
NOBODY IN THE VILLAGE REMEMBERED WHAT STARTED IT, ONLY THAT THE OFFENSE WAS RANK.
KKRRRKKKKLLL
LIVESTOCK WAS STOLEN AND BUTCHERED. PEOPLE DISAPPEARED. HOMES BURNED DOWN.
RRRNNCCH
BLOOD BEGAT BLOOD.

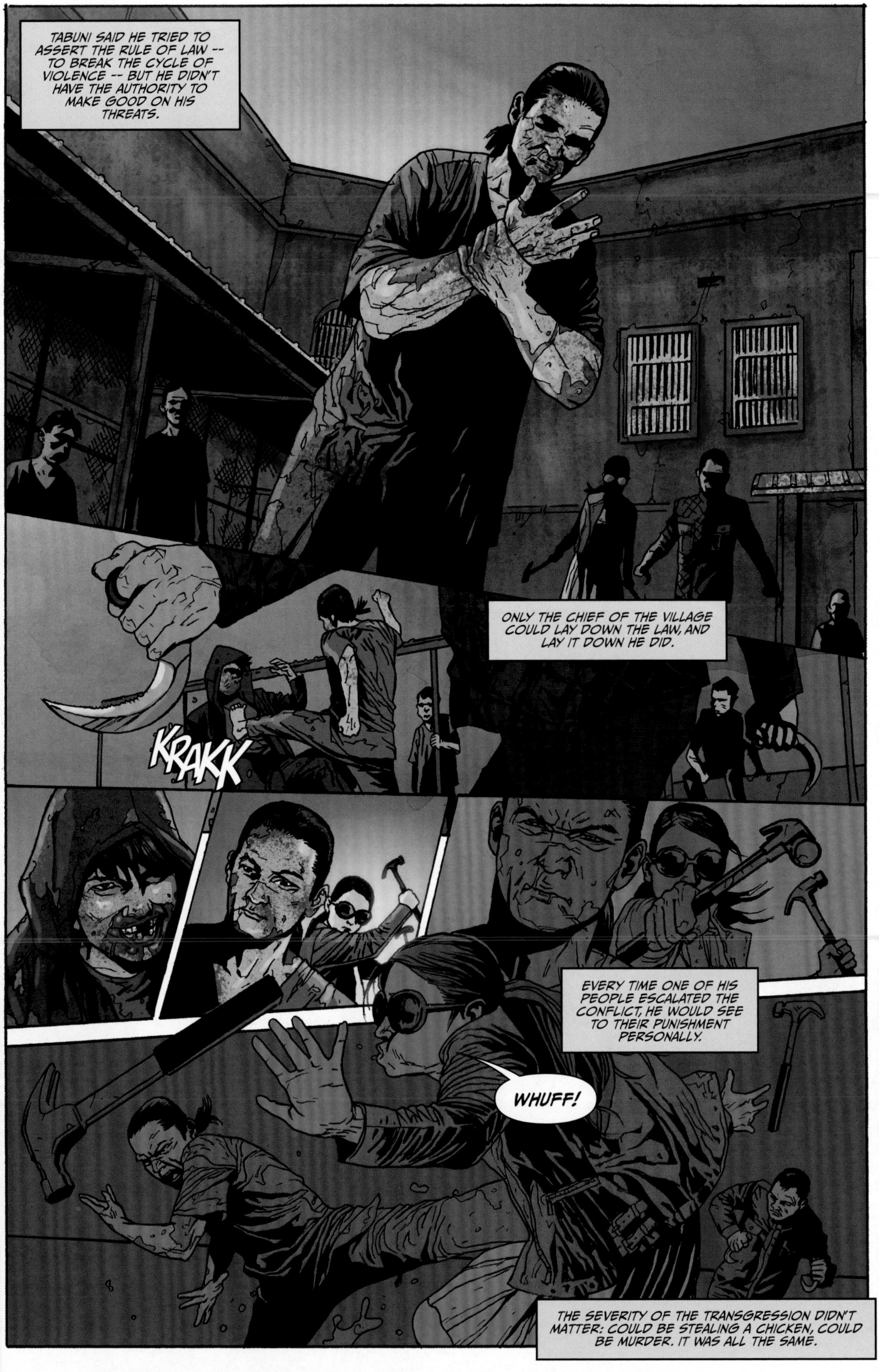
TABUNI SAID HE TRIED TO ASSERT THE RULE OF LAW -- TO BREAK THE CYCLE OF VIOLENCE -- BUT HE DIDN'T HAVE THE AUTHORITY TO MAKE GOOD ON HIS THREATS.
ONLY THE CHIEF OF THE VILLAGE COULD LAY DOWN THE LAW, AND LAY IT DOWN HE DID.
KRAKK
EVERY TIME ONE OF HIS PEOPLE ESCALATED THE CONFLICT, HE WOULD SEE TO THEIR PUNISHMENT PERSONALLY.
WHUFF!
THE SEVERITY OF THE TRANSGRESSION DIDN'T MATTER: COULD BE STEALING A CHICKEN, COULD BE MURDER. IT WAS ALL THE SAME.

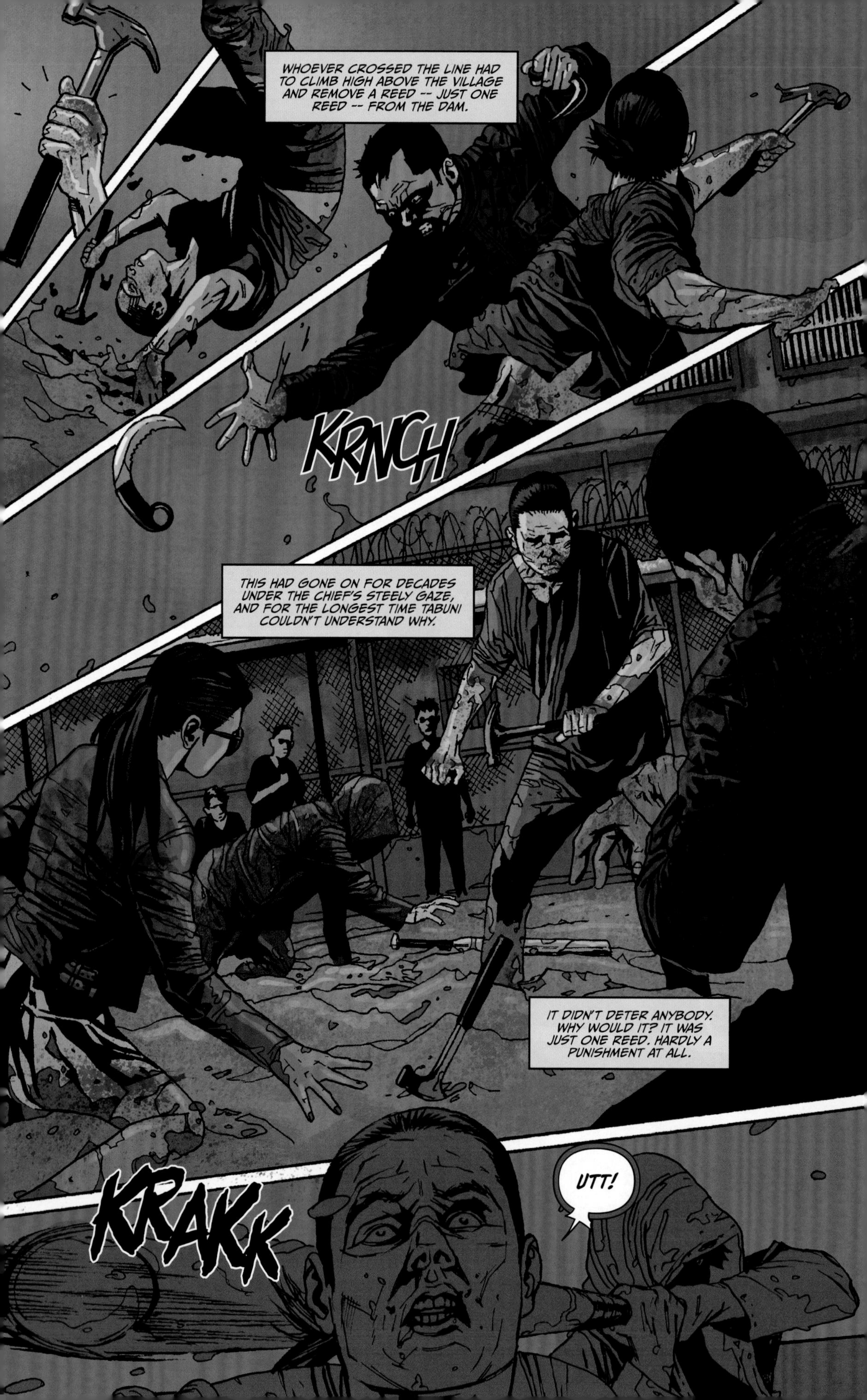
WHOEVER CROSSED THE LINE HAD TO CLIMB HIGH ABOVE THE VILLAGE AND REMOVE A REED -- JUST ONE REED -- FROM THE DAM.
KRNCH
THIS HAD GONE ON FOR DECADES UNDER THE CHIEF'S STEELY GAZE, AND FOR THE LONGEST TIME TABUNI COULDN'T UNDERSTAND WHY.
IT DIDN'T DETER ANYBODY. WHY WOULD IT? IT WAS JUST ONE REED. HARDLY A PUNISHMENT AT ALL.
KRAKK
UTT!

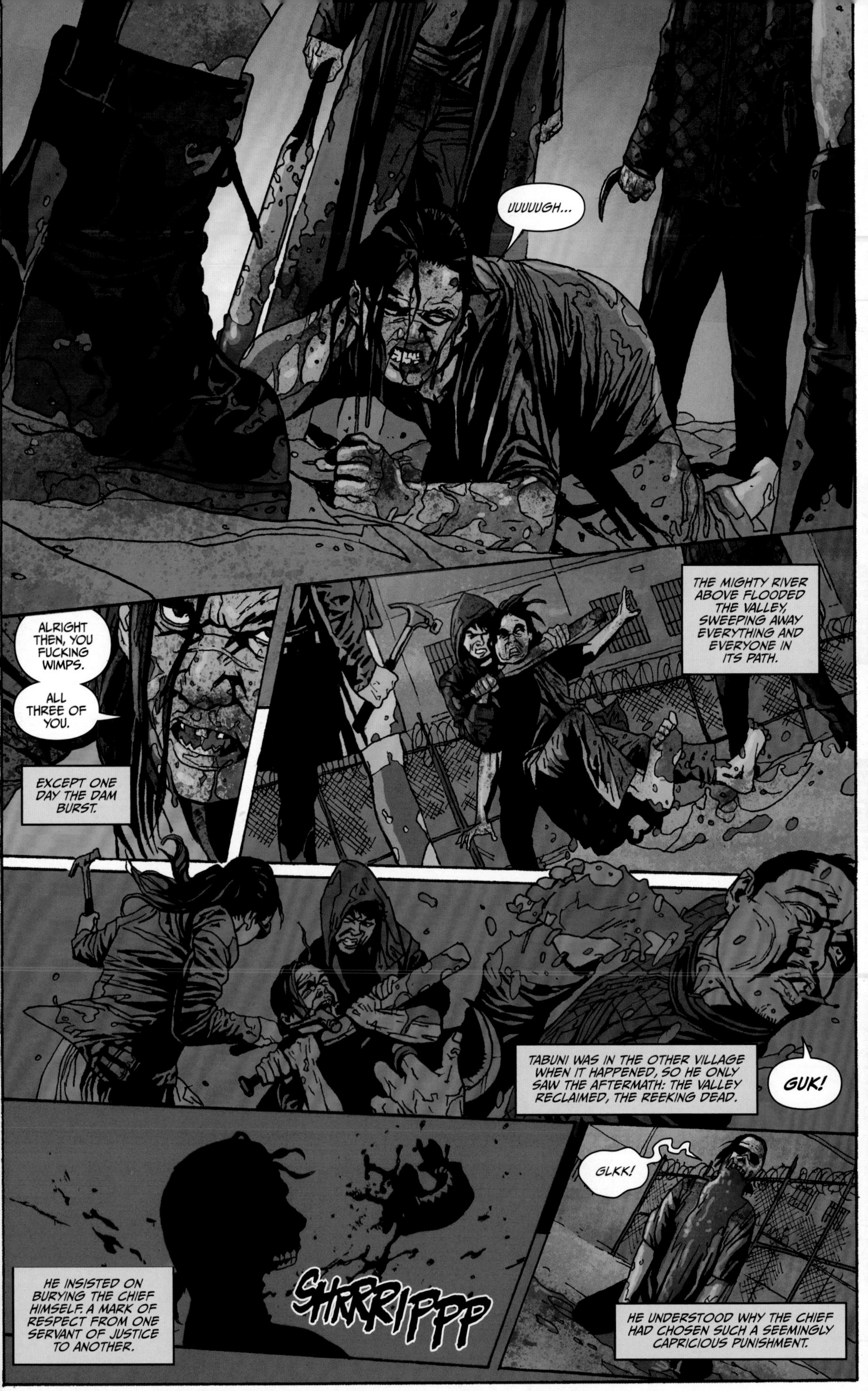
UUUUUGH...
ALRIGHT THEN, YOU FUCKING WIMPS.
ALL THREE OF YOU.
EXCEPT ONE DAY THE DAM BURST.
THE MIGHTY RIVER ABOVE FLOODED THE VALLEY, SWEEPING AWAY EVERYTHING AND EVERYONE IN ITS PATH.
TABUNI WAS IN THE OTHER VILLAGE WHEN IT HAPPENED, SO HE ONLY SAW THE AFTERMATH: THE VALLEY RECLAIMED, THE REEKING DEAD.
GUK!
HE INSISTED ON BURYING THE CHIEF HIMSELF. A MARK OF RESPECT FROM ONE SERVANT OF JUSTICE TO ANOTHER.
SHRRRIPPP
GLKK!
HE UNDERSTOOD WHY THE CHIEF HAD CHOSEN SUCH A SEEMINGLY CAPRICIOUS PUNISHMENT.

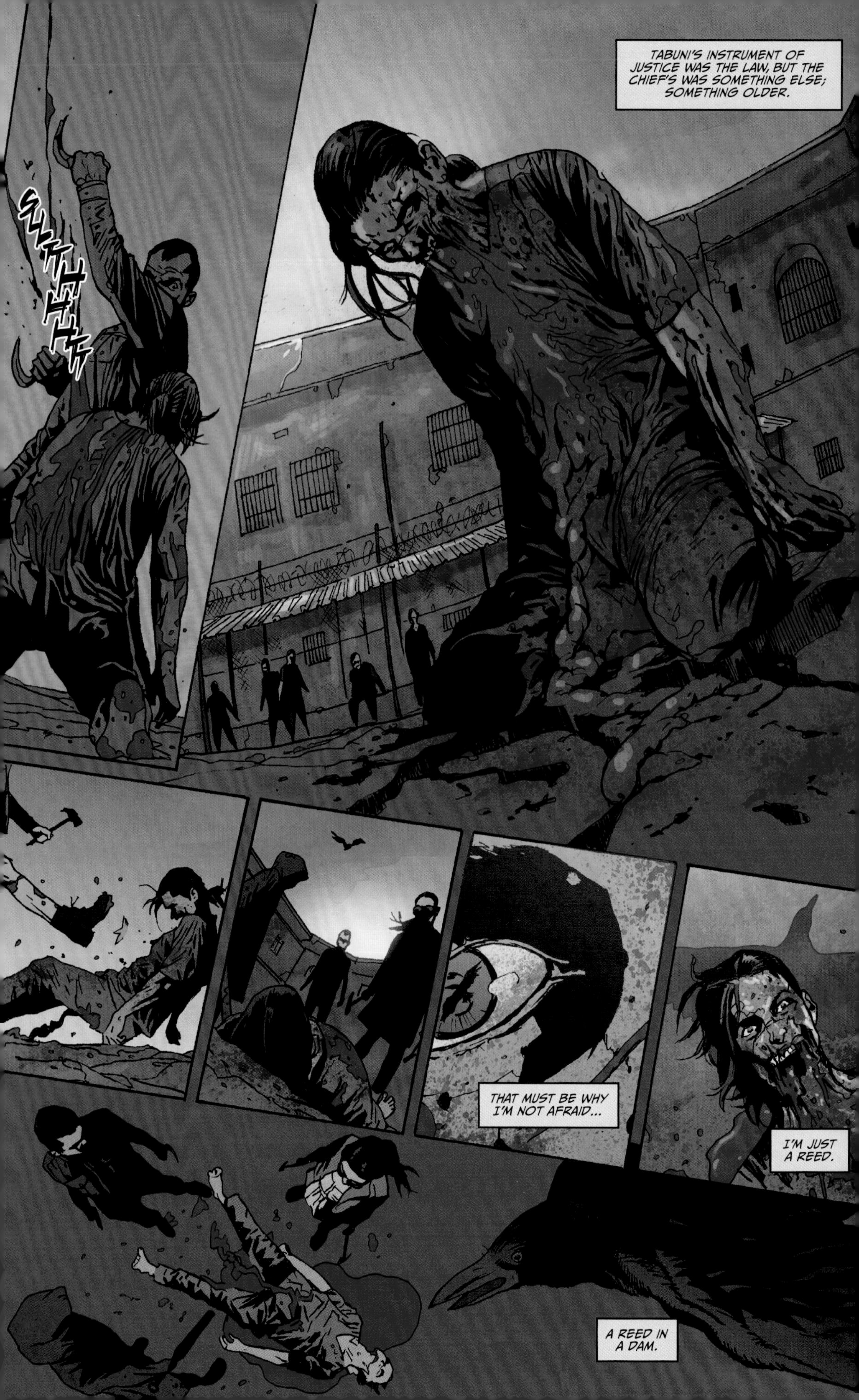
TABUNI'S INSTRUMENT OF JUSTICE WAS THE LAW, BUT THE CHIEF'S WAS SOMETHING ELSE; SOMETHING OLDER.
THAT MUST BE WHY I'M NOT AFRAID...
I'M JUST A REED.
A REED IN A DAM.

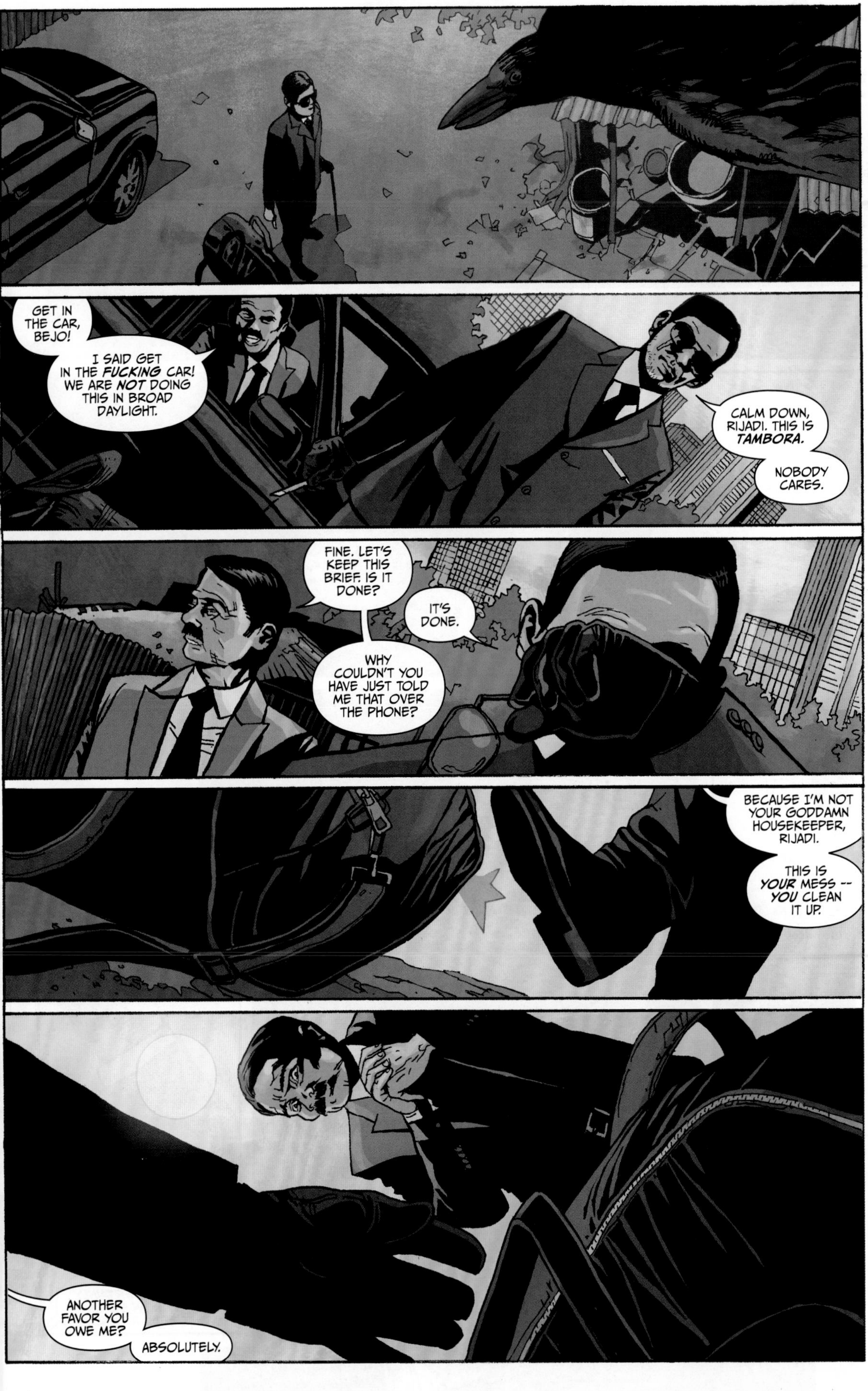
GET IN THE CAR, BEJO!
I SAID GET IN THE FUCKING CAR! WE ARE NOT DOING THIS IN BROAD DAYLIGHT.
CALM DOWN, RIJADI. THIS IS TAMBORA.
NOBODY CARES.
FINE. LET'S KEEP THIS BRIEF. IS IT DONE?
IT'S DONE.
WHY COULDN'T YOU HAVE JUST TOLD ME THAT OVER THE PHONE?
BECAUSE I'M NOT YOUR GODDAMN HOUSEKEEPER, RIJADI.
THIS IS YOUR MESS -- YOU CLEAN IT UP.
ANOTHER FAVOR YOU OWE ME?
ABSOLUTELY.

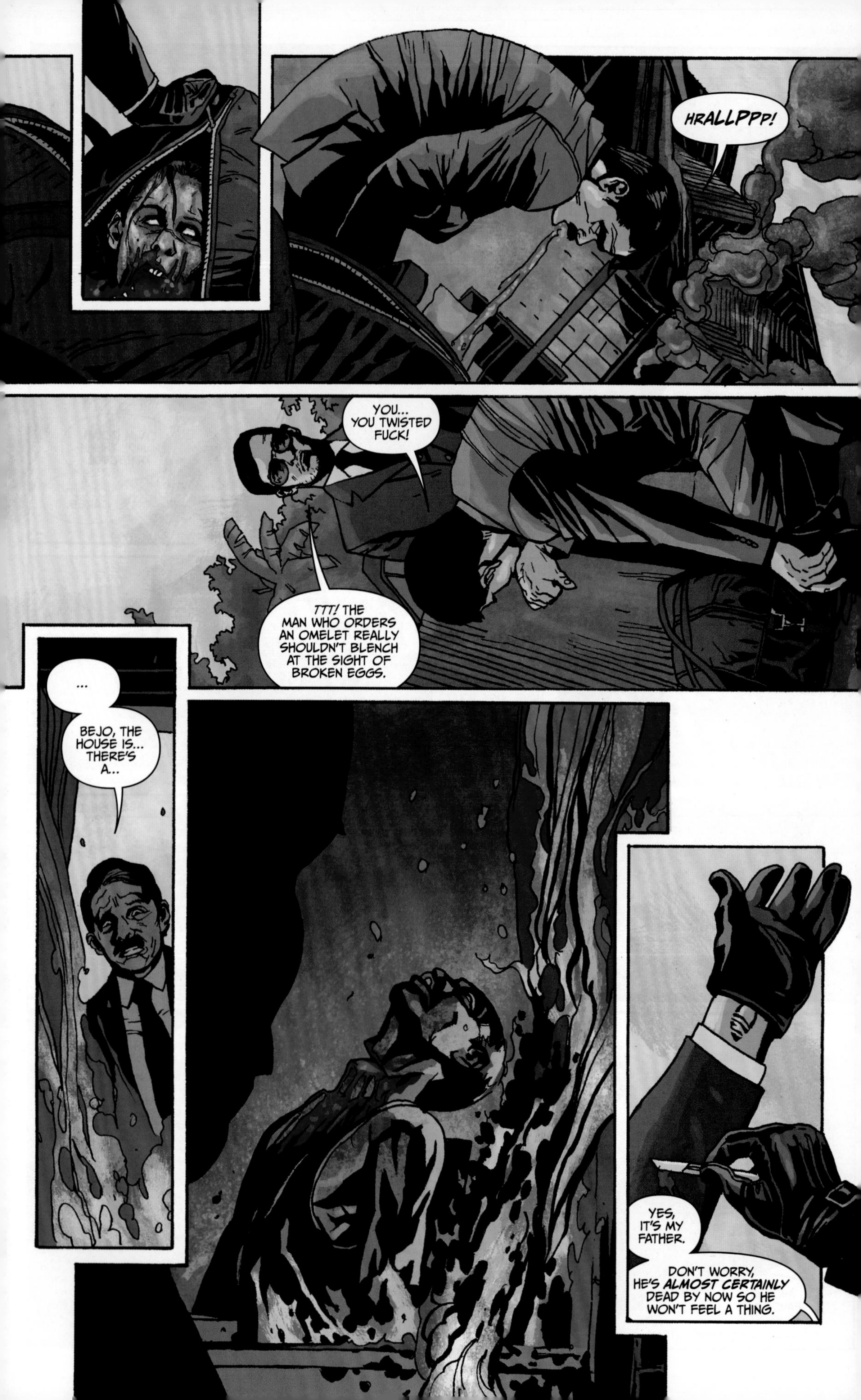
HRALLPPP!
YOU... YOU TWISTED FUCK!
TTT! THE MAN WHO ORDERS AN OMELET REALLY SHOULDN'T BLENCH AT THE SIGHT OF BROKEN EGGS.
...
BEJO, THE HOUSE IS... THERE'S A...
YES, IT'S MY FATHER.
DON'T WORRY, HE'S ALMOST CERTAINLY DEAD BY NOW SO HE WON'T FEEL A THING.

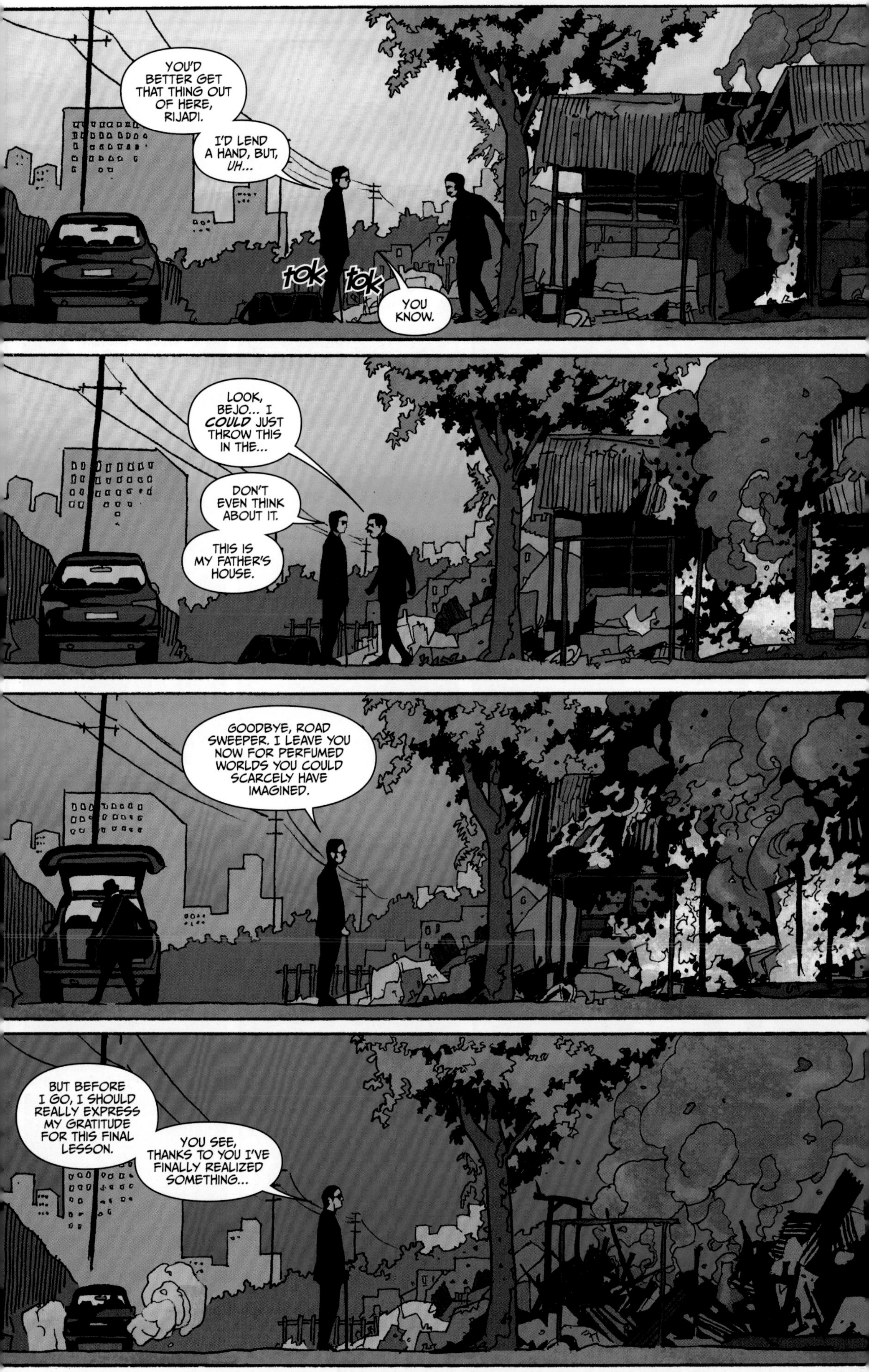
YOU'D BETTER GET THAT THING OUT OF HERE, RIJADI.
I'D LEND A HAND, BUT, UH...
TOK TOK
YOU KNOW.
LOOK, BEJO... I COULD JUST THROW THIS IN THE...
DON'T EVEN THINK ABOUT IT.
THIS IS MY FATHER'S HOUSE.
GOODBYE, ROAD SWEEPER. I LEAVE YOU NOW FOR PERFUMED WORLDS YOU COULD SCARCELY HAVE IMAGINED.
BUT BEFORE I GO, I SHOULD REALLY EXPRESS MY GRATITUDE FOR THIS FINAL LESSON.
YOU SEE, THANKS TO YOU I'VE FINALLY REALIZED SOMETHING...

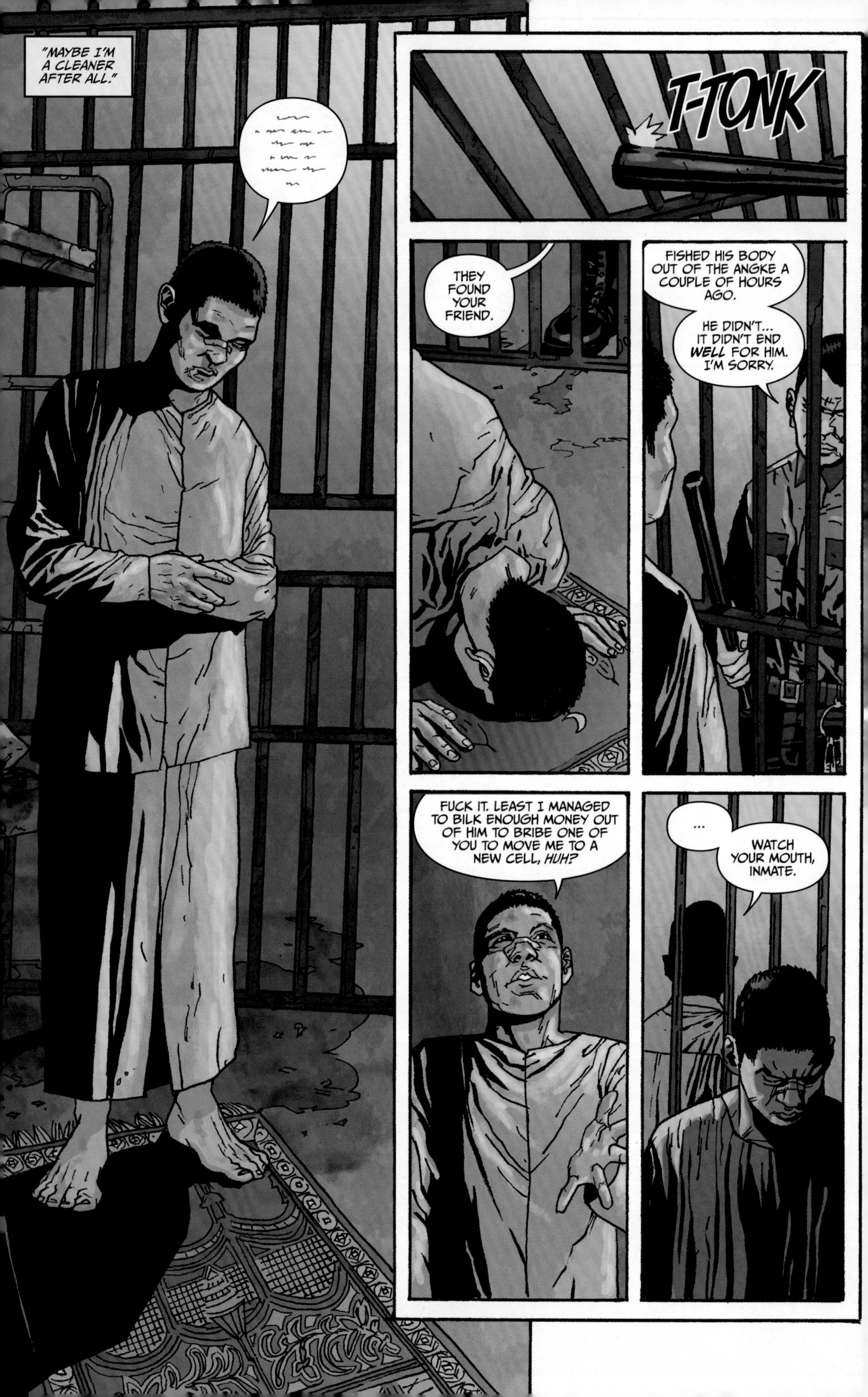
"MAYBE I'M A CLEANER AFTER ALL."
T-TONK
THEY FOUND YOUR FRIEND.
FISHED HIS BODY OUT OF THE ANGKE A COUPLE OF HOURS AGO.
HE DIDN'T... IT DIDN'T END WELL FOR HIM. I'M SORRY.
FUCK IT. LEAST I MANAGED TO BILK ENOUGH MONEY OUT OF HIM TO BRIBE ONE OF YOU TO MOVE ME TO A NEW CELL, HUH?
...
WATCH YOUR MOUTH, INMATE.

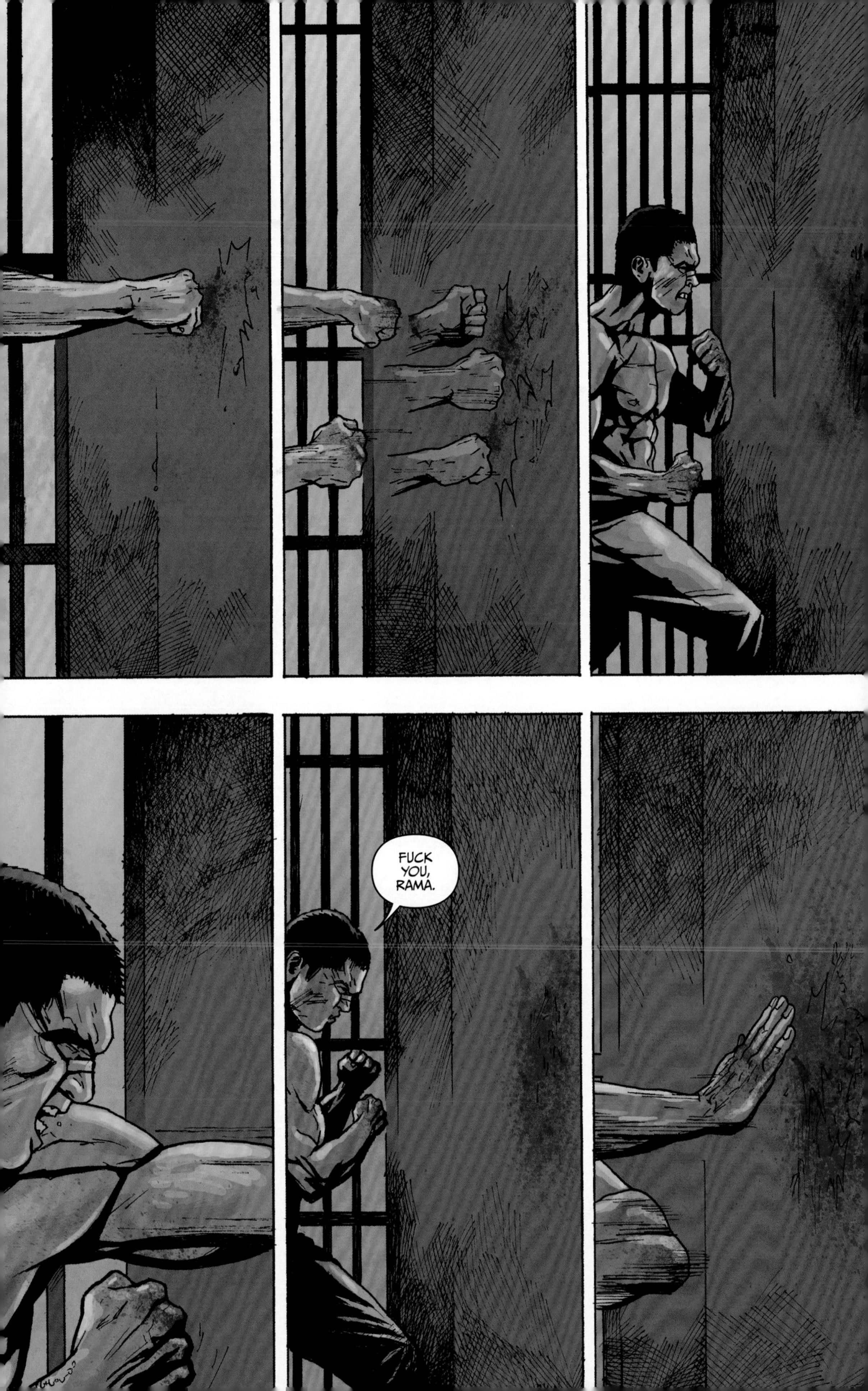
FUCK YOU, RAMA.

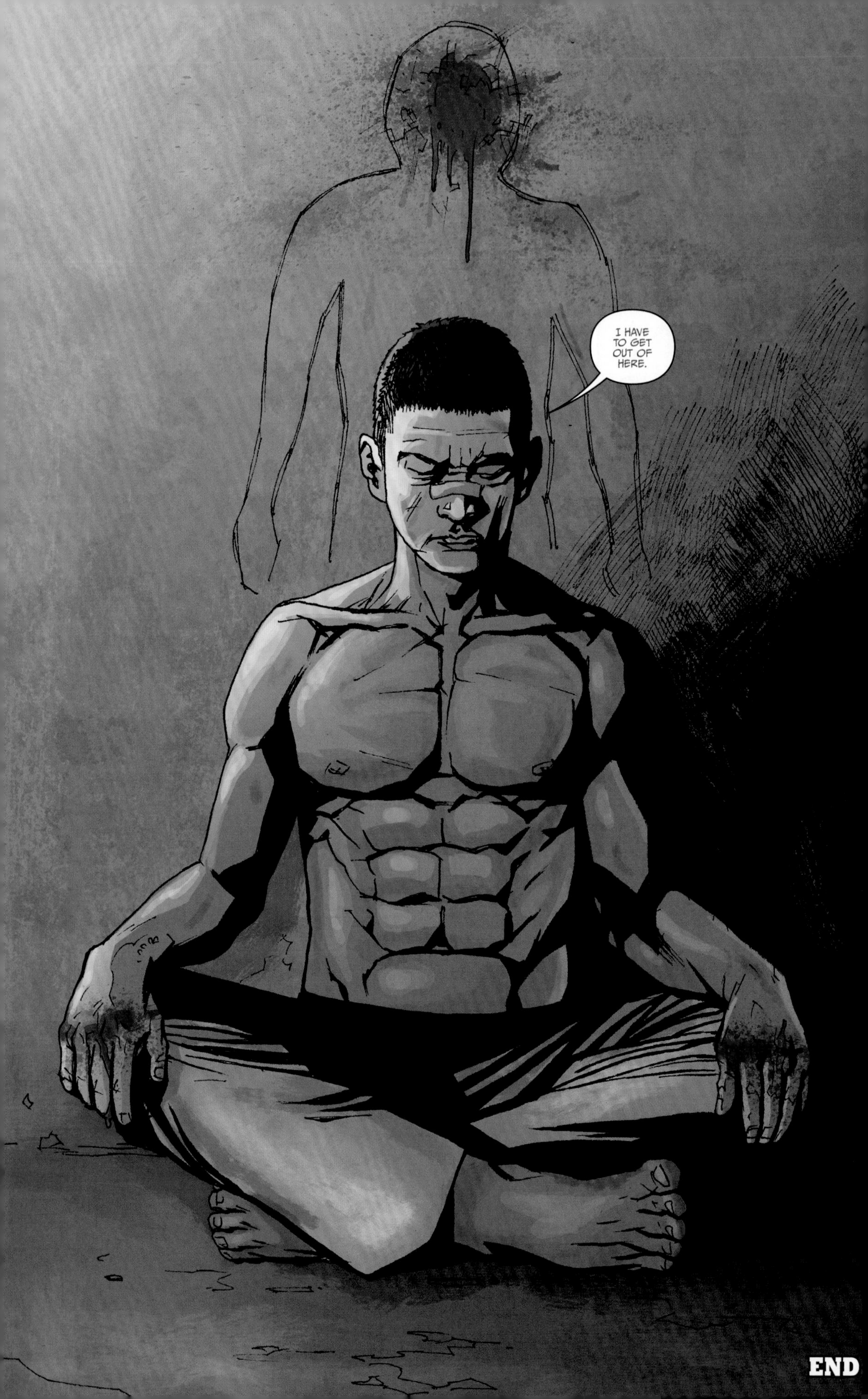
I HAVE TO GET OUT OF HERE.
END

EXTRA COVERS

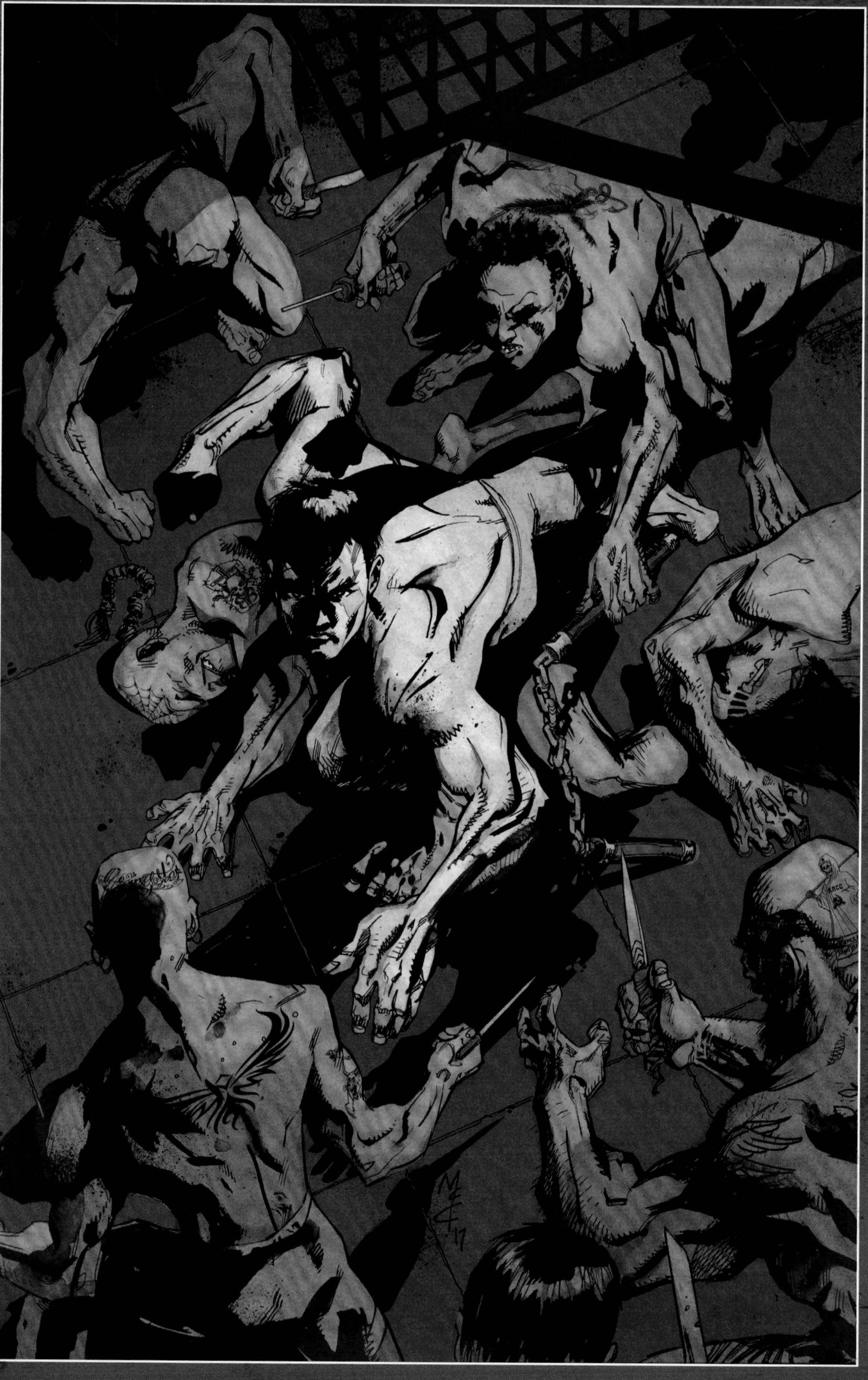

Cover 1d by **John McCrea**

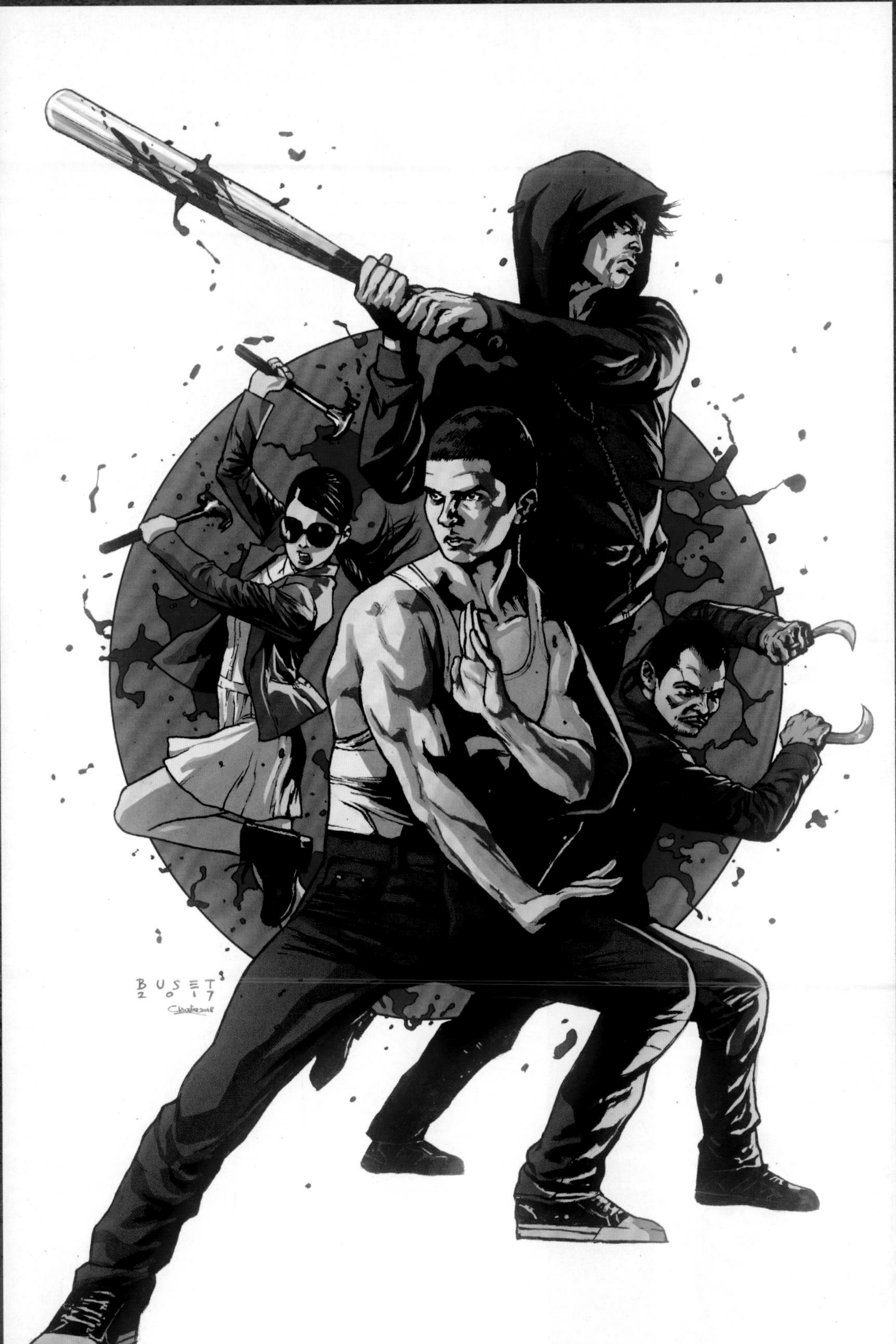
BUSET
2017

Cover 1e by **Budi Setiawan**

SKETCHES AND CONCEPT ART

SKETCH/CONCEPT ART FOR *THE RAID* SERIES' COVERS...

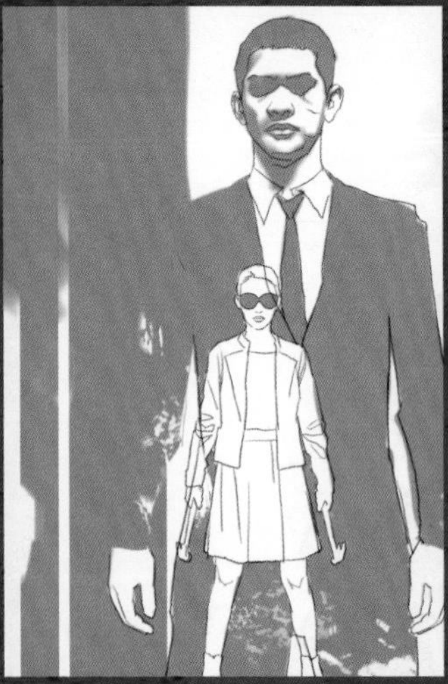

Cover 1a sketch by
Ben Oliver

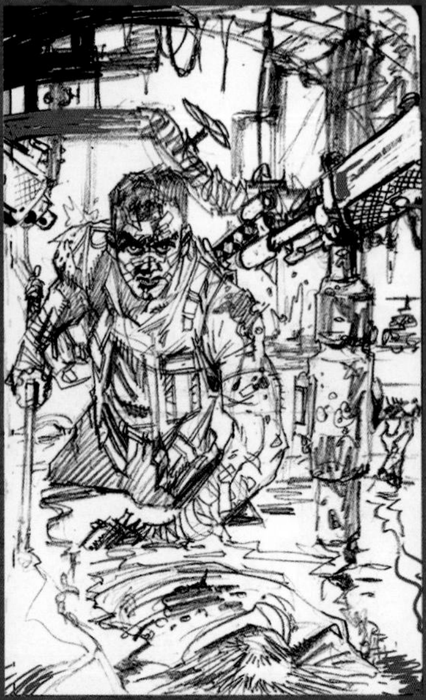

Alternative, unused sketch by
John McCrea

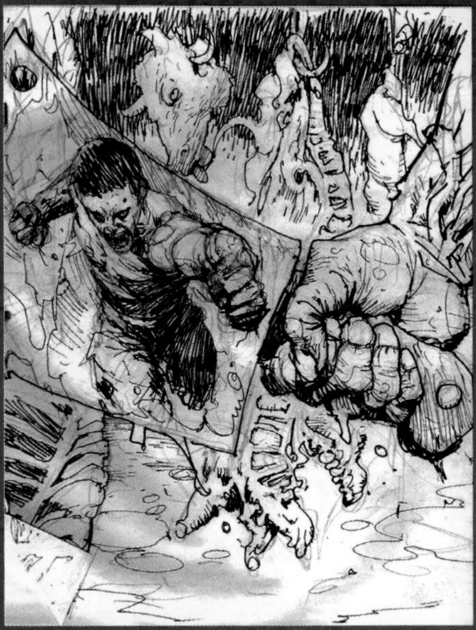

Cover 3a sketch by
Roy Allan Martinez

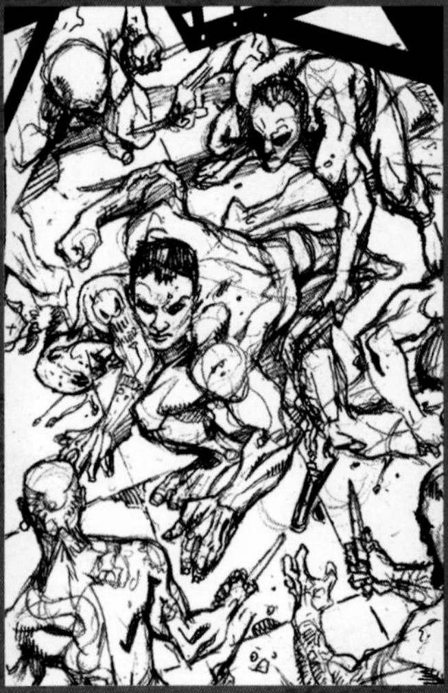

Cover 1c sketch by
John McCrea

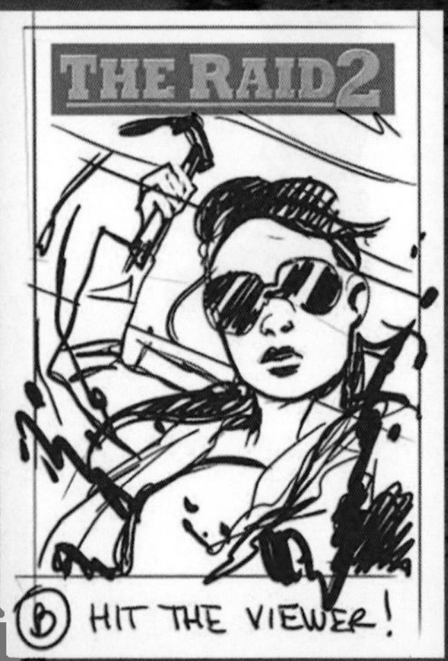
THE RAID 2
B HIT THE VIEWER!

Thumbnail sketch for cover 2a
by **Claudia Iainiciello**

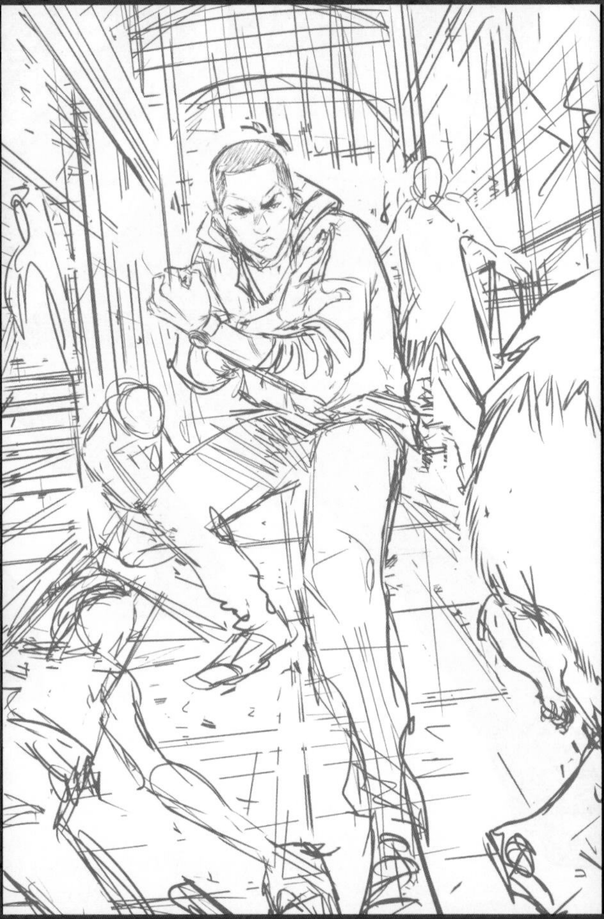

Cover 4a sketch by
Rhoald Marcellius

BUDI SETIAWAN – UNUSED SAMPLE PAGE

HERE IS AN EARLY *RAID* SAMPLE PAGE DRAWN BY BUDI SETIAWAN WHEN WE WERE DECIDING ON AN ARTIST FOR THE SERIES.

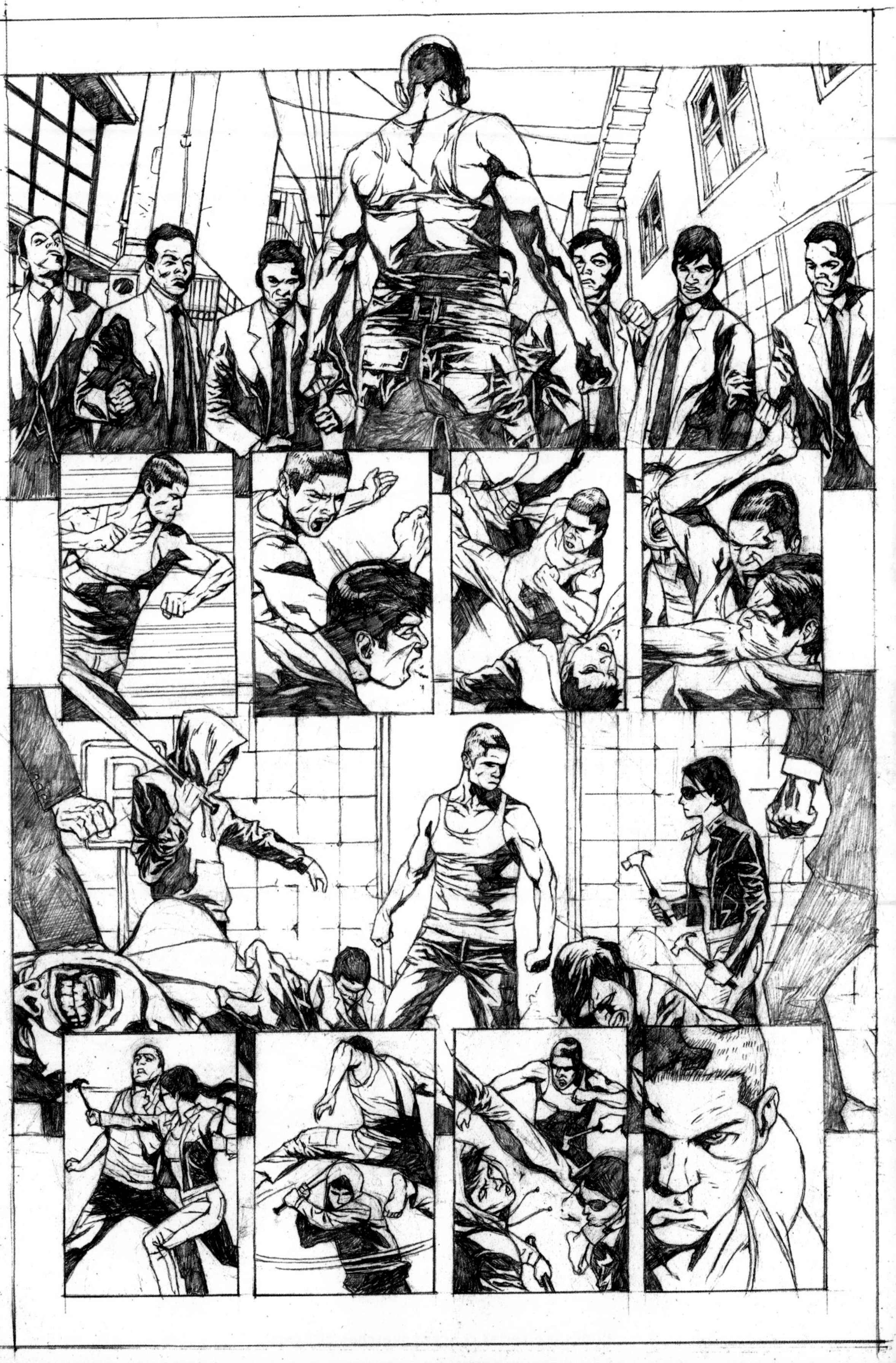

BUDI SETIAWAN
CONCEPT ART AND SKETCHES

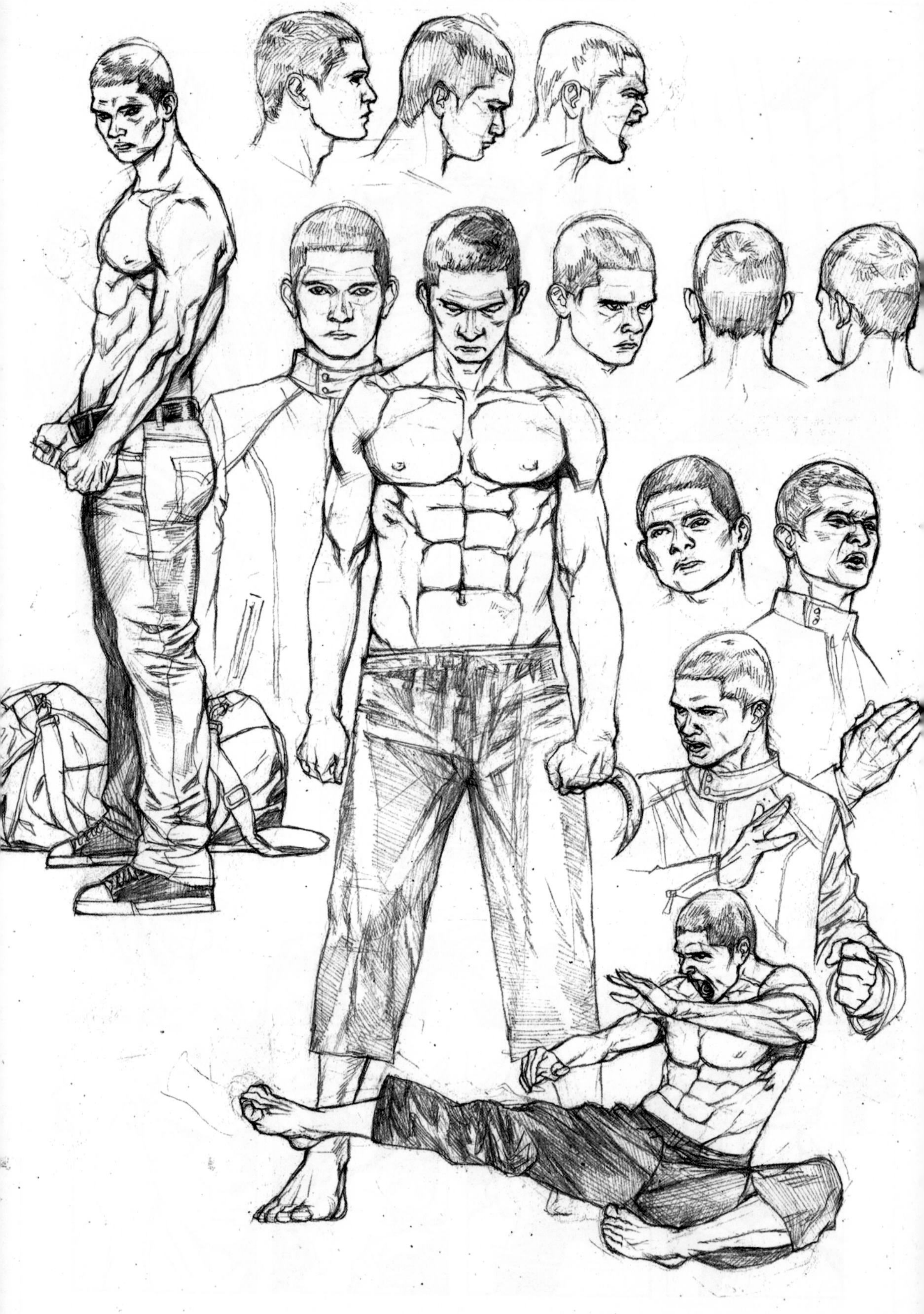

Budi's pre-series concept sketches of Rama

Budi's pre-series concept sketches of Hammer Girl and Baseball Bat Man

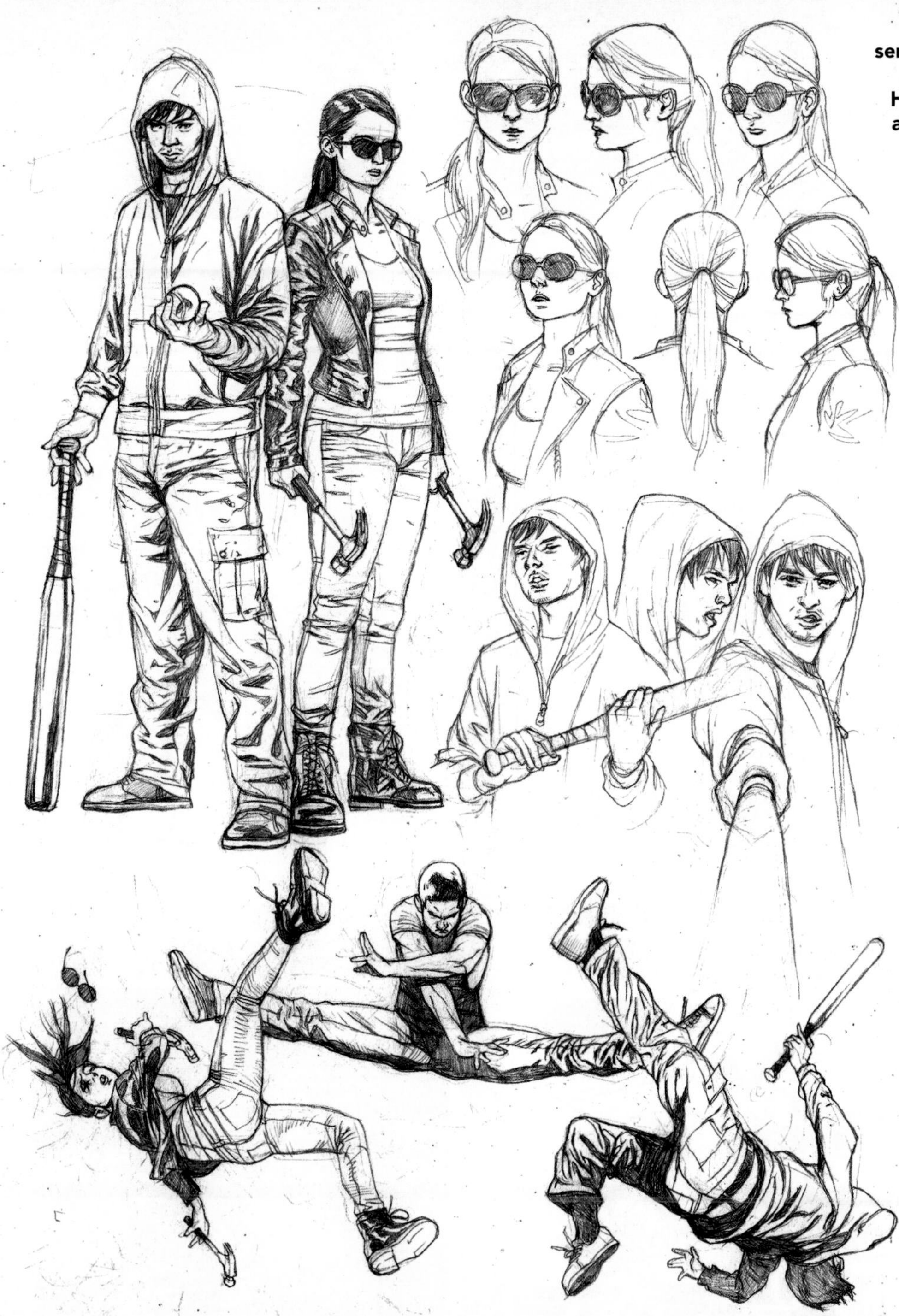

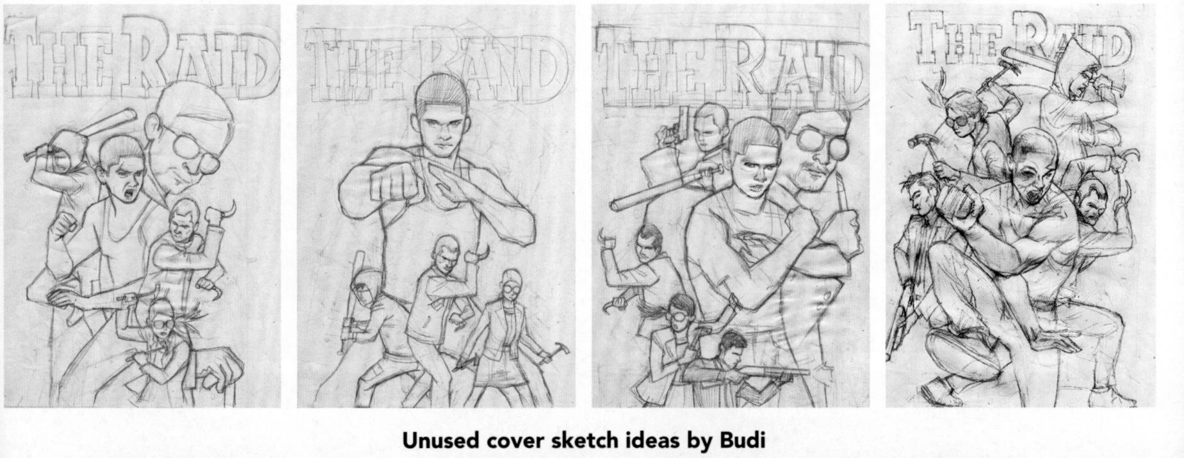

THE RAID
THE RAID
THE RAID
THE RAID

Unused cover sketch ideas by Budi

THE RAID COMIC PROCESS

HERE'S HOW A *RAID* COMIC PAGE IS CREATED!

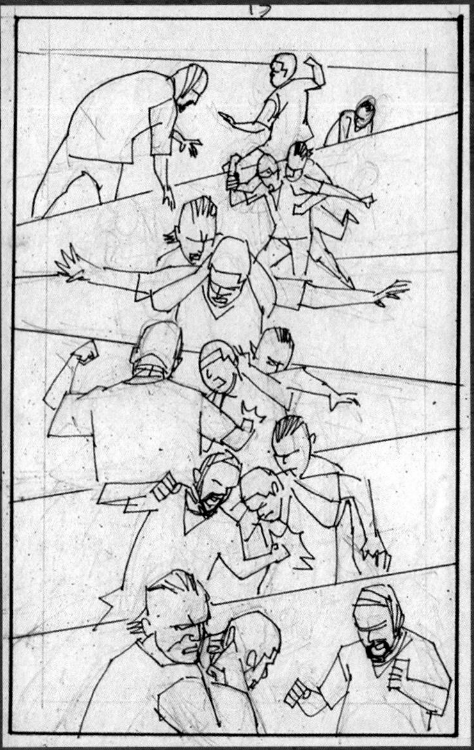

Thumbnails by **Budi Setiawan**

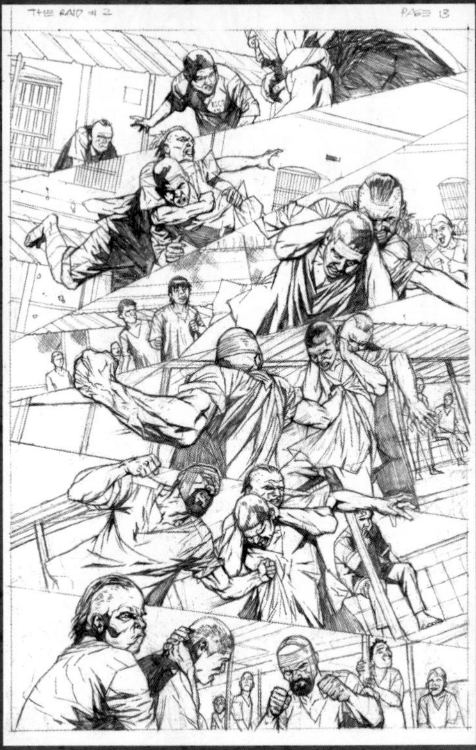
THE RAID # 2
PAGE 13

Pencils by **Budi Setiawan**

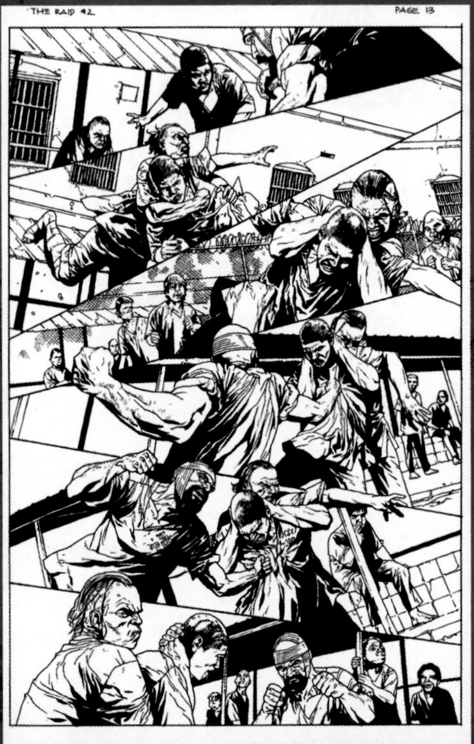
THE RAID #2
PAGE 13

Inks by **Budi Setiawan**

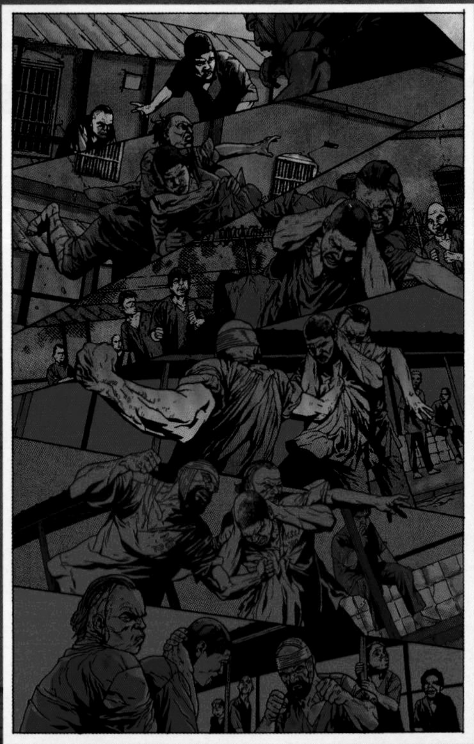

Colors by **Brad Simpson**

THE RAID BIOS

OLLIE MASTERS

Ollie Masters is a writer whose work includes *The Kitchen* (currently being adapted into a movie), *Snow Blind*, *Sons of Anarchy*, *Wonder Woman*, and *X-Men*.

ALEX PAKNADEL

Alex Paknadel has written *Doctor Who*, *Assassin's Creed*, *World War X*, *Little Nightmares*, and *The Raid* for Titan Comics, plus *Arcadia*, *Turncoat*, *Kino*, *Friendo*, and *Incursion*.

BUDI SETIAWAN

Indonesian artist Budi Setiawan came to prominence in 2007 when he was nominated for the Russ Manning Most Promising Newcomer Award at the Harvey Awards. Budi has also drawn *Rex Royd* for Titan Comics.

BRAD SIMPSON

Brad Simpson's stunning color choices have appeared in *Deadpool*, *Vengeance*, *The Amazing Spider-Man*, *Bloodborne*, *Godland*, *Sex*, *Sovereign*, *30 Days of Night*, and *The Witcher*.

JIM CAMPBELL

Jim Campbell has lettered Titan Comics' DreamWorks titles, including *Kung Fu Panda* and *Dragons: Riders of Berk*, and has provided lettering for several other comic companies.

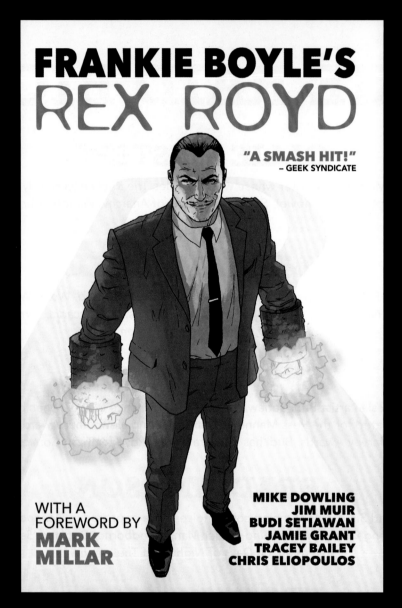